WORKING WITH DRUG FAMILY
SUPPORT GROUPS

Also by Paul Lockley

COUNSELLING HEROIN AND OTHER DRUG USERS
Free Association Books, 1995

WORKING WITH DRUG FAMILY SUPPORT GROUPS

Paul Lock

FREE ASSOCIATION BOOKS / LONDON / NEW YORK

Published in 1996 by
Free Association Books Ltd
57 Warren Street, London W1P 5PA
and 70 Washington Square South,
New York, NY 10012–1091

ISBN   1 85343 336 5   hardback

A CIP catalogue record for this book is available from
the British Library.

Impression 01 00 99 98 97 96   5   4   3   2   1

Produced for Free Association Books by
Chase Production Services, Chipping Norton, OX7 5QR
Printed in the EC by J. W. Arrowsmith, Bristol.

CONTENTS

PREFACE

There are many different Drug Family Support Groups which offer help to their members, persons who are close to illegal drug users, persons such as partners and parents. Unfortunately, many Groups spring up only to fade away after a few months. The hopes and expectations of its members are dashed, and those involved can feel cheated and resentful. Yet such Groups do not come to an end for no reason at all, and there does not have to be an unhappy ending. Other Groups soldier on, yet the amount of support they actually offer is very limited. By gaining an understanding of Support Groups, both the quality of support and the life time of such Groups can be increased. But such understanding is useful only if it is put into action. There has to be planning, from the setting up of the Group, through its operation with the attendant changes in membership, the monitoring and reviews that accompany the support work. This book, providing a combination of group and family theory with my own experience of eight years working in Support Groups, is intended to encourage Support Group members or those thinking of setting up such groups to review their own thinking and practice. This will work best if the readers are actively involved or about to be involved in Support Group work, so they can then check out for themselves the ideas contained in this book. Nothing should be taken for granted. Groupworkers have to find their own understanding of what happens in Groups and how best they can operate in them. There is one point that perhaps needs stressing. Books about groups can be de-skilling for some workers about to involve themselves in helping Support Groups. They might feel, 'I couldn't do that, there seems so much to remember and so much to do.' In practice we all make mistakes – though we rarely write about them. Progress can be measured by the number of risks taken, and this entails the likelihood of errors. The important thing is to be aware of one's mistakes, and be prepared to correct them and ensure that they do not occur again. In the pursuit of groupwork reality, I have used quotes from meetings, which give a flavour of what has happened and highlight some of the Group processes.

In the preparation of this book most thanks go to the members of the Family Support Group in Dundee which came under the aegis of the Drug Problem Centre, and the Family Support Group in Edinburgh which was associated with Scottish AIDS Monitor. My thanks also go to Joanna Morgan, Training Officer of Adfam, Hatton Street, London, for reading through the early manuscript. Thanks as ever are due to Gill Davies for bearing with me in the production of this book.

Paul Lockley

1 ANXIETY, HELP AND SUPPORT

PERSONAL CONCERN

Initial considerations

Illegal drug use is of concern to everyone nowadays. Drugs can be bought almost anywhere, and are not confined to deprived metropolitan areas. Up to a third of all school children have tried illegal drugs, and there are drugs awareness programmes in schools. There are also groups in the community and clinics in cities to help drug users. All this reflects the fact that drug use is endemic in our society. Even if we do not use drugs ourselves, we are likely to know someone who does. In addition, we may have friends and acquaintances who are using drugs, although we might be unaware of the fact.

So drug use is not something that happens only to other people. It is a fact of modern life, and none of us can claim that we will never be affected. For every person who takes illegal drugs, there are at least another two or three non-using people directly affected by that use: parents, partners, children, brothers or sisters.

Living with drug use

All those affected have to learn how to live with another person's drug use. This can be a long and difficult process, starting from the moment drug use in the family is first recognised. Illegal drug use usually begins in teenage years, and it may not be recognised for some time. Many of the signs associated with drug use may also characterise a young person growing up and becoming an adult: sleeping late in bed, inviting friends into the bedroom and acting secretively, having people phone at all hours, wearing clothes which parents find outrageous, colouring their hair, being moody and not talking, having what are regarded as dubious acquaintances coming to the house. These might be signs of drug use or they may simply be a mark of teenagers being teenagers.

However, most parents simply do not imagine that a member of the family would ever take illegal drugs. Adolescent behaviour might seem strange but it is seen as part of growing up, something others have to put up with, something parents even have to allow. Children need increasing freedom to become independent, they have to be allowed to rebel, 'kick over the traces' and find their identities as people. And all the while families have to try to live together. Family members have to get on with one another and accept each other's behaviour, even if that is not easy. There has to be respect for personal change, differences and boundaries. Indeed, personal privacy for adolescents becomes an important road to their emerging individuality. All of this points to illegal drug use being behaviour that is likely to be unknown to the family for some time.

Finding out

Nevertheless, there will come a time when what is happening can no longer be hidden. This is a mixed blessing. The person's odd and perhaps worrying behaviour can now be explained. On one hand this may be a relief – it breaks down fantasies that there is something seriously wrong with the family member, that the person may be mentally disturbed or turning against the family. On the other hand, parents or partners may well see drug taking as the most frightening of all possible causes for a son's, daughter's or partner's strange behaviour. The explanation might increase rather than decrease anxiety, and the rest of the family can feel at a total loss. As one parent admitted:

'Neither of us knew what was going on, except Phil had changed. Then someone, I forget who it was, suggested drugs, that Phil might be on drugs. We were devastated!'
'And what did you do?'
'We didn't know what to do at first. We had absolutely no idea at all!'

Nothing has prepared parents or partners for drug use in the family, so they have to try to find their own solutions. They have to come to terms with the fact that there do not seem to be any solutions. As one mother said:

'It was very painful, the way that Jane changed and seemed to grow away from me. I remember first finding out. She was sleeping on the couch and an arm was hanging down, out of the covers. With my nursing training, I recognised needle marks straight away. I was shocked but I tried to get her to talk about it. I would listen to her for hours, but it didn't do any good. Then I threatened her, I even hit her, but that was no better. Nothing worked and I could feel myself losing her.'

Often outsiders comfort themselves, imagining that no one in their family is likely to take drugs. However, drug use is not something that is restricted to any particular type of family. The only differences are in how families see the situation and how they react. Usually, the immediate reaction is to cover up what has happened so no one else knows about it. But this works only for a time.

'It was in the paper, so everyone could read it! The neighbours must have known. "Head girl breaks into chemist's shop." My daughter! I did not dare show my face outside the door.'

For parents there are two separate aspects that require their attention. First, someone in the family is using illegal drugs. Parents are expected to be able to deal with whatever the children do, yet they find themselves at a loss to suggest what should be done. This affects how they see themselves as parents. Second, there is the less obvious but equally important point in that they also do not know what to do about themselves. Parents are not merely unable to act constructively, they are suddenly assailed by negative thoughts about themselves. Drug use changes not only the individual's behaviour, it may also affect the behaviour of others, and in time may alter the functioning and health of the whole family (Spear 1991).

Part of the difficulty in doing something positive about family drug use comes through the general tendency to view it in rather simplistic terms. Often driven by politicians and the media, drug use is taken out of its social context and vilified. Action against it is seen as a war against an enemy. However, most of the 'enemy's' closest friends are family members. We should remember that a drug user is somebody's child, often somebody's partner and a parent to children. Ironically, public talk about a war against drugs is no more than a political stance with very little useful substance (Gardiner and McKinney, 1991).

The concern

It may seem that anyone emotionally close to a drug user has reason enough to be worried about the situation, but there the matter ends. We are dealing with people worried about drug use by someone they know and care for, so the main problem is simply worry. The family worries about the drug user's welfare, and is anxious for everything to be all right. But this is nothing exceptional. Almost all parents tend to worry about their children; almost all partners are concerned about their 'other half'. The problem is really people who worry unduly.

However, this ignores the effects that drug use in the family can produce. Drug use can produce anxiety in family members that results in severe symptoms – physical, psychological and behavioural. Induced anxiety may even cause family members to end up in a worse state than the drug users themselves.

Actual anxiety symptoms

All those who come to the Family Support Groups with which I have been associated have shown signs of stress and anxiety, though there were differences in the ways each individual was affected. The symptoms noted have included a weight loss of over twenty kilogrammes after the discovery of a son's drug use. One parent developed a serious heart condition; another developed peptic ulcers. Not all conditions are so serious. One Group member suffered the return of her psoriasis, another found that her epileptic attacks had resumed. Generally members tended to be run down, often suffering from poor sleep patterns and other forms of physical distress, such as persistent headaches and back pain. There were other psychological symptoms such as heavy drinking, which tended to cause its own problems. One Group member had great difficulty coming to the meetings because of marked agoraphobia. Some Group members suffered from low-grade depression and one member attempted suicide.

It is important to differentiate between worry, which affects us all, and chronic stress, accompanied by anxiety, that can cause marked symptoms in sufferers. However, we should also realise that this high-grade anxiety and stress may be quite normal in the circumstances. If the drug use is taken away; if the drug user receives treatment, then the anxiety level is likely to be reduced, chronic stress relieved and the family as a whole is helped (Gibson et al., 1992).

GOING FOR HELP

Help

Following the previous point, it is quite logical that the help most parents and partners want initially is for the drug user and not for themselves. If the drug use is stopped, then both user and family will be helped. However, the only person who can end the drug use is the drug user. No matter how hard partners or parents may try, they cannot stop it. So the family suddenly finds itself powerless, unable to act as it should.

Though Support Group members usually say that drug use left them at a loss, we should remember that this represents how they *felt*. In fact, family members do try to change the situation, and they make efforts to cope. It is likely that parents or partners will have gone to the extended family or close friends for help. The action of coming to the Support Group is another demonstration that family members are not helpless; they have their own ways of trying to cope.

It is worth noting that family members often feel negative about themselves and the drug situation; they do not believe that they have achieved anything. They blame themselves rather than feeling proud of their persistence and commitment. This negativity has to be turned around. Also, they have to realise that it is they who deserve help. They should stop trying to change what they cannot change – the actual drug use. This does not mean that the situation is unchangeable. My experience has been that many drug users are quite capable of coming off drugs, and this includes addictive drugs such as opiades and tranquillisers. However, family members should seek help for themselves, as they now have their own problems and difficulties. Once these are managed, they can consider helping others and being supportive of any efforts to change on the part of the drug user.

Families and help

Although parents and others close to the drug user may look for help, we should not underestimate what they can do for themselves. Even apparent inaction may be helpful, as a temporary means of coping (Pearlin and Schooler, 1978). In times of high stress, temporary avoidance or denial of what is taking place may be the only method of coping (Lazarus, 1983). Once the shock has been overcome, family members are able to think straight and take action if the situation is seen as a crisis needing action (Rueveni, 1979). Family members actually often do the right thing, even when they are unsure what to do, and they should not lose all confidence in themselves.

Nevertheless, the opposite may also be true. Action taken may be well intentioned but ineffective. Part of the reason for this is that, in crisis, family members can become very involved, their feelings run high, and they become very judgemental (Wilcox, 1981). This makes good decision-making difficult. Their stress is not alleviated by ill-considered action; indeed, further stress can arise in response to difficulties brought about by attempts to manage the particular crisis (McCubbin and Patterson, 1982).

What families are confronted with may be situations which are beyond their experience. They try to cope as best they can, but may not be successful. As a result they see themselves not only as unsuccessful in coping, but also as unsuccessful persons. This perception is fed into the overall situation and becomes part of the problem.

Outside forms of help

If families feel they cannot do very much, they may turn to the extended family for help. This is always a risky step, as those family members not in constant touch with the drug user are likely to share the general public's frightened and discriminatory reaction to drug use. So, feeling too embarrassed to share the fact of the drug use (Sarnoff and Zimbardo, 1961), the family might prefer to tell friends or acquaintances. However this is also a dangerous option, raising the fear of social rejection (Teichman, 1973).

So those affected by drug use may well look for official help from professional persons who will respect confidentiality. The difficulty is in knowing who best can help and who is acceptable as a helper. Social Services are not an attractive option, as they are seen as favouring family breakup through the taking of children into care, an image held by most Family Support Group members. Apart from this, there are doubts about how well qualified most social workers are in the field of drug use (Harrison, 1992). This is a common problem that applies not only to social workers but also to other professional helpers (Schlesinger, 1986).

The most obvious person to turn to for help is the family doctor. The difficulty can be in marrying up personal needs with the help that is on offer. If parents and partners want help for the drug user, then the doctor is the best person to provide it. However, the doctor can do little if the user does not cooperate. Also we have seen that those affected should ask for help for themselves rather than the drug user, but the difficulty is that any medical assistance is very much directed at the person with the identified problem – the drug user – and seldom directed at anyone else.

'It's OK for those who take drugs – they get help. Doctors give them this and give them that, but who bothers about the family? Who cares about us, who have to live with drug users for twenty-four hours a day? If you are a mother then you get nothing!'

However, some doctors would like to help family members and try to do so. Yet their training is very pharmacologically orientated, so they often resort to chemical means, such as prescribing tranquillisers, to relieve the anxiety of family members. In fairness, the lack of individual consultation time allows for little other medical input. In the short term, this medical help appears to be a solution. In the long term this is debatable. The effects of such drugs are very short-term, and after a few days they are of questionable value. More importantly, the use of drugs for treatment reinforces users' belief that people cannot live without drugs (Schwartzman, 1975) and can further lock them into their drug use behaviour. In addition, illegal drug use is likened by the drug user to the relative's or partner's use of prescribed drugs. Both are using drugs and this is seen as undermining the prescribed drug user's moral position, at least by illegal drug users, who make little distinction between legal and illegal drug use.

The alternative is for doctors to treat drug users and bring them off illegal drugs. Some doctors are not keen to prescribe or help drug users, having indifferent or mildly antagonistic attitudes to having drug users as patients. This is not a simple prejudice, as such attitudes have to be put in the context of drug user behaviour and drug user attitudes toward doctors (Telfer and Clulow, 1990). Even worse, these negative feelings towards drug users on the part of doctors may also include drug users' families or partners. Again, this may arise from family members being split between loyalty to the family member taking drugs and a desire to see change in that member's behaviour. Also, doctors tend to see drug use in families when there is a crisis and consequent family disunity and strife. They may thus have a biased and negative view of such families, overlook the family strengths and discount what families can do to help (Heller, 1979).

A different option is that drug users attend a drug clinic, but this tends to lock them into a drug using identity, should they agree to such help. In fact, drug users are unlikely to agree unless they are to be prescribed drugs to help them 'come off' illegal drugs. This 'coming off' can take months or years, which might be acceptable to the users but is little comfort to the family. The clinic's stress on harm reduction rather than coming off; of needle exchanges and prescribed drugs, rather than stopping, makes sense in that it prevents the spread of HIV infection. But this is of questionable comfort to those having to deal with a family member's drug use every day.

Professional help and families

Taking into account the drawbacks of going for help, many families prefer to deal or cope with the drug use themselves. And sometimes the crises can have a positive effect, bringing the family together and getting it to work as a unit. But for families with other problems, families that are dysfunctional or isolated, crises can have a negative effect (Gottlieb, 1983). Nevertheless, they might have little choice but to cope with the difficulty alone, as they may receive little support from friends, or their attempts to get support locally may be rejected (Turkat, 1980).

It seems that whatever families do, there are likely to be drawbacks and further problems. And although this may be only the perception of the families involved, there is much truth in it. As a result, those who finally come to Support Groups may have a history of setbacks when trying to obtain help for themselves. This will be just one type of difficulty that members will bring with them to the Group.

Reframing family perceptions

So far, a rather negative picture has been painted of action in the face of drug use. It should be remembered that most families do cope with it, albeit with difficulty. Even when help is sought outside the family, matters are not easy. One very common comment by new members of Support Groups is: 'You would think it would be easy to get help, wouldn't you?' As a result of such a difficulty, families feel angry and confused. They are unsure of what to do, and so, it seems, is everyone else. Social work, the medical profession, the family and the general public can all seem indifferent, obstructive and uncaring. However, the unhelpful attitudes, beliefs and behaviour are not likely to alter, so the emphasis has to be on what can be changed, and what can be changed are the families themselves.

It may seem somewhat strange that families should have to take action when the problem is the drug user. However, they are not asked to change their attitude to drug use or drug users. The only change is that families say precisely what it is that they want. This might seem a strange requirement for families that have been demanding help, but because of their high anxiety and the strong feelings involved, what they want may be unclear. Yet if people are clear about what they want, their needs are more likely to be met.

Family members have to let go of the negative aspects, the arguments in the family, the indifference of helpers, and turn to positive action. This positivity comes from formulating precisely what it is they want and how it can be realised.

GETTING SUPPORT

Stress

When trying to define the needs of families affected by illegal drug use, it was noted earlier that they were subject to high stress and anxiety. So one approach might be to work on such stress. This does not solve all difficulties, but by concentrating on one specific area, a start is made to lessen the distress arising from the drug use. By relieving the symptoms of stress, family members are helped, even if the causes of stress are not eliminated.

To achieve the best results, the process of becoming stressed has to be understood and appropriate steps taken.

The process of stress

The cause of stress in general can be put down to three major determinants:

1. Causes in the environments such as illegal drug use.

2. How the person interprets the causes; how drug use is viewed.

3. How the person reacts to stress items such as drug use.

There are many difficulties in life. Whether these cause anxiety, fear, or some kind of personal pressure depends on how the situation is interpreted (Kelly, 1955; Mischel, 1973). The same situation may be seen quite differently from one person to another, from one family to another. However what does seem to be common is that if the situation is little understood and hard to manage, then it causes anxiety (Lazarus, 1966; Bannister and Fransella, 1980). Also, everyone reacts differently to stress according to their genetic make-up and their past life experiences. Some people deal easily with stress, seeing problems as a challenge or a source of excitement; others may see similar problems as threatening or experience them as tiring and depressing. In addition, there are feedback mechanisms (Cox, 1978) which monitor how well a person deals with a situation, and this in turn affects the interpretation of the event. Seeing a situation as threatening but then finding that it is in fact manageable, is likely to alter how that situation is perceived.

From a helping point of view, it can be seen that although the ultimate cause of stress, the drug use, cannot be changed by outsiders, there is an opportunity to deliver help through modifying how the illegal drug use is seen and deciding how it is understood, and how best to cope with the situation and factors relevant to that coping.

Initiating stress relief

What is needed is some form of relief for personal anxiety, upset feelings and lack of understanding. There may be various ways of providing such help, but the help considered here is that of mutual support, the provision of emotional and practical assistance. Such support has been selected because it provides assistance for all the difficulties of those affected by drug use. Personal support is a logical answer to the experienced personal needs.

Nature of support

The immediate task is to work out how to give appropriate support, but first we must clarify what this means. Some of the difficulties that can occur in Support Groups arise through having different ideas as to what constitutes support, so clarification is very important. If we review the nature of support then there are five main categories, and these are:

(a) emotional support;
(b) material support;
(c) self-esteem support;
(d) informational support; and
(e) companionship.

If we turn to the greatest sources of support, then these are to be found in marriage or a similar relationship (Cohen and Wills, 1985), or a parental relationship in the case of children. Loss of such close relationships can lead to extreme stress along with psychological and medical symptoms (Berkman, 1985). Indeed, most people would see the five aspects of support listed above as normal parts of such close relationships. This is important as it points to support being something that is required not just in emergencies, but as something common to everyday circumstances (Kahn and Antonucci, 1980). This normalising of support means that the supported person does not have to be 'bad', 'mad' or 'ill'. Persons to be supported do not have to think of reasons or construct excuses to obtain and be given support. Nor does it mean that people have to fear that support might suddenly be taken away from them when they are 'well' or 'all right'.

Support needs

There are good arguments for making sure that the existing support systems – be they families, neighbours, communities, or professional services – are allowed to do their job, and Support Groups should not lessen or negatively interfere with such ongoing help. Support does not have to come from Support Groups. However, account must also be taken of the nature of a person's support network and whether it is likely to be helpful (Gottlieb, 1983).

If we try to work out where Support Groups might be useful, then first we must determine why support might be needed. There are four main reasons:

1. Support goes towards the formation of personal identity, reflecting the fact that people are social animals and support is helpful towards making all of us who we are.

2. Support helps with the process of change, and those changes which occur thoughout a person's life (Kahn and Antonucci, 1980).

3. Support helps all of us to cope with the difficulties that happen in life (Hirsch, 1981).

4. Support can give a sense of well-being, even when there is an absence of stress or difficulties (Kessler and McLeod, 1985).

The need for support is a normal requirement for all of us in life. And the required support is usually forthcoming from natural systems. However, it might happen that such support is not forthcoming.

Lack of natural support

Some people do not have adequate support systems and find it hard to cope with the difficulties that life presents them. There can be four main causes. First, support might not be available. Individuals may be isolated physically from family and neighbours, especially if they live in rural areas or are comparatively new arrivals in the community. There can be a tendency to isolation as parents grow older and the children leave home. A further cause of isolation may be death or separation from a partner. In fact, the availability of support in life varies generally according to age, lifestyle, gender, whether employed or not, and other variables (Leavy, 1983; Wills, 1985). Very often people come for help because they do not have anyone with whom they can talk things over (Argyle, 1981).

Second, it can happen that the support given is inadequate. This may be because the would-be support givers are themselves caught up in difficulties and want support. Also these supporters may themselves be in conflict, so that they cannot give unbiased help. Also, support may be given but prove to be inadequate as it is unrealiable (Boyce et al., 1988).

Third, difficulties can arise in that the person needing support is seen as unlikely to accept any help offered. This might reflect actual past experiences of help-giving, or general attitudes displayed, particularly of men who maintain a macho image and see taking help as a form of weakness (Lewis, 1978). Some people may have personalities which make it very difficult for them to take help or to be seen to take help (Kobasa et al., 1985), and thus may be self-isolating. A less obvious type of self-isolation occurs when support is taken but never or seldom returned. In time, supporters resent one-directional interactions and may eventually cease giving any assistance.

Finally, support may not be given where there are special difficulties, such as drug use in the family. In their study of mastectomy cases, Lindsey and Norbeck (1981) found that help came more from those who had undergone the same experience than from those in close relationships. Another area of special need was that of carers, who looked after others in need of help (Orford, 1987; Gilhooly, 1987). As they were carers, it was assumed that they did not need support themselves.

The basics of support

Thinking about support is easier if its nature becomes clearer and if we have a more concrete idea of what it is, so it is assumed that basic support comes through talking matters over with other people. Just talking can make people under pressure feel better and less stressed. This in turn can bring marked benefits. Feeling better is not necessarily a temporary phase but can bring about long-term results. For example, those who are part of a wide interactive social network where they can talk to many different people have a lower mortality rate than those with restricted social support (Berkman and Syme, 1979). A lack of social support is also associated with a decline in health (Patrick et al., 1986). Although this gives the general picture and is not confined to those affected by drug use, it does provide evidence of the real benefits of support. There are further advantages of support, but this requires specifying how support may be maximised.

First, those who are highly stressed have to talk about what is worrying them, how they feel and what difficulties they have experienced. Though this might seem self-evident, the abilities of those under stress not to talk, to mention only trivia, to talk about other issues, or not to show their feelings can be surprisingly great. And those who do not self-disclose are not only no better off; they are worse off. Non-disclosure increases stress and is unhelpful (Pennebaker and O'Heeron, 1984).

The most benefit comes from 'high disclosers', those who include their feelings in what they say, those who can let go emotionally (Pennebaker et al., 1987). Although this can be intimidating at times for both speakers and listeners, appropriate full disclosure is to be recommended. Simply talking through situations can lessen self-talk, that is, running through the situation in the mind and eventually resulting in obsessional thinking (Wegner et al., 1987). The talking-through may be done several times. This allows the talker to begin to make sense of what has happened (Silver and Wortman, 1980).

Other advantages of this talking-through process include the raising of the person's self-esteem (Wills, 1985) and the giving of a greater sense of control (Sarason et al., 1990), which in turn makes planned action easier.

When just talking does not help

It would be wrong to imply talking to others is all that is necessary to make one feel better. Self-disclosure about future events and what might happen, tends to be unhelpful (Costanza et al., 1988) so it is necessary to return to what has actually happened. Also, a total preoccupation with feelings while ignoring thought and behaviour can turn potential help into a negative experience (Sarason et al., 1990). Getting caught up in one's own negative feelings without looking at the positive can also prove unhelpful (Archer et al., 1982). In addition, the reactions of the listeners are equally important. Too cheery a reaction by listeners can feel dismissive of a person's deep feelings and may not only fail to lessen stress but may also irritate the speaker (Coyne et al., 1988). So talking does help, but to ensure that everyone involved feels better, the process must be done correctly.

Who gives good support?

The principal support givers tend to be either partners or parents. If these are absent, then support can be gained from close friends, who comprise a person's support network. This is best if the network is not a series of one-to-one relationships but a more complex setup, where the support persons also have inter-relationships. A lattice of interconnected relationships (Tolsdorf, 1976) lessens the liability of one-to-one dependency or over-involvement. As was noted in the mastectomy cases, special situations may need special supporters, so the nature of a person's situation and difficulties may be very relevant.

USING A GROUP FOR SUPPORT

Introduction

Those who are anxious and under stress might find that talking to someone is helpful but have little opportunity to do so, or they may discover that the number of people who will actually listen is not large. The Support Group provides that audience – and much more. The mere fact of being a participant in a Group can make its members feel better. They have a feeling of belonging (Hagstrom, 1965). By taking part, by contributing, the members begin to change. They acquire a new self-image (Freedman and Fraser, 1966) and start the process of diminishing personal anxiety. Accordingly, members feel less distressed and begin to gain a sense of power and control (Cobb, 1976) which goes towards building up their self-esteem (Linn et al., 1985). All this produces not only a feel-good factor – the resultant lack of stress can lower the incidence of members' medical problems (Berkman and Syme, 1979).

It might seem that being part of a Support Group is the magic cure for families under stress. This is not the whole picture. If the rest of the Group is stressed then an individual member is likely to feel worse, not better (Shaver and Liebling, 1976). If the support is given incorrectly – such as 'cheering up a person' – then this can also aggravate stress (Dakof and Taylor, 1990). In addition, negative support such as criticism or over-involvement (Hooley et al., 1986) can affect the particular individual more than positive support (Rook, 1984).

Support Groups

Using the previous information, it can now be seen that Support Groups usually provide four of the five aspects of support. They provide emotional and informational support; they provide a source of increased self-esteem, and they provide companionship. They tend not to provide material support, though they usually provide information about how to obtain such support.

Support Groups offer both the giving and receiving of support and provide a reliable source of support from persons who are in broadly similar situations. Even those immersed in their own difficulties and seemingly unable to make headway may want to help others and are able to do so. The nature of Group helping is such that the incidence of possibly dependent one-to-one relationships is minimised. Instead, the richer multi-personal relationships are formed.

Support Groups are not the perfect answer to those experiencing stress and difficulties in their life. Natural support systems usually prove adequate. However there will be situations where support is not present or not present in the required form and amount. In such circumstances Support Groups can be helpful.

Support Groups and emotional support

What Support Groups offer mainly is emotional support through the relationships that form within the Group; through the feelings that develop between members. And feelings are important.

Those affected by family drug use may come to the Group because they do not know what to do about their drug using partner, or they may have discovered their son is injecting drugs, or their pregnant daughter is living with a drug user. However, these situations do not cause concern unless feelings are involved. Having a drug using partner is a cause for action, a stimulus to come for help, because feelings are involved. Having a drug injecting son is painful, a worry, and possibly makes parents feel guilty and inadequate. It is such feelings that initiate the search for help and it is such feelings that require attention. But the feelings do not die. They have to be confronted, and the Group is where feelings exist and can be worked on.

Support and problems

Family Support Groups have their own special nature. Not only do they give support to Group members, they must also work with what, in the main, cannot be changed by those members. Acceptance of their different individual situations forms a large part of the work. Often members will come to a Support Group in the hope that someone can give them a 'magic' answer; tell them how drug use can be stopped. There is no magic answer. What the Group can do is to help members accept this fact. The real task is coming to terms with the situation and then helping members decide how best to act in the light of that acceptance.

However, we should also be aware that acceptance is not a negative action, pointing out the limitations of what can be done. In fact, acceptance of a situation can lead in turn to a more active approach to coping (Schussler, 1992). It requires the Group member to work with feelings, to take on other perspectives, attitudes and beliefs. It requires members to come to terms with themselves and their own lives.

Support and relationships

Identifying the essence of support and the need to attend to feelings moves us on to look at relationships. They are the channel through which we may deal with feelings and so deliver emotional support. To ensure those relationships are good, person-centred qualities and skills are needed as a solid working basis. These include empathy, or the ability to see the world from another person's point of view and sense how others are feeling. Also, acceptance of others, being able to deal with them in a non-judgemental manner and to see others as having a positive worth, whatever their past or present behaviour. For good relationships, people should be themselves and not hide behind roles, such as those of clients, patients or victims. Finally, there has to be honesty and a firm sense of reality.

The second required aspect of good support is good communication between the relevant people. This refers both to the ability to communicate clearly and precisely with others, affectively and cognitively, and to the ability to be a good listener. Both these aspects of support – relationships and communication – help to define the nature of good support. However, there is still more we need to know.

Refining ideas about support

To determine the nature of support more precisely, it is useful to clarify possible misunderstandings. First, support may be given but it also has to be taken. Taking support is an active process, in which those seeking support have to participate.

Second, support is an interaction involving giving as well as receiving (Maton, 1988). Those wanting to be supported do so best if they let others know how they feel and what they are thinking. This not always possible. There will be times when Group members are 'down' and feel unable to give much to others. This is no great problem as others feel 'up' and able to contribute. Over time, members are likely to go through both positive and negative stages, but overall these are likely to balance out (Clark, 1983).

Third, support does have its own area of work, its own boundaries and limitations. It is not intended to help everyone bear the unbearable. It does not solve all problems nor help all people. However, neither does it reinforce, condone nor simply accept painful situations, distressing relationships and antisocial behaviour. Support does not have to embrace the status quo, take life as unchanging or unchangeable.

Finally, support as described here has its own humanistic value system, which should be explicit and shared by the Group.

The experience of being supported

Saying how support should be is not always very helpful to potential Group members: they want to know what support is like. The following may give more of a feel for the nature of being supported.

- Support is not simply being nice to people nor always agreeing with them. It should be honest, and those supporting should be themselves.

- Supporters should keep personal boundaries, and not be overwhelmed by situations but be able to comment on them. They should suggest options and challenge the person being helped if this is appropriate. Support may even be considered somewhat unpleasant at times, as those supported have to face themselves and the actions of others close to them.

- Being supported can involve personal change, and any form of change may be disconcerting and potentially upsetting.

- Support is not feeling sorry for someone, as this can merely reinforce someone who sees the world in a negative way. Nor is it trying to cheer up those needing support, as this fails to acknowledge and deal with how that person feels.

- Support is not telling people what they should be doing. It is entering into a formal relationship with individuals and helping and being helped through those relationships. The assistance has to be given in a structured way (Moos, 1974) to be really useful, ensuring mutual interaction through good relationships.

- Support is not a process where one person is always receiving support and another is always giving it. Such one-way help is more likely to engender personal dependency and to diminish personal responsibility.

How others may see it

After such a list, it may seem that support is a rather arbitrarily defined source of personal help. We should never forget that the definition of appropriate and useful support depends on how it is seen by those involved, by members of Support Groups and by those affected by drug use and asking for help for themselves. We should not assume that we automatically know what constitutes support, as it varies between people, subcultures, ethnic groups and cultures (Giordano, 1976; Williams, 1993). Support has to be decided with reference to those involved.

For example, when a Support Group was asked what they wanted from support, the answers were:

1. *Feeling better*. This covered feeling less worried or anxious, being more content, and being able to have fun. It meant waking up in the morning and not automatically starting to worry.

2. *Not being 'wound up'*. This meant not always feeling angry or frustrated, being able to let others know how one felt and being able to talk about things. It meant being free of feeling that everything was boiling up inside and then being afraid of exploding into violence or saying things that would later be regretted.

3. *Getting on better*. Relating better and not arguing all the time with the rest of the family and with the person who was taking drugs. Being able to talk with family members without one's comments being seen as criticism.

4. *Being able to do something*. Not always being in the same situation, feeling that nothing can be done and feeling trapped. Having a say in the situation and being able to influence events.

5. *Doing what is best*. This covers what is best for the whole family: for the rest of the family, for the children, for the partner and for oneself. Getting the needs of everyone into some sort of order.

6. *Being able to help others*. To feel again like helping others; being able to tell others what can be done; hearing that things have gone well for them and seeing them looking better. Not being upset when things do not work out.

7. *Being able to get out and meet people*. To feel like getting out from time to time; not feeling trapped in the house; having the ability to to go out and enjoy oneself and not to feel guilty about having a good time.

Everyone wants slightly different things for themselves and their families, so the above is not a definitive list, merely a list composed by one particular group of people affected by drug use. However, it does indicate what these people would like for themselves and others, and areas that a support service should try to cover. What is noticeable is that feeling better was listed as being the most important aspect of support. Indeed, some new Group members could say little more than that they wanted to feel better. Part of the task of the Support Group is to ensure that feeling better is a long-term, as opposed to a temporary, state. And a long-term feeling of betterment is associated not only with feelings but also with positive thoughts, having a more optimistic outlook (Scheier and Carver, 1992). There is no set model of what should be provided by way of support, only a synthesis of what Group members want and what is likely to be supportive.

The image of support

Describing aspects of support might make it sound out of the ordinary, yet support is normal, a part of everyday social behaviour. Everyone experiences support in their lives, whether from partners, family, work colleagues, their social circle or other sources. In fact it is so normal that we tend only to notice support through its absence (Barkow, 1977). As a result, asking for support is seen as abnormal, a sign of weakness or an admission of failure, rather than being something to which everyone is entitled and which everyone needs (Fisher et al., 1988) In fact, one of the aims of the Group is to normalise the idea of receiving and giving support.

Those thinking about coming to a Support Group should see their action in a positive light; see it as a source of revitalisation, a way of helping them carry on. Those who come to the Group need to gather energy for themselves. This perception does not mean people are dependent on support. Dependency is a form of helplessness, a learned condition which allows people to seek help without any commitment from themselves (Seligman, 1975). In the long run, this is counterproductive, both for themselves and others.

Support through Groups

Helping others is an important way of increasing self-esteem in that members discover they can help and be positive, and so give range to their own abilities. This does not happen immediately. Initially, members help by simply being there. This is enough to start the process of feeling better. Later, with a slightly increased self-esteem and self-confidence, new members can begin to participate more fully in the Group and further increase their self-esteem.

A Group can give a range of options and different experiences. Each member can take out what is relevant to them. Equally, each member is helped through relating to someone else, and the Group provides a wide range of persons to whom each can relate. All these points are reinforced by having persons with similar experiences in the Group, persons with whom there are common links allowing a shared understanding and empathy.

Further support through the Group

The Group, by allowing members to help each other, enters into a delabelling process. Members can work towards ridding themselves of labels such as 'victim', 'client' or 'patient'. They can begin to see themselves as capable of improving their situation, rather than being dictated by the family drug use and other difficulties. The fact that the Group mirrors the family setup is also helpful. It provides a suitable place to discover what happens in families and how best to take action.

As the Group lives and continues after individual members have left, this can result in it building up its own expertise, history and culture. The Group can be used to retain relevant experiences and actions, and these can be passed on to other members. In this way, it is more than the sum of its present members. The Group represents all members who have ever attended. It has a culture of its own that interacts in turn with present Group members.

Perspectives on power

For those not involved in support work, the idea of getting a group of needy people together, people in various stages of anxiety and crisis, and expecting them to solve their difficulties and feel better may not seem a very logical action. Of course, all of us find it easier to deal with the difficulties of others as opposed to those of our own. Nevertheless, there still seems little reason why those in difficulties should be able to help others.

However, two separate points should to be taken into account when faced with disbelief about the usefulness of Support Groups. First, support is an active process and is effective only through action. Action starts with members coming to the Group. Further action comes with the interaction between members. Thus, supportive action is self-reinforcing: if members of the group feel just a little bit better then this allows them to achieve more and so be more mutually supportive. What the Group can do at the start may be very limited, but this grows in time.

Second, Group members may come together because of what they see as unmanageable feelings, which in turn reflect the members' vulnerability. Though vulnerability might bring about difficulties in coping and what are seen as crises, yet it can also be a strength. Vulnerability involves sensitivity, caring, hope and a certain ability to be realistic, even if this involves having to cover up or deny what is known to be true. All of these can be useful: they can be the basis for better family functioning. Part of the problem for those affected by drug use in the family is not only that they might feel bad about themselves, but also that others may reinforce such negative feelings. But once they come together and they can be helped to see alleged weaknesses as strengths, then they can begin to use the qualities and abilities they possess.

Getting into it

What most of those interested in the task of providing support and forming a Support Group want to do is to get out there and start one; to get down to the job of helping others. Unfortunately, the idea that 'at least it won't do any harm', when applied to helping and support, is not true. Those in distress come with expectations of feeling better. If this does not happen then they feel worse than before. Their expectations are dashed, and they may go away convinced that there is nothing that can help them.

For this reason we should take time at the initial stage to plan properly, think about what we are doing and what exactly we want to achieve. All of this requires having some idea about support. Wanting to help is not enough. People can be damaged through the kindness of others, and people can also damage themselves through wanting to help.

2 PLANNING SUPPORT

INITIAL THOUGHTS

What form of help?

There are many ways of helping: for example, individual counselling, groupwork, family therapy or befriending. All of these approaches, like Group Support, have their particular theoretical underpinning and reasons why they are chosen. Support Groups, as a means of helping families where there is drug use, are chosen as they are useful in meeting their specific needs.

When providing Group support, we have to pay attention to those asking for help, to what they want rather than what can be offered. This may not be so simple a matter in practice. For example, the following scenario followed my visit to the home of a drug user. What was said by the participants is as I remembered and recorded that evening.

Father: 'You'll have to take her. And you (turning to daughter), get out! You're not staying here! (turning to me) Her mother hasn't slept.'
(Mother, looking depressed, is staring at the floor. She nods.)
Bev: 'It's hard when you are withdrawing.'
Father: 'She lies in bed and shouts at her mother to do this, do that.'
Bev: 'Well ...'
Father: 'Get out! I don't want to see your face in this house ever again. Get out now! You had better get her out. I'll strangle her. Get out!'
Me: 'Come on, Bev, I think we had better go.'
Father: 'Out you go! ... Have you got anywhere she can go?'
Me: 'No.'
Father: '... Well, she can stay the night.'
Mother: (Whispers) 'I just can't cope.'

An examination of this scenario can help us orientate ourselves to drug use in the family. High feelings are aroused: the father's anger, the mother's depression, the daughter's guilt. Then there are the feelings towards others, such as the father's concern for his wife and his ambivalence about his daughter. We might judge that the most pressure is felt by the father and the daughter, the main protagonists. However, their participation and release of feelings gives them a degree of relief. The person most under pressure is the mother, caught in the middle between husband and daughter. As a result only she actively wanted help, even if her articulaton was indirect.

If we are looking for help which matches the mother's needs, then helping all three would seem the logical answer. Attractive though the idea might seem, there are complications. In this example, all three persons involved would have to agree to total family help or therapy. In fact, the disagreements in the family were echoed in disagreements as to whether to seek help for themselves. Yet if all three are not seen together, then the situation cannot totally be resolved. No matter what is said to the mother, her actions in the family may well be undermined or sabotaged by either her daughter or her husband.

Group support

The example was introduced to show that often there is no easy answer to family difficulties. Helpers have their own agendas and want to demonstrate that what they have to offer is the 'answer', but we should be realistic and honest enough to admit to limitations. What can be done in the above example is not going to be a perfect answer, merely the best under the circumstances. From the beginning, help has to be seen realistically, as help, and not as a solution.

Group support is not the ideal answer but is often the most realistic answer to the pressures that arise through family drug use. We should realise that there are likely to be difficulties or disadvantages, as well as advantages, in using a Group for support. The task is to maximise the advantages and lessen the disadvantages.

Further thoughts about the Group

A Support Group, being composed of people who have experienced difficulties with drug use in the family, makes talking about personal feelings and the family easier. There is less feeling of stupidity, guilt or embarrassment when others have had similar experiences. This is more important than it might seem initially, as those needing support are likely to have very low self-esteem, which makes talking to any stranger difficult. However, there is a drawback in that it can be embarrassing to talk to strangers, even if they have had similar experiences. More to the point, the thought of talking to strangers is likely to be intimidating, so those in need might not even try talking to others.

With a group of peers, it is easier to have a common understanding and so learn from them. There are likely to be fewer personal agendas which get in the way, such as status or people having an expert role. A group of peers can set its own pace and agendas. The drawback can be that others in the Group can reinforce dysfunctional behaviour or the Group can be unhelpful as a whole. Also, the Group allows members to be positive, to give something to others in a safe environment, and to begin to discover that they have a strength within themselves to act constructively. The drawback can be that of expecting Group members to help others when they feel unable to do so.

A start to planning

What may be gathered is that Group support, where everyone helps each other, seems a viable idea though there are potential drawbacks. Planning is essential to increase the benefit of any support system. Help, if poorly considered and delivered, can be counterproductive and make a person's situation worse. The success of the Group largely depends on initial planning and what happens before it actually starts (Douglas, 1970). Planning is also required for ethical reasons. It seems incorrect to allow people to be exposed to an ill-judged form of help, especially as those exposed are likely to be very vulnerable.

INTO PLANNING

At the beginning

The very first step is to create time for planning. It is tempting to rush into action, to provide immediate support, especially if there are people asking for help. People under pressure and highly anxious are likely to demand immediate action. Yet to omit proper planning at this stage would be counterproductive, resulting in time being lost later on – time taken in clearing up misunderstandings and undoing what has taken place.

Without common understandings laid down in the planning stage, contradictory messages will be given in the Group and confusion will result. Members might 'do their own thing' and end up pulling in opposite directions. Without agreed rules, it becomes difficult for new members to pick up what is the usual functioning of the Group and to know when someone is infringing normal Group practice. What may seem to be the holding back of help is actually essential for the running of any group.

Some preliminary work

At the very beginning, time can be taken to read up on how to start and run a Group. Members can visit local Support Groups. These act as sources of information and can provide the addresses and names of local resources. They also provide encouragement and practical tips. Doing such work at this stage is important as later on there might not be the time.

Going ahead

If someone decides that there is a need for a Drug Family Support Group, then the immediate task is for that person to draft in a sympathetic and relevant co-worker, someone to share the task of setting up the Group. No one person is likely to be able to do everything sufficiently well. In addition, Support Groups are about sharing and working together, and the sooner this is put into practice, the better. Founders of groups and organisations are often people with a lot of drive but not always good at sharing, and in the Group sharing and cooperation should be the norm.

Establishing the need

Before proceeding, the founding members should try to determine whether there really is a need for the proposed Group. A very rough idea can be formed by obtaining from the police an estimate of the number of illegal drug users locally. This will give a very approximate figure of those affected by drug use, but little idea of the numbers that might come along to the Group. Another method is to put a small notice in a local paper advertising a meeting to discuss families and drug use. Such meetings can then be used as a recruiting ground for those interested in providing and obtaining Group support.

Founding members should find out whether there is already a similar Group locally. This need not stop existing plans, but for future good relations it is best to inform the other Group of what is intended. Also, a discussion could minimise difficulties with overlapping membership or people going to both Groups, and lessen the chance of the new Group being seen as a threat to funding. Joint approaches and cooperation should be the aim.

Areas of planning

There are two main areas which require careful planning. The first is that of working out the Group's aim and objectives, what the Group is all about and what it is going to do. The second is the management of the Group covering items like administration, use of premises, recruiting new members, dealing with other agencies, and all financial matters.

Often these areas are managed by the founding members on a basis of assumed common understandings. This is fine, until a contentious issue arises. Then everyone concerned in the Group suddenly appears to have had very different ideas. So agreeing and writing down Group business is necessary. This might sound very bureaucratic and the relevant records might be referred to only rarely, but this does not invalidate the process and sets a good precedent for future working practices.

Aims of the group

The founding members have to decide what the Group's main purpose is. This aim may seem obvious and not worthy of discussion. None the less, such discussion represents the first time Group members have had to work towards a common understanding of what they are trying to achieve, and how support can be delivered.

The aim in its final form should be agreed and written down. It might be similar or equivalent to: 'The aim of a drug family Support Group is to provide group support for those affected by illegal drug use in the family.' There is no need to make the aim any more complex than this. The simpler the aim, the easier it is to remember and ultimately to achieve. However, the statement of the Group's aim does need some definitions of the various important terms used.

It has to be agreed what the drugs alluded to are. In those Groups in which I had experience, the drugs referred to were illegal drugs or substances, and the usual one was heroin. However, the particular drug taken is not so important; most drug users take a variety of substances (Perera et al., 1987). What is important is that those affected by the use of drugs have similar experiences to share.

The meaning of family also has to be determined. This term might include partners, relatives or even very close friends. The main point is not who can come to the Group, but whether everyone knows and agrees who can come. Sometimes there are unspoken rules, such as there being a lower age limit, so children are not allowed to come to the Group. However, it is preferable to discuss formally all rules, whatever their nature.

It is worthwhile going over and agreeing what support means. Usually, support is for the members of the Group and not for the drug users; it is mutual, emotional and of a practical nature. Support should be differentiated from Group counselling or from drugs education, from drugs campaigning or from a social group for those affected by drug use. One of the major reasons why Groups fail is because there is no clear agreement about the nature of the aim. This can result in members pulling against each other. They move towards their own private aims and objectives, only to find that the Group as a whole is not serving their purpose.

Objectives

How the Group's aim is carried out is described in the objectives. These can be many and varied, and analysed until they can be and are written in operational terms, describing exactly how the aim is to be carried out. For example, the aim of providing Group support may be seen as coming principally from Group meetings, and this objective can be further analysed into the sub-objectives of expressing and sharing feelings, sharing information and experiences, discussing personal problems, planning coping strategies and increasing self-esteem.

All of these sub-objectives have to be subdivided into operational statements. For instance, the sharing of information might be accomplished through participation in training sessions, inviting professionals to talk about drugs and answer questions, ensuring each new group member is given a booklet covering drug issues, getting members to describe their own experiences and checking this out with similar experiences to be found within the Group.

Different members' perceptions

Although members may have agreed to adhere to the Group's aim and objectives, these are likely to be perceived differently from person to person. Usually agreement on the aim is not difficult, but how the objectives are to be carried out is likely to be the subject of some debate. Often there are assumptions about how things will be done and different views are not apparent. Yet there has to be consensus on how the objectives are to be carried out.

Carrying out the objectives

Giving and receiving support can best be done by the members meeting as a Group and discussing their experiences and problems. However, we should not ignore the fact that other forms of support can be given at the same time. Networking, or members keeping in touch with each other by phone or through meeting, has limitations as any benefit is usually restricted to two or three persons rather than the whole Group. However, it does relieve feelings of isolation and provide some support between meetings.

Networking has other advantages in that it diminishes the influence of the more powerful people in the Group, who can inhibit other members. Also, networking means that members are operating outside the meetings and are able to talk about relevant matters outside the Group and closer to the family, so members might want one of the Group's objectives to be that of networking.

SETTING UP THE GROUP

Group naming

At this stage it might be useful if the founding members decide on a name for the Group as this helps to put the proposed aim and objectives into a more concrete a form. However, naming may not be so straightforward. Too vague a title might not attract members, but too exact a title, such as 'Relatives of Drug Users Support Group', can make confidentiality harder to maintain. Nevertheless, deciding on a name does help members to become more precise about the nature of the group.

Management

Group management may be divided into various categories. First, agreeing on how decisions should be made. Initially, when there may be only two or three in the Group, there seems no need to consider decision making systems; decisions are made on an informal basis. Indeed, it would seem to show a lack of mutual trust if they were made in any other way. However, with a greater number of members, a system becomes necessary. Even with just two members, it is helpful to get into the way of management and decide on a system. This might involve no more than declaring that any decision requires agreement by both parties in order to be valid. As numbers increase, there has to be agreement as to what issues require decisions. Practicality demands that petty decisions do not require the consent of all the members, so the system has to categorise those decisions that need Group agreement.

Second, Group members tend to have slightly different recollections of what is said and agreed, based on their own understandings and interpretations, so recording agreed decisions is important. As the Group grows, there has to be more specification, such as whether decisions are still to be made by general consent or by majority, the number of members that compose a quorum, and what procedure is required to overturn a decision.

The third management step might be to allot Group members various responsibilities. These can vary from opening up the premises for meetings, bringing along coffee and tea, sending out notices of meetings, recruiting new members, or bringing them to the Group. A balance has to be achieved between having what may seem a very regimented set-up, which can get in the way of an informal atmosphere and easy discussion, and having too relaxed an atmosphere, which can result in work or practical arrangements not being accomplished or one or two members having to do all the work.

Fourth, finance is not a necessity for Groups, as a room can usually be obtained free or for a nominal amount. The cost of tea and coffee can be defrayed by those attending paying on the night. Some Groups might avoid money matters altogether and be content to stay as small local Groups. However, where there is to be funding, management means more than taking care of money. It can involve a strict accounting of money with adequate and proper financial systems. To obtain charitable status requires a written constitution and a Board of Management, so application can be made for funding from local authorities or charitable bodies.

Fifth, it should be noted that funding gives the Group greater resources and abilities to contact and help local people. It can also bring a different atmosphere to the Group. Members come for support and might well be quite uninterested in issues of management and financial control. They do not want to come to meetings where talk is about money matters. A common solution is to have separate meetings: one for those managing and one for those members who come simply for support. However, the result can be a split in the membership, and usually members who deal with the finances become more powerful. For those having to deal with drug use in the family, and feeling powerless in the face of the associated difficulties, having to deal with powerful Group members can reinforce their feelings of of powerlessness and inferiority. Part of the management of the Group involves balancing its support aim with the other needs that arise.

Finally, there can come a time when those involved in the financial matters will have a major say in Group affairs. In fact, they are likely to end up running the Group. This may demand so much of their time that they want paying for their trouble. If this happens, then there may be further tensions between those members who want to be paid and those who do not, or those who are paid and those who are not. Management has to attend to tensions that develop in the Group and to decide how the Group can resolve them.

FOUNDING GROUP MEMBERS

Carrying out the planning

Often Support Groups are started by one or two people; they begin in a very small way. The job that confronts the founders seems quite simple: they have to set up the Support Group. Yet what happens at these early stages sets the pattern for later developments, so thought should be given to all relevant aspects.

For instance, founders have to try and get support for themselves, at least until the Group meetings begin. This may not prove so easy. Group founders are often people of strong personality, who see others needing help but not themselves. Also, it is easy for them to get caught up in the demands of forming the Group and this can divert them from thinking about what is happening in relation to the Group and themselves. Indeed, part of the way they alleviate their anxiety and concern is by burying themselves in the business of setting up the Group.

Personal agendas of the founders

People decide to start Drug Support Groups for many reasons. Some parents want to do something because they discover a son is taking drugs, or a daughter has died from a drug overdose, or perhaps a close friend who used to take drugs has died of AIDS. Some relatives are angry that there seems to be a lack of services for drug users; others resent there being so little help for themselves. Whatever the reason for wanting to start a Support Group, the founders should look at themselves and acknowledge their own motives and needs. Founders have to ask themselves whether the Group is directed mainly towards their own needs, or whether it is sufficiently open and flexible for others to join. Even if such openness has been agreed, what actually takes place may be rather different. If friends are invited along, then a cliquish Group might be formed, making the inclusion of outsiders more difficult.

Founders and consultation

To help founding members of a Group, an outside person can be used in a consultative capacity. This person would not take any part in the meetings, but would act as a helper to the founders. The role might be twofold. It could involve enabling the founder members to acknowledge what has already been achieved amd providing positive feedback – necessary in the initial stages when there may be difficulties in getting the Group off the ground. The other task would be to help the founding members to direct their attention to the different areas of work required to be done. Consultation can be done on an informal basis and is helpful in the Group's earliest stages.

Founders have high expectations and tend to want to do everything as quickly as possible. Getting them to take some time to relax, slow down, and reflect a while can be useful in the long term. Some of the self-inflicted pressure can be relieved if they realise that success is not the only consideration. They can permit themselves the idea of the Group taking longer to set up than expected; that self-imposed timetables can always be adjusted. Plans can be broadened, so starting up the Group is not the only consideration. In fact, founder members cannot provide everything that is required. They need other members with different skills, such as administration or dealing with finance. Also members with different qualities are helpful, being complementary to those already in the Group. Above all, the Group, which is so important to founding members, has to move from an individual to a group perspective, a necessary but not always easy step.

GROUP COMPOSITION

Initial thoughts

Who comes to Group meetings will largely be defined by the Group aim and objectives, though it is always worth discussing specific terminology and criteria. If we mention partners then what is meant by this term? Do they have to live with each other, and for how long? And what happens if their relationship to the drug user ends, so they are no longer in contact with drug users? Similarly, if we talk of family members, then what is the definition of family? And are different generations to be invited, for example, children, partners, parents and grandparents? Although the process of definition was mentioned earlier, it is increasingly important to continue the process, so that all members have a clear and shared idea of the Group and its functioning. As long as there is clarity, then the Group can begin to take shape.

Special consideration might have to be given to the partners of drug users who want to come to the Group. They are younger than the parents present, more closely involved with drug users, and may be at some degree of risk of taking drugs themselves (Taylor et al., 1966). If they start to take drugs, this has implications with regard to entry criteria and continuance in the Group.

The question of cannabis use by Group members is one that is often ignored or left unresolved. It is an illegal drug but one that is fairly widely used. How members see that use and how they think others will see it, may vary between Groups. This problem has no 'right' answer, but should be debated and decisions taken as to how the Group should react.

Group size

A paramount task for founding members is to get others to join the Group, thus little consideration is given to what would be the optimum group size. In practice, if an intimate Group meeting is required, then five to eight members is a good number. This does not mean the Group itself should be confined to a maximum of eight, as not all members are likely to attend at any one time. In fact the maximum group number can usefully be placed at twelve to fourteen. More than eight members at a meeting increases the likelihood of subgroups forming, which might present difficulties (Hartford, 1971). The minimum number of the Group should be kept at around eight; thus if two or three members do not come to a meeting it is still viable. In a meeting of four or less, the small size can become an issue, detracting from other personal concerns.

The advantage of the small Group meeting is that it is possible to have easy eye contact with everyone present, for feelings of intimacy to occur, and for all those present to have the chance to talk. As will be shown, this universal self-disclosure does increase trust in the Group. In larger groups, the number of active speakers declines (Stephan and Misler, 1952) and a small functional group of core members emerges. This can produce difficulties, causing the rest of the group to become less participatory. Generally, the larger the group size, the more likely it is to be dominated by one person (McGrath, 1984), a factor that mitigates against a democratic and sharing group.

Sexual composition

Another issue is whether the Group should be single sexed or not. Some women, especially those who have been abused in the past, find it difficult to speak openly in the presence of men. However, as the Support Group is a family group, my feeling is that a mixed group is best, with the proviso that there is a greater number of women. This allows their empowerment in the Group (Davis and Proctor, 1989). In fact, the usual difficulty is not excluding men but trying to get them to come to Support Groups, so rules of composition need not be devised too early.

The Group founders also have to work out whether they are reinforcing stereotypes by arranging that referrals will be more likely to favour one class of persons. For instance, are women being favoured against men, reinforcing the stereotypes of men being uncaring and of women being family carers? Are men asked to come to the Group with sufficient persistence? Often a wife will say that her husband would not come and the matter is left there, without bothering to involve him further. Or do the founders accept the reply of fathers that there is no need for them to attend if their wife will be going? My own reaction is to stress that both parents are important and both are welcome to attend. The matter should not be pressed, and the couple should be allowed to decide who comes to the meeting. Also, the fact that only one partner comes to the meeting might reflect an uneven marital relationship, and trying to get both to come to the Group might be unhelpful all round.

Men in Support Groups

As mentioned, involving fathers and male partners has always been difficult where there is drug use in the family (Wermuth and Scheidt, 1986), and this is in part a result of their reaction to the family drug use. But mainly it is the product of the differently perceived roles of men and women, and fathers and mothers, combined with the degree to which they can talk about themselves and their feelings.

Role differentiation starts at an early age, and women are accustomed to self-disclosure (Youniss and Smollar, 1985). Men continue to maintain their male or macho image, so they are much more concerned about possible negative consequences of talking about feelings (Petronio and Martin, 1986). The situation is aggravated in that women also tend to view men as better adjusted if they do not self-disclose, whereas women are seen as being better adjusted if they do talk about themselves (Chelune, 1976). The outcome is that it tends to be assumed that men are not interested in talking about their feelings and being self-disclosing (Derlega et al., 1985).

There is a case for trying to get fathers along to Support Group meetings, though this may not be easy. It may also be that such involvement is assumed to be difficult and therefore it is not even seriously attempted. The Group is not immune from such perceptions, and may even think male attendance to be unimportant (cf. Satir, 1967).

What can also be difficult at times is a man being in a Group that is otherwise all women; the reverse can happen but I have not come across any examples in Support Groups. For a lone man to attend a Support Group can be interpreted by some people as an undermining of his male identity, and this can become an issue in itself (McNab, 1990). When changing from a single sex group to a mixed group, it might be useful to wait for two men to agree to come and then their gender might be less of an inhibiting issue. However, practicalities tend to act against such plans, as getting two men to come to a Group at the same time is very difficult to arrange.

General variations in composition

The same consideration can be said for gay men and lesbians coming to a Group of heterosexuals, ethnic minority members coming to a white Group, or young members coming to a Group with older members. This does not mean that there should not be mixed Groups, merely that their composition and any attendant feelings should be acknowledged. It is helpful if the Group is not completely homogeneous as this results in a lack of dynamism, while too heterogeneous a Group means that the differences get in the way and there are not enough commonalities (Bertcher and Maple, 1977).

Preferred composition

Usually the number of persons coming to a Support Group is low, so there is no real choice as to who comes. However, the question of composition is still relevant, because referring bodies often ask whether there are criteria for admission to the Group. There is also a possible hidden agenda here, as agencies or organisations that take anyone are seen as being unselective, even unprofessional. This can result in few or no referrals being made to the Group.

The Support Group should have an agreed approach. The admission of people to the Group should depend on their having an illegal drug user in the family, rather than trying to say who will or will not benefit from help. Of course, the aim is that all members will be supported and will benefit, but the Group aim has to be distinguished from Group admission. It is not the role of Group members to decide who they would prefer or who they think would benefit most. Generally, I would suggest that there are criteria for people likely to benefit less than others from Groups (Fink, 1981). The criteria are:

1. Persons who are strongly self-centred.
2. Persons with very rigid personalities.

3. Persons who relate only on an intellectual plane.
4. Persons who are over-controlled.
5. Persons who lack insight.
6. Persons who see the drug use as the only possible problem.

Such people are not candidates for rejection but should be seen as a challenge. It might be easier for groupworkers to insist on working with the potentially more receptive parents and partners, but there are ethical reservations about denying support to some applicants and not others. There are also practical reservations in that once a Group is seen as refusing admission then its whole image changes, and it may no longer be seen as supportive. The difficulty at times is getting other organisations and persons to recognise that the Support Group's strength is that it does take all applicants.

Open or closed Groups

One important consideration is whether the Group is to be open, new members being allowed to join and to leave when they choose. Alternatively, the Group might be closed, having a fixed membership and timespan. The separate natures of closed and open Groups result in a different dynamic to their functioning. Closed Groups take on a greater intensity as they operate without the disruption of members entering or leaving, causing a regression in members' progress. However, at the end of the Group's time, members have to be self-supporting if they do not want to revert to their former unsupported situation. For this reason Support Groups are usually open.

Practical considerations of open and closed Groups

Although open Groups have the disruption of members joining and leaving the Group, this can be turned into an advantage. Members can learn from the experience of new beginnings and endings, and having to deal with change and the difficulties of loss. Another advantage of open Groups is that the throughflow of members does bring a greater amount of differing experiences, perceptions and possible action options. However, this throughflow can also lead to there being new members and 'old hands', which may lead to the latter forming a subgroup.

The Groups with which I have been associated have been open, a reflection in part of the many problems of the members and their long-term nature, requiring members be supported over a long time. Also, because Support Groups have links with the local community, the closed Group would not be appropriate if people were excluded.

Time and frequency of meetings

The frequency of the Group meetings is best decided on a provisional basis, but an initial fortnightly rate is reasonable. At first, members will have difficulties and crises they want to unload, to talk about, and see a lot of meetings as necessary. However, once much of this initial anxiety has been reduced through coming to two or three meetings, the need for so many meetings becomes less. However, it can be difficult for new Groups to negotiate a reduction in meetings at such an early stage, so the high rate of meetings continues with possible absences. Accordingly, it is preferable to start off with a low frequency of meetings. This allows members sufficient time to absorb what has taken place at a meeting. Too many meetings allow a greater expression of feelings and experiences, but allow less to be taken in and acted on. Also, very frequent meetings can build up a degree of dependency, where attendance is more important than quality and outcome. Having many sessions seems to be a legacy of highly reinforcing treatment (Palazzoli, 1980), and such control is unnecessary in Support Groups. Of course, the Group can always discuss the frequency of meetings after a few months to decide whether it should be altered.

The time and the day of the meetings usually has to be juggled to suit the potential first Group members. Evening and weekend meetings do allow those who are working to come along. However, the fact is that no day or time will necessarily suit everyone, so some potential members will not be able to come to the Group. For this reason the founders should think of alternative help that could be offered to such people. Offering support and then not being able to provide it, for whatever reason, can be unsettling.

The length of the meeting is best set at an hour and a half. Some Groups run for much longer than this, but the ability of anyone to concentrate fully for longer, even with a break for coffee or tea, has to be doubted. What can happen in over-long meetings is that they become repetitive, the talk tends to go round in circles, and members begin to feel frustrated.

Venue

The venue for meetings may be seen in ideal terms, but what tends to happen is that the Group founders have to settle for whatever is available. Nevertheless, some points are worth considering despite a possible lack of options.

The venue should be accessible, and should be on a bus route. Adequate lighting outside the building where meetings are held is helpful; this can become an issue in mid-winter, when going home in the dark can be intimidating.

The actual accommodation for meetings should be capable of ensuring confidentiality, which means no interruptions from people coming in or from phone calls. However, a telephone on site is useful, so members can phone to say if they have been delayed in coming to a meeting. The accommodation should be comfortable: poor accommodation reflects a lack of importance accorded not only to the meetings but also to the members as well, to parents and partners who have to live with drug use in the family. Moreover, a homely feel to the meeting-place is beneficial for any Family Support Group.

Endings

It might seem strange to consider the topic of the ending of a Group before it has even started, but it links up with that of open and closed groups. In practice, Group members often have difficulty in thinking about endings, as so much emotional investment is put into keeping the Group going. However, we also have to be aware that Groups do end or fade away, or they change their remit to ensure continued existence.

There are two points to be considered. First, Groups can usefully extend their working life by careful planning, and this can include building in breaks. Just as working people have holidays, so the whole Group can benefit from having occasional short breaks from the meetings. This allows members to regain energy, gives them time to absorb what has been said in the meetings and avoids personal dependency on the Group. Such breaks might result in people not coming back to the meetings, but this has to be seen as a positive development. The intention is that members are supported and are able to deal with family difficulties. If they can do this outside the Group, so much the better.

Having short breaks in a Group does introduce another dynamic, that of mild separation anxiety. Concern about ending results in members feeling under some pressure and they are more likely to produce new material in the meetings. On the other hand, the breaks should not be too long as all members tend to have concerns about possible loss, and these can be unduly intensified by a long break.

REFERRAL SYSTEM

The system

A referral system, which brings in members to the Group, should be devised as early as possible, as without one there is likely to be a lack of Group success. With any established open Group, there is likely to be a slow decline in numbers over time. If members leave and are not replaced, the loss of membership can become a preoccupation to the exclusion of other matters.

The referral system is aimed to secure new members but it should also promote the advantages of the Group, not just as a resource but as a resource that can be of use both to clients and to professional helpers. For instance, the most prized referrals are self-referrals, those affected by illegal drug use who decide to come to the Group themselves. What is offered to these potential members is the chance to feel good again, to obtain relevant information, to gain greater control over their lives, and to put an end to persistent feelings of isolation and hopelessness. Now it might seem surprising in a service that is meant to be client-led, that immediate reference is not made to what clients want. However, what is often wanted initially by potential members is an end to drug use in the family. Yet for the Group to make such a promise would be fundamentally unrealistic and dishonest, as there is no way it can stop the illegal drug use. So, from the very beginning, from the initial referral, a move is made to change perceptions to ensure that real support will be forthcoming.

The main source of self-referrals comes from word of mouth, so members have to be conscious of what benefits come from the Group, and this includes not only the regular meetings but also all the other relevant matters. There has to be an informal and fast response service. The visiting of potential new members by existing

Group members can allay anxiety, and the accompaniment of recruits to their initial meeting can ease entry into the Group.

Referrals from professional agencies

Many referrals might be expected from agencies and professional helpers, especially as they often complain of overwork and excessive caseloads. When seen, professional workers and helpers are sympathetic to the aims of Support Groups. They will often allow the Group's advertising to be left on the premises and they do promise to refer clients to the Group. Unfortunately, this rarely happens.

Some agencies such as health centres are reluctant to refer patients to a non-professional agency or even bring the patient's attention to the Group, seeing such referrals as being unprofessional. Even more importantly, however, is the fact that the medical way of thinking, the underlying medical paradigm, consists of linking symptoms with organic causes, and then treating and counteracting those causes. So if the cause of the members' problem is illegal drug use, then the cure lies with treating the drug user. Those affected by drug use are of passing interest only. This does not mean doctors are unsympathetic to parents and partners affected by drug use; they will treat their symptoms of severe anxiety and associated medical conditions. But the drug use and the anxiety, being related to different patients, are treated as being quite separate.

There are different theoretical approaches to helping people. This means there is a possibility of misunderstanding between adherents of the different methods. Moreover, mutual misunderstanding can lead to unhelpful attitudes and behaviour if either is unprepared to accept the other's approach.

Further misunderstandings

Differences and misunderstandings can also extend to the Group's remit and criteria for referral. Outside agencies have their own ideas as to the aims and nature of Support Groups, and who can or should attend. This means that the Group has to be sure to compose a brief guide to referrals for the benefit of outside agencies. In addition, face-to-face meetings can defuse a lot of anxiety and other feelings that might exist on both sides.

One feature of drug use treatment is that professional workers can try to privatise their patients or clients, and refuse the assistance of other helpers. This may not be obvious as it may be covered up by an expressed appreciation of the work done by others, even by Family Support Groups – yet there are never any referrals. This can mislead Groups who fondly expect referrals, who hear statements like, 'Yes, Mrs Smith could do with some support. I'll get her to contact you when she is feeling a bit better', or, 'I don't think Mrs Smith would be interested, but I'll put it to her.' The professional worker acts as gatekeeper and can stop further access to help or present help in such a way that it is likely to be turned down.

Rather than reacting against such behaviour, the Group has to look and see whether there may not be good reasons why the professional worker is being so negative. Unfortunately, inter-agency disagreements and conflicts do occur and the Group should always be tactful in its dealings, whatever the situation. Non-cooperation may reflect feelings that the Group is unprofessional, that too many helpers are already involved with the client or patient, or that the Group will not be of any help. When dealing with professionals it can be helpful indirectly to mention possible difficulties (for the professionals!) to ease the passage: 'I just wondered if there were any patients in the practice who might benefit from the Group. We have noticed that anxiety symptoms have been reduced by attendance and would appreciate it if this could be confirmed with your professional cooperation.' Alternatively, the role of gatekeeper has to be bypassed. This can be done by requesting professionals to pass on written information, including information about the Group, to possible members. The information sheet is given in a sealed envelope and handed over by the professional worker, thus maintaining the confidentiality of client or patient.

From the Group's point of view, there has to be an ongoing referral system and this does require being able to deal constructively with professional workers. This is useful in itself as professional workers are directly or indirectly part of the life of those affected by drugs; they might even be part of the problem. Thus the interaction of the Group and professionals has implications beyond that of mere referral.

Possible professional agency practice

Some agencies will refer patients or clients who do not fall within the Support Group's remit. Outside agencies may have a great many patients or clients requiring help and they may be tempted to offload the most persistent and irritating ones on to any agency willing to take them. And sometimes outside helpers simply do not know what to do about certain patients or clients and so refer them on. Support Groups still have to apply their normal admission criteria of members having a drug user in the family and being prepared to come to the Group, and both to give and to receive support. People are accepted into the Group as usual, however members may feel about the motives for the referral.

Difficulties of referral do not simply lie with outside agencies. Sometimes agencies are reluctant to refer because they see the Support Group as having poor rule enforcement; and they may be correct. So Support Groups should look to themselves and be responsible without compromising their own aim, nature and integrity. There are likely to be differences between the Group and other agencies, and members have to be aware of them. For example, the rules of confidentiality between the Group and a particular agency may be different. What has to be borne in mind is that both want the best for the members or clients involved; this is the basis of any understanding. Then the different aims and objectives have to be related to those rules. Support Groups have to respect other agencies just as much as they respect their own members – provided other agencies keep to their rules.

The last point about differences between helping bodies or agencies points to ways of improvement. In particular, the referral system needs constant servicing. There should be occasional but regular meetings of some Group members with those from a potential referring agency. This should be known to all Group members and the limits of confidentiality set and observed. In practice, being able to talk anonymously is reassuring for both parties and helps to break down agency barriers to the betterment of client services.

Finally, no one should expect referrals to be a one-way process. For instance, if the Group never makes a referral to an agency, then there is little chance of getting a referral in return. If a referral is made to the Support Group and there is no feedback, even if only to say the person is now attending, then, again further referrals are unlikely.

Voluntary agency referrals

Referrals from other voluntary agencies are also difficult to obtain, but for different reasons to those applicable to professional agencies. The concerns of voluntary bodies may be mainly about increasing the Support Group's numbers and so increasing the likelihood of its obtaining finance – to the possible detriment of the referring agency. In fact, voluntary agencies sometimes see themselves in direct competition with each other and behave accordingly, rather than attending to what is best for their clients or members.

For this reason, good relationships should be encouraged between voluntary bodies. Joint meetings and joint work can go towards cementing those good relationships.

Advertising

Advertising is a somewhat underrated feature of providing help for clients, so it usually receives little consideration. However, if persons locally do not know of the service, then the service is failing them. As to the form of such advertising, then the following suggestions may apply:

1. The form of the advertising reflects the service agency, so spending money to produce a professional product is important.

2. Initially the lack of money will preclude professional work. Rather than relying on the Group's amateur efforts, it might be better to get semi-professional help, such as students from the local Art College. This may go towards producing a product that will not seem embarrassing after a few months.

3. Care should be taken with putting up advertising, which should be done with permission and should be checked at regular intervals, as posters may be torn down. Potential referring staff should be asked how advertisements could be made more effective, a way of making them more interested in the Group. Also, if new notices are used to replace old ones, then all old copies should be taken down.

4. Consideration should be given as to the best place to put advertising notices, including the likely time they will last in situ. Such information can be gained from the periodic checking of the notices.

Other forms of advertising

As noted, word of mouth is the most effective way of recruiting new members, followed by referral from agencies which are part of a proper referral system. Advertisements in local papers, usually free if connected to an accompanying article about the service, are less effective but are still worth the effort. Advertisements on local radio and spots on local television can also be obtained free, and can be effective. As a rule, if a free spot is given in one medium then this excludes free spots in other media, so advertising should be planned as an overall package.

THE REFERRAL PROCESS

General considerations – commitment

If a person is referred by an agency, then that person must be seen by a Group member to ensure he or she really is thinking about coming for support, has not been pushed into the idea, and does not have serious reservations. It should be remembered that those in need can be vulnerable, and very open to suggestion, and may have unrealistic expectations of the Group.

The first requirement is that the person shows some commitment to the idea of the Support Group, and both the receiving and the giving of support. The giving of support is something the potential Group member may not be capable of delivering at first, but it is important that the giving of support is known to be an expectation.

The client's expectations should also be checked out. Sometimes it is difficult for new members to accept that the support is for them and not for drug users. Often members will have spent years trying to help the drug user and the rest of the family, and so the idea of help for themselves comes as a radical change.

Further commitment to the Group comes through regular attendance at Group meetings. Even if members feel that they are not in any special need of support, they should attend to support others. The act of attending and listening to others is itself very supportive.

Confidentiality

The subject of confidentiality should be raised and the rules of the Group explained. It is worth taking a bit of time in this matter, as non-professional people do not always have a good understanding of what confidentiality means, even though confidentiality is necessary to make the task of talking to strangers, to other members in the Group, easier. A copy of the rules of the Group, including those relating to confidentiality, should be left with all new members.

Other factors

It may be worth asking potential Group members whether they have received any help in the past. Generally, the answer is negative, but the question can be worthwhile; if they have been helped they may expect the same kind of help from the Group. Alternatively, they may have bad memories of previous assistance. Knowing the situation allows misapprehensions to be corrected and acknowledgement made of past difficulties. Also it is a good idea to point out that there are limitations to the help that can be given, and some of these limitations come from Group members. What they are likely to get out of the Group is directly related to what they contribute to it.

Potential members can ask about the Group in general terms, but specific information is confidential. Asking whether the Group is a mixed-sex group is quite legimate. Asking whether a named person attends the Group is not a question that will get a direct answer. However, it is worth saying that any new member might meet one or more people they already know in the Group. This might be taken as good or bad, often depending who the members are.

Partners

If there are partners to potential new Group members, their feelings about the Group are worth investigating. Often husbands will insist that going to support groups is 'women's work' and will not come themselves. I always make it plain that partners are very welcome to come along and this minimises any suspicion as to what might be going on. Even if partners do not attend, it is helpful if members feel they have their support. Sometimes the idea of a 'partners' day', when partners can come along, can be helpful.

Admission to group

Whether a person is asked to come to the Group depends on whether the person really wants to come, agrees to abide by all the Group rules, and falls within the Group criteria. As long as both the person and the Group will potentially benefit from the new member, then the candidate should be admitted. The procedure with some Groups is that such decisions are left with existing members. They see the person and discuss whether he or she should be admitted. This is intimidating for new members and seems far too judgemental a method. Only those cases which are debatable need be referred to the Group, and these are very unlikely to occur. However, cases of serious mental illness, for example, might be referred to another agency as this might be more appropriate.

Also to be decided is who sees potential Group members. This can be done in rotation by the members, or one or two people may be given the responsibility. As all people wanting to come to the Group tend to be accepted, who actually sees new recruits first is less important than the process being well done.

In conclusion, any referral should be done as quickly as possible. As people approach Support Groups often at times of crisis, their idea of what constitutes a reasonable period to wait for acceptance into the group is likely to be a very short time. Any referring agency should be informed in writing of the accepted referral or alternative arrangements.

Coming to the group

Coming to the Group for the first time can be very intimidating. One couple I know of went seven times to the building where the meetings took place before managing to walk over the threshhold, so having a Group member to accompany new members on their first time is helpful and supportive. New members should be reminded just before the meeting that they can take their time, and that they do not have to speak. And of course formal introductions will be made to ease the passage of entry.

3 FACILITATION

GENERAL INTRODUCTION

Whether members receive adequate support from the Group depends on its functioning. Getting people together with little in common, except having an illegal drug user in the family, does not ensure they will be supported. The Group has to function usefully. This requires that members feel safe, surrounded by trust, and then they are able to learn more easily and comfortably about themselves and drug use in the family. They can feel the warmth of positive feelings, and can express their feelings and let go of their anxiety.

This requires structure to be introduced. There also has to be an ability to deliver a quality service. Group members have to be aware of what sort of service is being provided, be capable of assessing it and ensuring the Group aim is being achieved. This sounds a heavy demand for ordinary people, but it can be done. In fact, Comstock (1982) noted that some self-help groups were more supportive and effective than professionally led therapy groups. So the aim must be to ensure that all self-help groups exhibit such effectiveness.

GROUPS AND FACILITATION

Introduction

However much men and women want to help each other, it does not follow that they will do so. In fact, any form of personal help can be potentially harmful, either to the helpers or to those being helped. Just as no one would trust themselves to an untrained doctor, so Group members have a right to feel concerned about being helped by those who have an incomplete understanding and lack technical skills in what they are doing.

Of course, Group members are likely to have some group understanding and skills, as all of us belong to groups even if only a family. Such expertise can be increased with training, and this is needed for reasons both practical and ethical.

The need for expertise

Often, Support Groups spring up but do not last very long. The length of survival is to some degree a measure of how well-run they are. Although the aims of those starting up Support Groups are well meant, knowledge of working with groups finally outweighs good intentions (Hinrickson et al., 1985). For this reason, my inclination is to advise Groups to use someone who is experienced and knowledgeable about groupwork: they should use a facilitator. It should be added that many self-help groups do welcome professional participation in groups (Lieberman, 1990), and such participation has been found to be helpful (Borman, 1982).

However, there is often a fear that professionals will take over self-help groups, a fear not unfounded in the light of what has happened in the United States with regard to Drug Rehabilitation Projects (Mowrer, 1984). Concerned people set up helping groups, then professionals take them over and get paid to run them. So there are deep concerns about professional workers having anything to do with self-help groups. Not only do these professionals not meet the usual membership criteria, but also their training and professional values make them more inclined to interpret the Group as one for treatment rather than self-help (Katz and Hermalin, 1978). This means that any professional helper must not only be unprejudiced and non-judgemental, but aware of existing professional attitudes and beliefs, such as the therapeutic perspective (Wills, 1978), which is inapplicable to work with Support Groups.

How to use professional help

In what capacity and role may professionals be used by the Group? An indirect role (Comstock, 1982) or a non-directive role seems most appropriate. This does not mean the professional helper joins in a laissez-faire regime, as this is likely to be unhelpful (Lindenfield and Adams, 1984). The helper has to be active, but not directive.

The reaction of most Groups is likely to be positive towards professional help, just as long as it really does help the Group to be what it wants to be (Levy, 1982). However, for those Groups that have reservations, there are other possible assistance resources such as the tapes available from the California Self-help Center at University College, Los Angeles. Although the idea of professional help or facilitation will be described, it should not necessarily be assumed that facilitated Groups are better than self-directed Groups (Coyne,

1974). Nevertheless, provided there is a bond between Group and facilitator, professional help brings considerable benefit.

Facilitators

Facilitators are experienced groupworkers whose role in Groups is to make them run efficiently and usefully for the members. The facilitator is an outside person who can take a more detached view of the Group; a person who understands its functioning, who can increase the interaction of members, who has ultimate responsibility of keeping the group to its aim and objectives, ensures ground rules and safety are maintained, and takes care that no one becomes emotionally damaged.

Facilitators have overall responsibility for the building of trust in the Group, of honest interactions and useful work, and the working through of issues. They should be a guarantee of quality work being done during the meetings.

Facilitators and leadership

One of the difficulties of facilitation is that it is often confused with leadership. The founders of the Group feel they are being asked to give up their special position to an outsider. However, facilitation is for the good of the Group as a whole, helping the Group to run itself. As for leadership, there are two aspects to be considered.

Leaders are not born, but are people able to contribute to others in certain situations (Fiedler, 1967). As the situations change, so different leaders may arise. This applies to Support Groups, which change over time, thus allowing different members to take up the leadership role. In fact, there can be more than one leader in the Group and this can reflect the separate needs of members. One member might lead the tasks of the Group and another member might satisfy the feelings and relationship demands (Bales, 1958). Both the facilitator and the rest of the Group have to accept and come to terms with the fact that facilitation and leadership in Support Groups not only are different but should be different.

Choice of facilitator

The choice of facilitators is important as they should be sympathetic to and identify with the Group's aim and objectives, be prepared to adhere to the Group norms and have groupwork expertise. All of these requirements will help in getting the best from facilitation (Hollander, 1982). It is not essential that the facilitator knows much about the likely subject matter of the Group, for example, drugs or HIV, as members can provide their own expertise. However, relevant knowledge by the facilitator may well prove helpful. To some extent, facilitators become a model of behaviour, so they can help to set not only the tone but also the identity of the Group.

Unfortunately, facilitators for self-help Support Groups are not common, so there is a certain lack of choice at present. This lack of choice can result in a few people doing a lot of facilitation, and it is worth finding out what other work the facilitator does; too much facilitation can turn the work into a professional routine with consequent loss of quality. To counteract possible poor work, the best plan is to have facilitators on six-month probationary contracts with a final review to decide on a possible renewal of contract.

The facilitator and the Group

From the very beginning it is important that there is a clear understanding of the nature of the facilitator's role in the Support Group. The facilitator is part of the Group meetings but not part of the Group. There is a balance to be maintained between being distant and taking up a 'professional' role, and that of behaving like the Group members. This detachment extends to all facilitator dealings, whether in meetings or not. The facilitator has to be even-handed as regards the Group functioning and be very aware of the facilitator's role.

For instance, those who have been members for a long time tend to try and form alliances with the facilitator which, if permitted, can distort the Group's functioning. To prevent this happening, the facilitator has to keep a slight distance, as this gives space to allow a tactful adjustment of relationships.

Disadvantages of facilitation

There are disadvantages in employing outside facilitators in Support Groups in that they might not have someone close who is affected by drug use. This somewhat alters the nature of the Groups, which were set up on the understanding that all those attending the meetings should possess this admission criterion. On the other hand, this

lack of personal experience does allow a degree of emotional detachment, and an ability not to take sides in Group debates but to work
towards solutions. This detachment or neutrality can be annoying at
times to members who expect backing when they are 'in the right',
but in time it gives a feeling of reassurance. There is someone in the
Group who will not be overwhelmed by feelings, someone who can
act as an anchor and bring stability to members who might feel that
their life is very chaotic.

Another potential problem is that employing a facilitator
introduces an expert into the Group who can exert considerable
influence, if not power. This goes against the basic approach of
self-help. However, the facilitator is only an expert in groupwork, not in the family aspects of drug use. Here the rest of
the group are the experts.

Facilitation, leadership and payment

The fear of the facilitator becoming the leader in the Group can be
minimised if care is taken to delineate the aims and expectations
of facilitation. The latter is done by both the facilitator and the
Group, so mutual expectations can be satisfied. It should be
pointed out that devolving power and not becoming the leader of
the Group is part of the facilitator's remit and expertise.

Finally, facilitators are professional persons who are likely to be
paid for their work, and the Group might have to pay. In voluntary
groups the presence of a person who is paid for attendance, while
members are not, can be a source of resentment. However, being
paid means the facilitator has to attend and this does introduce
desirable reliability into the Group, which is essential for members
with very low self-esteem who are accustomed to rejection and do
not really believe that the rest of the Group wants them. It should
be added that the question of payment does introduce difficulties,
but as the Group grows over the years some members of the
group may also get paid. In practice, financing of the Group should
include a facilitation budget, which is seen as a necessary com-
ponent of proper Group management.

The disadvantages of having a facilitator in the Group can be
minimised and may indeed be minimal. However there are likely
to be disadvantages, even if they are not apparent or mentioned.
This means some work should be given to reviewing facilitation
and for difficulties to be made known and discussed.

OVERALL FACILITATION

Introduction

Facilitation is generally invested in an outside groupworker but one of the members or even the Group as a whole can carry out the task. My preference is for a professional facilitator to do the work and it has been assumed that this will be the plan, but it does not have to be the case.

The overall facilitation has been divided into:

1. General nature of facilitation
2. Theory
3. Chairing
4. Skills
5. Understanding
6. Controls
7. Group safety
8. Reviews
9. Support

GENERAL NATURE OF FACILITATION

Professional facilitation

Initially members come to the Group meetings and talk about their own past experiences in relation to drug use in the family. They can express their feelings and everyone begins to feel better. However, after this initial rush of feelings which have stayed unexpressed for so long, there can come a slowing down, almost a halt. The Group seems to lose its way and members cast around for direction.

The facilitator can help the Group find its way, look more closely at what is happening in the meetings, help members expand the accounts of their individual situations at home, and increase members' understanding of themselves and what might be happening at home. By having a facilitator, the Group can largely avoid the meetings becoming repetitive, shallow or unduly negative.

Nature of facilitation

Facilitators have to work on a variety of levels, and this is not easy. It is even more difficult for ordinary Group members to work in such a way, while having to deal simultaneously with their own concerns.

One level at which the facilitator operates is that of the actual content of what is being said, and listening to Group members. This is the level or area involving all members and there is the danger that the facilitator may become engrossed in what is being said, instead of listening both to the content and to the nature of that content. This requires trying to identify the various members' attitudes and beliefs, and relating them to the difficulties those members are experiencing. In addition, the facilitator assesses the quality of communication as exhibited in the meeting, both speaking and listening.

Facilitators have to observe members' non-verbal language; what is being communicated but not said. This is important as people can control what they are saying, but find it much more difficult to control their physical gestures – their body language. The truth of a person's feelings may be revealed at times more obviously through physical reactions than through speech.

Interactions in the Group – who tends to talk to whom – are also of interest. In particular, note whether any member is being excluded or being scapegoated, or whether a member or small group of members is dominating or controlling the Group. These can be counterproductive, make mutual support more difficult to achieve and may even be damaging for members.

Facilitators have to have a feel for what is happening to the Group as a whole, its stage of development and how the Group as a whole is feeling. At times there can be general feelings such as frustration, anger or depression, and it is important that these are identified so that appropriate measures can be taken.

How the members are reacting towards the facilitator in the Group is also of interest. This is not just a matter of what is said, as little may be said directly, it is also a matter of how members are reacting and what feelings the facilitator is picking up from them.

What happens is that facilitators move in and out of these different levels, a task requiring great concentration. As a result, facilitators seldom have time to relax; the job is very demanding and draining. Indeed, my preference is not to come to the Group straight after other work, but to make time for myself before meetings to prepare, and afterwards to take time to wind down.

All of this points to the difficulty of any member, when hampered with personal worries, trying to facilitate the Group.

Facilitation and power

Although facilitation and groupwork are both forms of working in Groups, members should be clear as to the difference. Facilitators have to allow members to exert power as people in their own right and to take responsibility for themselves. This requires facilitators not taking power for themselves: they have to give power back to the Group. This is often equated with being non-directive, the facilitator not telling Group members what they should do. In fact, much more is involved. Many groupworkers imagine that they are being non-directive and are not acting as leaders, whereas the opposite is true. Training in groupwork can make a person better able to understand what is happening in groups. It can also make workers want to change things for the better, and this can lead to being directive.

The difference between groupwork and facilitation may be seen in an example quoted by Edelwich and Brodsky (1992) in their book *Group Counseling for the Resistant Client*. The following extract comes from the counsellor who is wearing a three-piece suit, whereas the other group members were either in work uniforms or casually dressed. The group counsellor reacts to a question about his suit:

> Good question. Some of you have uniforms; well, this is my uniform for my daytime job, from which I come directly to group. I wouldn't necessarily put on a suit like this for group, but I could, and so could you. It doesn't violate any of our expectations here to wear a three-piece suit. Does anyone else feel the same way about it? I'm asking for feedback now. Is this so important? Is my suit the issue here? (p. 45)

This directive approach may be admissible in group counselling but it is definitely not appropriate in facilitation. The extract represents the unconscious assumption of power – represented by the suit. Everything that follows is a justification for the possession of power and the counsellor ends by being quite aggressive. A more facilitative reply to the question might have been: 'You're right, John, I am the only one in a suit here! I wonder how everyone feels about that fact. John is a bit uneasy about it, so I am wondering if the rest of you have feelings about it.'

The point is that the facilitator, like everyone else, is allowed to make mistakes, to be wrong or insensitive. This means there is no point in being defensive or having to be self-justifying. The Group exists not for the facilitator but for everyone present, which means mainly the members. What the facilitator has to do is to build up credit with the group (Hollander, 1958), and this comes through the work done, even if the work is studied non-intervention. In the Group, attention is as much on the facilitator as a person as on the facilitator's role.

Accordingly, facilitators should monitor and vary their roles to avoid behaviour that is unhelpful to Group functioning. By being non-directive, being aware of what is happening in the meeting and getting honest feedback, facilitators minimise potential drawbacks and substantially increase the benefit of members being in the Group. Facilitators also have to be clear that being non-directive is a constant balancing act, an active process. For instance, giving advice is unhelpful, but making suggestions is acceptable (Sainsbury, 1975). Indeed, without the ability to make suggestions, the role of the facilitator would be minimal and largely redundant. It is not merely a matter of what is done; how it is done is equally important to the role.

The final point is that the facilitator should work towards apparent redundancy; for the Group to function with as little intervention as possible. This means that some of the functions of the facilitator, in time, should be identified, understood, and taken over by the members.

Facilitator intervention

To obtain a further insight into the nature of facilitation, it may be useful to look at the practice of intervention. Facilitators have the final responsibility with regard to Group functioning, but this does not mean that they should be directive and constantly intervene, however well intentioned such actions may seem. Rather they should hold off to let members intervene, thus avoiding dependence on the facilitator. All members should be brought into the Group process, and the facilitator should recognise that on occasions Group members themselves might be of more help in the meetings. Groups contain a multiplicity of different relationships, and any one of these can be the one which another member finds the most helpful.

'It was Donna who helped me the most the first evening.'
'But I hardly said anything!'

'You were listening, you were paying attention and I thought, there's someone who is sympathetic, someone I can talk to.'

Facilitators have to give members the opportunity to be active and to take ownership of their Group, even though ultimate responsibility lies with them. Naturally, this does not exclude members being responsible for themselves and for others: by accepting such responsibility they get full support for themselves. However, if it seems that Group members are not going to intervene then the facilitator may consider taking action. This is still a matter of judgement, of assessing whether anyone is going to intervene, whether members are leaving it up to the facilitator and whether a lack of intervention is going to be harmful. There are also the longer term considerations. Too frequent interventions will destroy the flow of the meeting and the provision of support. Insufficient necessary interventions can leave the Group anxious and less likely to take risks.

Facilitators and self-disclosure

Group meetings are set up for the support of the members, not the facilitator. Members talk about themselves, their feelings and thoughts, but the facilitator does not. The Group belongs to its members: the facilitator has no such ownership. There has to be an acknowledgement of such differences, which have to be worked through. Only then can work with the Group be carried out successfully. For example, the lack of facilitator self-disclosure has to be balanced by its effect on members. If the facilitator's silence and lack of self-disclosure become an issue in the group then appropriate self-disclosure is advantageous and not a drawback.

What does become clear is that facilitation involves a distinct and separate role. Group members cannot be expected to take up this role easily, even if they are trained, as they would then be moving forever between roles as facilitator and Group member. This would make effective work very difficult indeed.

THEORY

Introduction

The facilitator must have a consistent and coherent method of working with the Group. This requires adherence to a theoretical approach. Though an atheoretical approach has the advantage of the worker not being blinded by theory and so full of constructs that what is taking place is not properly observed, this assumes that there is a neutral stance in relation to human behaviour. In fact we all have to make some assumptions and rely on constructs to understand the world. So the task is to take on a theoretical approach, but one that is appropriate.

Choice of theory

The theoretical approach is chosen to be complementary to the aim and objectives of the Support Group. In broad terms we see three major characteristics of the Group.

1. It is not a therapy group. Its members are not ill and are not weak or failing in some way. They are merely coping with a situation that they find almost unmanageable

2. The Group should be empowering and this is hardly possible if the facilitator is directive. Members have to take responsibility for themselves, as they have to carry what they gain from the Group into their family life.

3. The Group should be mutually supportive, and this is made more difficult not only if the facilitator takes a central role, but also if there is a lack of acceptance and respect in the Group so other members do not seem worth supporting.

The logical choice is a Group person-centred approach, based on core qualities of empathy with the client, respect for the individual, people being themselves and not hiding behind a role or facade, and acceptance of people, whatever their past or present associated behaviour. The method is non-directive, empowering and relies on individual responsibility.

The person-centred approach is most often used in individual counselling, and it should be remembered that there is no simple transition from individual counselling to group facilitation; in fact some individual counsellors are not suited for the latter.

My own approach has been modified with regard to advice-giving. The usual practice would be to insist that advice is not given, that members have to suggest their own answers. However, there are two points that have to be considered. First, the person-centred approach is very much designed for individual counselling: it is not a group method, nor is it a support method. If members in the Group are giving each other advice this means that the Group is finding its own answers and being mutually supportive. In fact, even in counselling, clients find that making suggestions can be useful, despite theoretical expectations (Murphy et al., 1984; Elliott, 1985). There are times when members can be so overcome by grief or so highly anxious that they want someone to tell them what to do: they are incapable of making any decision for themselves. They might not take up any Group suggestion made, but they do feel supported, which is very much what they want at this juncture. Suggestions carry an affective as well as a cognitive message.

Specific theoretical areas

The person-centred approach also needs supplementation when dealing with drug use in the family. This approach is related very much to working with feelings, and there should be a proper balance. Human behaviour involves thoughts as well as feelings, so account must be taken of both aspects.

There are three areas which require special consideration: drug use, family dynamics and group dynamics, where experience and a theoretical overview are likely to be helpful. It is not necessary that Group members should take on theory, as it is used by the facilitator to isolate and identify what may be important events, thoughts, feelings or behaviour. How these are interpreted is the concern of the Group, which may include the facilitator, but they are not dependent on the theory used.

FACILITATION AND CHAIRING

Introduction

Facilitation has some similarities to the chairing of meetings. Indeed, in non-facilitated Groups one member often takes up a chairing role: this resembles facilitation to some extent, but there are aspects that differ.

Facilitative chairing is performed in a manner much more subdued than that of most chairpersons. As noted, interventions are made for the overall good of the Group and have to be finely judged. Interventions are more likely when a Group is newly started or is being facilitated for the first time. In this way, facilitation can set a model of a well functioning Group, a style which members can soon pick up. This in turn reduces the need for overt chairing.

Facilitators may or may not carry out certain duties and actions, but they have the responsibility of ensuring they are carried out. For example, meetings should have a formal beginning. Generally, there is some social chit-chat when members arrive. A formal beginning ends the social aspect and moves towards the business of Group support, discovering who is not at the meeting and relaying any apologies for absence. It is important to get the tone right, so the opening might be on the lines of: 'Well, we are all here except for Betty. I think she said last time she was going to be late tonight. Has everyone got their tea or coffee? Right, if you all agree, we will make a start.'

Important points in the meetings

There are points, incidents or stages in the meeting that require special attention, and for which the facilitator has the final responsibility. The formal opening is just one such point. The next step is to pick up any outstanding business from the previous meeting. As facilitator, my preference is to mention such business, as there is a tendency for members to be reluctant to introduce old concerns. Yet following through concerns to some sort of conclusion is a necessary aspect of work in the Group.

Behaviour in the meeting

Chairing in a facilitative way involves giving control to the Group as a whole. The facilitator is present to ensure each person can tell their story and be heard. There has to be appreciation for whatever has been said, as this shows respect for the individual.

So there has to be a measure of control where self-control is lacking. The Group is controlled to the extent that all members have their say and are allowed to mention things that might seem strange, outlandish, dubious or ridiculous. The facilitator is not there to judge but to encourage; not to say what is right but to enlarge the number of expressed thoughts and feelings. Members have to be allowed to say what they want to say, not what they think they should say. This requires structuring in the Group and control to promote freedom.

Personal anxiety and feelings can make orderly meetings

difficult at times. Some members are not accustomed to order and will interrupt others without thinking. Even worse, sometimes a person can be so anxious as to monopolise the floor, talk incessantly and prevent others from speaking. Usually, waiting for a gap in the flow and then asking others for their views is all that is required. However, there can be times when there is no gap and the rest of the Group becomes restless. The facilitator might have to force a way into the stream of talk and not wait until everyone is no longer listening.

Ordinary chairing involves merely the bringing to order of meetings, the sharing of information and the making of decisions. Facilitative chairing involves enabling members to learn from each other and from what is happening in the Group. The learning is then to be used not just in the meetings but also outside the Group. For these reasons, intervention should be gentle and to some degree explanatory in nature, so everyone can learn from it. At other times, intervention is very much a matter of putting points back to the Group. For instance, if a member keeps inter-rupting a lot, then the facilitator might remark: 'I get the feeling that this meeting is becoming very disjointed and bitty. I wonder if anyone else feels the same?' Alternatively, it might be more useful to put the question to the person who is interrupting, and say, 'Joan, you seem to be wanting to say a lot this session. I am wondering if there is something that is worrying you and if the Group can help.'

The facilitator can help by encouraging members to talk and giving them time. Sometimes a bit of patience is needed as members can be anxious and almost be overwhelmed by their feelings, or they need time to find the exact words to describe those feelings. A slowing down of the pace of the meeting can bring greater self-control and diminish anxiety, to the advantage of everyone.

Patterns of communication

Facilitators are likely to appear as powerful figures at first. Often questions will be directed towards them, or the Group will wait for the facilitator to pronounce on some topic or to give the final deciding word on the subject. This should be resisted. If asked a question, a facilitator should consider putting it back to the Group and asking what members think the answer is. At times, the facilitator will have to fight hard to resist pressure to lead the Group. Staring at the floor or avoiding the gaze of members can be one way of making members look to someone else, to make them take responsibility for themselves.

Regular patterns of communication soon spring up between members. In discussions one member may address what is said to everyone, but actually direct what is being said to one or two people in the Group. This is quite acceptable unless patterns become too fixed, and one or more members feel they are being excluded. This can often be remedied by asking the member who might feel excluded, how he or she feels about what has been said. This brings that person into focus in the Group, including the recent speaker, who may realise that a member was being excluded. Sometimes a stronger measure is required; perhaps a simple statement such as: 'John, I notice that when you speak, you usually speak to Iain.' The advantage of a simple statement is that it leaves matters open for John to say whatever he wants, and there is no criticism. This contrasts with the question: 'John, why do you usually speak to Iain?', which can be interpreted as criticism and puts pressure on John.

Further points

Everyone should be given their chance to speak at the meeting and be encouraged to do so, even if only for a short time. Sometimes very anxious members will want to speak and others may feel that what they have to say is less important, or even unworthy of comment. Not only are they not being supported, but the content of the Group can become distorted, giving the impression that the world has little more to offer than difficulties, crises and personal pain. Hearing that a member is doing well, that little has happened and that life can be relatively unexciting, is also of importance. The Group should not concentrate on disaster stories while ignoring improvements or the good aspects of life.

Of course, new members do not have to speak, but their presence needs to be acknowledged. For this reason a statement such as, 'Well, Irene, this is your first time. I hope it has been of some use ...', will give Irene the chance to say something neutral, or she may see it as an opportunity to join in and talk about her situation.

Sometimes members sit in a circle and turns are taken to talk about their situations by going round the circle. My feeling is that this is not always the best formula. Waiting for their turn to come can make members unduly anxious and gives a rather mechanical appearance to the meeting. However it is important that everyone is given the chance to speak and that one or two members do not dominate. For instance, members of higher social status are more likely to be very active and powerful in the Group, and this can diminish the benefits for the others (Hare, 1962).

On track

If the meeting is to get down to serious work, it must adhere to its aim and objectives and keep to the business in hand. This means that members should keep to the subject and refrain from indulging in gossip or speculation. Also the Group should be listening and paying attention.

There are three points be made. First, keeping on track is often seen as talking about matters directly relevant to drug use. This is too limiting. The aim of the Group is to deliver mutual support, and talking about drugs is one way of doing it. But this is not the only way. Indeed, talking only about drugs may even begin to be counterproductive if it reinforces the members' feelings of their lives being dominated by drugs. Members want to know that there are other things in life besides drugs, they want to be able to function without constantly referring to another person's behaviour or to a person's drug use.

The difficulty for the facilitator is knowing how to arrive at a balance. Are members avoiding issues by not talking about drugs or do they simply want a rest from the subject? And is it correct to see avoidance as a necessarily negative form of behaviour? Might discussing non-drug issues be a form of members exerting control over the situation, doing what they want and talking about their own topics? By insisting that members stick firmly to one broad topic, the facilitator may be excluding other possibly more relevant issues. This does not mean drug use is unimportant, but what is of greater importance is allowing members to live more rewarding lives.

Another point is that thoughts and feelings about drug use can be painful and distressing to express and consider. Energy is required to carry through the associated work, and the facilitator has to judge the energy level in the Group. Is it sufficient? In addition, the level of Group acceptance has to be monitored, to ensure everyone is not so overwhelmed by feelings that they are unable to concentrate, act and be mutually supportive. Working through serious issues has to be balanced against the energy and concentration factors in the Group.

Finally, it is not always easy to identify what is relevant to the meeting. What seems irrelevant may prove to be of relevance later on. Recognising the repetitious and the circular is comparatively easy, but other unhelpful aspects of the Group's discussion are harder to spot. And it should be remembered that what is said by the members and the Group belongs to them. Talk that does not seem relevant and is serving no apparent purpose can be used by the facilitator. For instance, in one Group I attended members started discussing a programme on television, a programme unconnected to the business of the meeting. As facilitator, I decided to use what had been said to move towards the substance of the meeting. By turning the Group's attention to the relationships, the family issues and the feelings portrayed in the programme, it was possible to link up with members' concerns. Admittedly, this constituted a rather artificial linkage, but this was no great defect, as members spotted the artificiality and recognised that they had been off-track.

The example illustrates how facilitators have to be flexible in their attitude and begin to get a sense of what will be of interest to the Group and what will be irrelevant. They have to be able to keep to the Group aim and objectives, yet be responsive to members' present and future needs.

Quality of talk

The nature of what is spoken can reflect some of the difficulties that members might have outside the Group, so the facilitator should be sensitive to the quality of communication. For instance, do individual members take responsibility for themselves? Do they own what they say? Instead of being vague and saying things such as, 'People say ...', 'What I heard ...', 'When this happens to you, you ...', members should recast the statements in the form, 'I feel ...', 'I think ...', and 'I did ...'. Once members get into the habit of owning statements in the meeting, it becomes easier to do the same outside the Group.

Another aspect of monitoring language is ensuring that feelings are not omitted from members' talk. Both the affective and the cognitive aspects of speech have to be included. The cognitive aspects should be concrete and as specific as possible: vagueness is unhelpful. However, members should be allowed time to search for what exactly they are trying to express. This applies particularly to affective issues, when it may be difficult for members to identify and express exactly how they feel.

Facilitators listen to what is said by members to pick up individual attitudes and beliefs. Those of interest are characterised by stereotyping and labelling, instances which are stored away for possible future discussion. This is not a matter of inflicting some form of political correctness, rather it is a matter of identifying examples of loose thinking.

The form of language

The kind of language used also can be a subject of debate. Facilitators should be non-judgemental and their language should reflect this. However, the difficulty is knowing how to react to members who are not only non-judgemental but also prejudiced in their language. Words such as 'Junkie' and 'Paki' are prejudicial words but may be the everyday words used locally. Should the facilitator insist on alternative terms? If so, what words should be used? Translation into other terms may seem strained for members if 'prostitute' has to be translated into 'sex worker', and 'drug addict' translated into 'drug user'. We also have to appreciate that whereas many Self-help Groups are middle class (Levy, 1981), Drug Family Support Groups are often local and working class with a slightly different set of attitudes and values, expressed in a different language.

Facilitators might want to state the reasons for their choice of language, but insisting on perfectly correct language will probably be counterproductive. By using non-judgemental language, facilitators are likely to bring about some change; not only in what is said but also in attitudes. This is important: without non-judgemental attitudes, information given in the Group may be interpreted to fit in with existing prejudicial attitudes and the final result can be misleading.

A similar concern may be given to the use of bad language. Such language has to be seen in context. Indeed, sometimes words like 'fuck' are used so often that they have almost lost their meaning. It is useful to open up a discussion about language and to see what members feel is and is not acceptable. For example, one group decided that calling someone 'a fucking ...' was acceptable, whereas calling any woman 'a ... cunt' was quite unacceptable.

Summarising

An important task of a facilitator is to summarise what has been said. This is not an automatic reaction whenever a Group member has finished talking, it is a way of underlining what has been said, and helps members to check out their understanding of a discussion and reflect on it. Summaries also show that attention has been given to the speakers and that their concerns have been taken on board. It provides an opportunity to assess the accuracy of what has been heard, and very often speakers will add to the summary as new thoughts arise on hearing a precis of what has been said. The rest of the Group might want to say how they see things as well.

Me: 'Well, Diane, if I have got this right, you are unsure whether Ray started using drugs again. You found some white powder in his bedroom and he said it was Beecham's powders as he felt flu coming on. Later, the two of you had an argument about money and Ray left the house. 'You are worried about his possibly sleeping out.'
Diane: 'Put like that, I know he was taking something. He looked me in the eye and said, "Mum, I promise you I'm not taking anything. Why can't you believe me?" I thought then, 'You are a bloody liar, Ray. I know you are lying."
Me: 'And because he is taking drugs again, you are worried about him.'
Diane: 'Yes.'

Summarising is important at the end of the meetings as this can be used to tie up any loose ends and defer outstanding and unfinished business until the next meeting. Without such reinforcement, what has been learned from the meeting is more likely to be forgotten.

GROUP SKILLS

Context

The facilitator requires various skills to be able to work best with the group. However these skills are of little use unless they are embedded in person-centred qualities. These qualities are useful not merely for the effective practice of particular skills but also for help in delivering assistance, care and support to Group members (Toseland et al., 1990).

The facilitator must be accepting of individual members and this includes whatever they bring to the Group. There has to be an acceptance of the stage they are at. There should also be acceptance of the Group itself with its aim of mutual support, as opposed to counselling or therapy.

Members of the Group should be seen as persons of positive worth, even when at their lowest and seemingly unable to cope positively with their situation. They are individuals in their own right, and not victims incapable of action. All members have the potential to better their situation, and coming to the Group is evidence of this fact.

Finally, the facilitator has to be empathic; capable of experiencing the world from the various members' points of view, not only cognitively but also through their feelings. This may not be so easy, as external and internal factors can interfere with such perceptions, for example, intruding thoughts and feelings both from the Group and from the facilitator.

Atmosphere

In line with the Group aim of support, the facilitator must set the right atmosphere to engender and build support. This requires the Group to be warm, friendly and welcoming, which in turn demands from the facilitator a positive belief in the potential of Support Groups. This belief will be translated into personal behaviour: the facilitator can then be honest and will not have to put up a false front by pretending to believe in the worth of the Group. It should be noted that although faith is put in the Group's potential, this does not exclude the occurrence of wrong directions, mistakes or misjudgements. These will happen because all human action and any progress carries a risk of going in the wrong direction, so members should be allowed to take risks in as safe an environment as possible, and this applies equally to the facilitator.

In fact, the Group should offer even more. Members should be encouraged to take risks to move into action. This may not be easy for them, tied down by their anxiety and inhibited by their low self-esteem. Mistakes seem like things to be avoided at all cost, rather than being a by-product of positive behaviour. This is not to ignore or excuse mistakes: it is to take the spotlight off them.

Facilitator honesty and the Group

Facilitators can contribute to setting the atmosphere by first look-ing to their own behaviour and being aware of how their actions contribute towards the overall Group feeling. This depends largely on everyone being themselves, which can be as difficult for facilitators as for members, as they have to be honest with themselves and with others. Nor should we assume that facilitators will be completely honest. Sometimes inexperienced facilitators feel the need to maintain a professional facade, while experienced facilitators want to maintain what they see as their professional status: in both cases this can be at the cost of the truth. This is a facilitative mistake which affects the whole Group atmosphere. In fact, honesty is a much better response, so the most useful replies are those such as:

'This is the first time for me. I'm not very experienced, so please bear with me.'

This example does mirror some important points.

1. Facilitators have their own part to play in setting the tone of the Group meetings, so they have to be self-monitoring and watch their effect on the Group, and alter their behaviour accordingly.

2. Power has to be shared in the Group. Facilitators in their unique role have the possibility of exerting considerable influence over members, and thus have to be especially careful to divest themselves of power – not easy when members expect them to lead the Group.

3. Facilitators can act as models in meetings, as their behaviour affects the whole Group. They do not have to be directive but they must accept that indirectly they will influence the Group. Also, they will be affected by the Group in turn, so they have to monitor their behaviour in relation to the members, as well as the members in relation to themselves.

Interventions

Within the context of a good Group atmosphere, facilitators can use their group skills to ensure useful interventions. Such interventions require attention to be given to the following:

1. The facilitator has to decide when to intervene. In a meeting, when a member is talking, there is little enough time to come to any decision, usually a second at most, so any decision has to be

made very quickly. This is done most easily if the facilitator foresees the need to intervene, which demands following the nature as well as the content of what is said.

As mentioned earlier, non-intervention can allow the members to intervene themselves and to assert their ownership of the Group. However, this requires reaching a stage where they feel able to do so, and where the Group has developed sufficiently to feel comfortable in doing so.

2. Non-action may be advisable if there have already been sufficient facilitator interventions. Even if intervening seems necessary, too much work by the facilitator is likely to be ineffective as there is only so much that members can absorb, apart from the Group becoming facilitator rather than member orientated.

3. Intervention is only likely to be of help if the Group can respond in a useful manner. This means there has to be a point behind the intervention and the Group must be able to deal with it. For instance, if the energy of the Group is low, making an intervention will probably be a waste of time unless it is addressed to the Group's energy level.

4. Interventions can always be deferred. This might be to accumulate further examples of the same point, so the facilitator draws attention not to an isolated item but to a pattern of behaviour. In addition, many possible interventions are not taken up immediately as the facilitator is unsure how things are going to develop or where a member or the Group is going. This can affect whether what was said is important or not, and thus whether it is worth intervening.

5. Those interventions made have to be well timed. Facilitator actions, especially if few in number, tend to have a large effect in the Group. They are like italics in a book, drawing people's attention – whatever the precise content. This means that undue significance can be given to relatively trivial points if the facilitator is not careful.

My own preference is that if there is any doubt, then do not intervene.

6. Apart from monitoring the energy of the Group, the facilitator should try to achieve the right balance. The meeting should be enjoyable, allowing easier learning and being supportive in

itself. However, if meetings are too nice, members can become unwilling to take risks, be over-defensive and fail to build up trust. There has to be a subtle blend of enjoyment and work at the meetings.

Necessary interventions

There will be occasions when the facilitator cannot let pass what is said or done in the Group, and so must intervene if no one else does straight away. For instance, a member might be aggressive and upset those present. In such circumstances, what is to be highlighted is not the particular member but the behaviour itself. The facilitator repeats what has been said and describes what has taken place. Then the Group is asked how they feel and then what their thoughts are. Any such incident has to be treated as a learning experience, something that can be applicable to anyone in the Group. The particular members are still accepted, even if their language, tone or general behaviour is unacceptable.

The facilitator has to balance Group learning against the feelings of the Group; to remember that the meetings are for support, and not just for education. At the end of the intervention the facilitator should establish how everyone feels, and give them the opportunity to give vent to their feelings about the incident and how it was handled. There has to be a public recognition of what has happened, so the Group can move on. Whatever takes place at meetings, at the end of the session members should feel better and not walk away burdened with negative feelings.

Work sharing in the group

Each member is expected to be allowed to have a share in the work of the Group, to have their say. However, the facilitator has to understand that some members may be reluctant to contribute – for whatever reason. This is acceptable to the Group in the short term but in the long term it can lead to resentment. It should be noted that people tend to imagine that they give more support than they receive (Buunk and Hoorens, 1992). Accordingly, resentment might be experienced even if the facilitator feels a member is contributing enough. What does help is if a discussion is opened on sharing in the Group and members' stages of confidence in being able to do so.

PARTICULAR SKILLS

The role of skills in facilitation

The skills of the person-centred approach such as active listening, speaking, probing, summarising and challenging may have to be modified for group use.

1. Listening is the most important skill and requires working on so many levels that facilitators should recognise they cannot listen to and remember everything. For this reason, mechanical recording of meetings is important.

2. Facilitators should listen to themselves and trust their feelings about how things might be or how they might be developing. Action in groups, as opposed to one-to-one relationships, is so complicated that it is often impossible to know what is going on, though this does not prevent participants from sensing it. The problem can then be having faith in one's instincts and not being afraid to be wrong.

3. Facilitators should listen a lot but speak very little: non-intervention is as important as intervention. Also, what is said should usually be for the Group, as opposed to being for the facilitator or the person who is the facilitator.

4. Sometimes interesting points arise and they can be usefully expanded. However, it is best if it is done by a Group member, with the facilitator as the fallback person, but one who helps the Group to be active and intervene.

5. Facilitation can require teaching members skills such as that of challenging or confronting others in a helpful manner.

6. Interpretation of members' behaviour has little place in facilitation, being the expression of the role of an expert. Also, interpretation is increasingly seen as irrelevant as a helping method (Meehl, 1960), even when the interpretation is correct (Garfield, 1990). However, when some enlightenment might be useful, facilitators may intervene and ask the Group what they see as the significance or meaning of what has just been said.

GROUP UNDERSTANDING

Introduction to general understanding

Facilitators have to understand what is happening, both to members in the Group, and in the lives of those members. The latter involves not being able to tell them what is 'really' happening in their lives, but being able to relate to them in a helpful manner. Attitudes are made more helpful if there is some understanding. This can be illustrated by what one member said:

'My friend, she tries to help but it's just her attitude. She doesn't really understand and it's all false. I find myself actually speaking to her in a different voice. I can say what I want to say here. I can be myself.'

It does not matter how much people want to help, and how open and kindly they may be, there has to be understanding if real benefits are to be gained. This is not always easy. Any understanding has to come from the Group as a whole and must not be confined to the facilitator. However, the facilitator has the responsibility of increasing understanding within the Group.

Reflection

One step towards understanding is to help Group members to take time to think, and not feel they have to respond or react straightaway. Members often do understand situations, but do not always employ that understanding and thus do not get the feedback that enables them to discover that they were right. This means they are less likely to trust their own abilities; to realise that they do in fact understand.

Making time for oneself and for others can be surprisingly difficult. Members have to be able to take their time, and the facilitator can act as a model. Then members see how reflection works at home, in the family. I stress that they should not expect any sudden change, as families get into certain patterns of acting and interacting which are hard to change.

'I remembered what you said about taking time and thinking about things ... Instead of snapping back at him, I thought what was really happening with Ronnie. He laughed at me and said

"Ah, lost for an answer then!" I said, "No, I'm not lost for an answer, just for the right answer." I took my time and for once he actually listened to me.'

Making time for thinking and reflection can be practised in the Group, where there is no pressure to respond with ideas or to answer straight away.

Directing attention to the present

To further Group understanding, the facilitator should ensure that what is said is connected with the speaker; not merely owned, but connected through feelings to the present, to how the speakers are feeling here and now. Members come to the meeting to say how they feel and what they are thinking, but often find it easier to give accounts as if they were history, secured in the past. Yet for most members matters rarely are completely finished. To close situations, speakers are asked to bring their accounts into the present, to express how they feel as they sit in the meeting. This reinforces the point that what does not belong to the past can be changed.

Understanding and drug theory

There is one issue that is relevant to the facilitator: whether it is necessary to have a theoretical overview of illegal drug use. On one hand it could be argued that such an overview is irrelevant and merely introduces preconceptions about drug behaviour into the Group. Moreover, the Group is for the support of those close to the drug user, and is not a drugs group to help users come off or use drugs more safely. However, if a greater understanding of drug use results in greater support for individual members, then this must be of benefit.

Understanding diminishes powerlessness, guilt and frustration, so it should be built up in the Group. There is no generally accepted theory of drug use; nevertheless, there are a few basic ideas that might usefully be shared. The following list of ten ideas may be discussed as a lead-in to the Group sharing its own ideas.

1. Drugs are used generally in society – drugs such as nicotine, alcohol, caffeine, over-the-counter drugs and prescribed drugs. The first two examples are the major life-threatening drugs, still

more lethal overall than illegal drugs. As members of society, we have to put illegal drug use into context; its main characteristic is its illegality rather than its life-threatening qualities.

2. Illegal drugs are primarily chemicals that alter the taker's moods. They may be taken for their beneficial and enjoyable mood-changing effects. Thus taking drugs is not irrational but may be a way of helping the person feel better in the short term.

3. These drugs often relieve anxiety and so may be a temporary method of coping with life. When life situations cannot be changed by the individual, the individual may use drugs to do the next best thing – cope with the pain the situations produce.

4. Young people will often try drugs out of curiosity, through peer pressure or for excitement. At this stage there might be little real appreciation of what drug use can lead on to and the difficulty in controlling the use. They continue to use drugs either because they are enjoyable or because stopping is unpleasant.

5. Taking drugs is a personal choice which may have unforeseen and dysfunctional consequences. Everyone has some choices and everyone can exert some measure of control over their own life. The problem is often that of controlling one's life rather than controlling one's drug use.

6. Stopping drug use can take a long time and relapses are likely. Group members should bear in mind the difficulty in changing one's patterns of behaviour; possibly even their own patterns of behaviour such as stopping smoking or drinking, the difficulty in dieting or other personal habits.

7. Not all drugs are physically addictive and not all drug users are physically addicted, despite what they might say. Even if they are, they can often come off by themselves, with support. However most drug users do not really want to stop their drug use, or they prefer to defer any such decision.

8. Medical help is no more than help; it is not treatment. It does offer the possibility of increased personal control and stabilisation, as well as the replacement of one physical addiction by another, but without the user's real desire to come off, it may offer little more than a free supply of drugs.

9. If drugs are a way of coping, then to stop the drug use is to take away a person's psychological crutch. This is acceptable provided other non-drug supports are offered and taken up. Without offering support, we are nudging the user back to drugs.

10. The drug subculture can have a strong influence over the user – it becomes almost a second family. Part of the difficulty is for the user to leave the local subculture, to avoid reinforcements such as other users, places where drug use is carried on and people who talk to them about drug use. However, users usually do come off finally and need help to rebuild their own identity, to become themselves rather than a drug user.

There is no grand theory in these ten points, as I do not think it useful to elaborate any particular theory of illegal drug use. However, I have found the ten statements helpful in discussing and broadening the Group's perception of drug use, lessening personal guilt and ensuring realism. They constitute a certain approach and set of attitudes which is useful for the process of Group support.

A more specific use of the general attitudes is when members ask why their partners or children take drugs. Questions as to why people act in certain ways are seldom very helpful. All that anyone can do is speculate and suggest reasons, which might not prove so useful for Group members. However, if some attempt is not made to answer the question then members are quite likely to blame themselves, the drug user or someone else. In fact, the whole process of blaming is very negative, so my preference is to get the Group to hazard answers, but to keep the previous ten points in mind and say:

• We all tend to take drugs, so the question is why take illegal drugs rather than socially acceptable drugs.

• Illegal drug use often starts in the teens, when children are looking for something new and exciting, even risky.

• Ultimately, everyone has a choice, and some children choose to take drugs. Often this is because their friends are doing it and they do not want to feel left out, scared or conformist.

• Illegal drugs, just like alcohol and tobacco, may be unpleasant initially, but soon seem pleasant. Illegal drugs can be enjoyable and exciting. Some reduce anxiety, making social interaction easier. They can give a feeling of confidence, and this can make the user feel better.

- In time other benefits come, in that the drug user meets many people who become apparent friends, feels part of a crowd or group, and begins to feel important.

- Stopping taking drugs can be difficult, not merely because of possible withdrawal syndrome, but because stopping might mean losing friends and the support of dealing with reality with the help of drugs. Also the presence of drugs locally and the people taking them means it is hard to get away from drugs. Finally, being off drugs can seem boring and not as good as taking them.

I always stress to the Group that I neither condemn nor condone drug use. It is more important to try to understand such use and its relation to life. Even if the drug user enjoys taking drugs, those affected may be very upset by such behaviour, and in life we all have to be sensitive to others. There are risks associated with drug use, but constantly reminding the user may not be helpful. Drug users are often well aware of the risks they run.

The important point is to get Group members to discuss drug use as this actually tends to diminish anxiety. As facilitator, do not expect members to agree with you, but in time the extreme views of some members may be modified.

CONTROLS

Group rules

Group rules are a public recognition of certain norms which have to be maintained for the benefit of the Group. Usually, as few are kept as possible. Too many rules runs counter to the intended informal atmosphere and feelings of acceptance of Support Groups. However, it is necessary to have a few rules, such as those relating to the criteria of Group membership and confidentiality. These rules are separate from any management and financial rules.

Group rules are for the Group's benefit, and for no one else. For instance, a Group member might invite a friend along to a meeting, although the friend does not have the required membership requirements. From experience, this does happen in Support Groups, and represents a breaking of confidentiality and an ignoring of the Group aim. Another example is when members are tempted to use the name of the Group to obtain special consideration from local doctors for drug users. Alternatively, the Group's name might be used in reports to Court concerning particular drug users. The remit of the Group is that of support, and going beyond this remit is likely to provoke difficulties.

Other rules that may be required are those covering confidentiality as applied to the advertising of the Group. Consideration has to be given by the Group as to what may be put into advertisements. This is especially important if there is going to be any contact with the media. Members often fail to appreciate that newspapers are usually not interested in help and support being given to families – they are interested in a story, in selling papers. For this reason, any interviews should be done with more than one Group member present and the final version to be printed should be seen beforehand (even though the newspaper interviewer might say this is impossible).

Rule enforcement

To be able to enforce the Group rules equitably and usefully, they must be written down and every member must have a copy of them. After the arrival of a new member to the Group, it may be helpful to go over the rules. This not only reminds members of their nature but also helps to define them. Members are not usually professional persons, so they may not have precise ideas of concepts such as confidentiality. They will also have differing interpretations of the rules. As long as the Group can work towards a consensual view, there should be no problems about possible misunderstandings.

Enforcement of the rules usually means reminding a member of the rules and pointing out an infraction. How this is best done may vary between Groups. There can be a difficulty in that breaking the rules can cause considerable upset, yet it can be awkward for members to say anything. My feeling is that the facilitator may be required to have a private word with the particular member or members. The member talking about the incident in the Group can even turn a mistake into a positive learning experience.

Although rules can be viewed rather negatively, they are a basis for trust and security in the Group, and have a positive role. They are likely to be better observed if presented in a positive light. For instance, confidentiality allows members to talk more openly at meetings. A lack of rules can lead to secrecy, as members adhere to their own informal rules, rules which are unspoken and not discussed.

Ethics

Ethics should be a concern of the whole Group, but especially of the facilitator, the professional worker in the Group. There are five areas that require special consideration.

1. Those who come to a Support Group are usually experiencing a personal crisis, feel themselves under pressure, and are vulnerable. Their searching for help, their low self-esteem, and a perception of the Group as an answer to their difficulties can make new members very suggestible. It is tempting to fall in with the members' expectations and believe the Group is everything, that what happens there must be for the good of its members. However, this is not the case: members' vulnerability means they can be easily damaged, and account must be taken of this fact.

2. Facilitators can only make assessments of what is happening in Groups if they are self-monitoring and know how they are affecting the other members of the Group. They have to be aware of their own personal and professional agendas so that these do not interfere with the facilitation.

3. The use of power in the Group should be avoided as much as possible, especially as members come from home situations where they have felt themselves to be powerless. The first step is for facilitators to monitor their own behaviour and role in relation to power in the Group. Only afterwards can they assess the use of power by others in the Group.

4. Groups are composed of individual members, who are all different. It is important that differences are respected, and that facilitators uphold the right of members to be different. This may mean supporting the expression of minority views.

5. A non-judgemental approach by the Group as a whole is the one

to be encouraged by facilitators. This should avoid any particular underlying beliefs, whether political, religious or psychological being introduced to Group members as an answer to their difficulties. Of course, it can be argued that the person-centred approach is itself a set of beliefs but, in my mind, they do not provide answers – only a way whereby each Group member can discover answers for himself or herself.

The ethical system used by facilitators is linked with values around individuality, power, choice, and vulnerability. The person-centred approach is taken as the basis of the value system, but even this is not beyond question. Moreover, ethics is not merely an intellectual apparatus but a system to be applied to the work being undertaken in the Group and difficulties that can arise.

For instance, the view that a professional in a self-help Support Group should recognise undesirable developments in functioning and counteract them (Kataschnig and Konieczna, 1987) requires a delicate balance to be achieved. Group members should be aware of the possible consequences of their actions and behaviour, but professional workers have no right to determine what is 'right', nor to take it upon themselves to move the Group in ways it does not want to go. All ethical problems are characterised by a lack of clear answers but need a balance of relevant different values.

GROUP SAFETY

Introduction

The facilitator has the ultimate responsibility for the safety of the Group, for ensuring that members are not damaged during the meeting. There has to be a differentiation made between members who get upset but work through it, and those who cannot work through matters and need individual help (Galinsky and Schopler, 1977). In time, the Group should be more responsible for its members and not have to rely on the facilitator. Members should be able to recognise when others are at risk and be able to help them appropriately, but sometimes this has to be learned. In the meantime, the facilitator has to attend to Group safety.

Sometimes the facilitator's role is seen as being that of preventing possible upsets and calming any upsets that do occur. However, the role is not so simple: the Group has to be allowed to take appropriate risks, and the facilitator has to make best use of what happens in the meeting. This results in the facilitator on occasions not being able to say what is likely to be unsafe, and waiting to see how matters develop. And the facilitator can be wrong. Yet, as always, mistakes can be steps to learning if they are identified, admitted, and worked on in the Group.

Personal confrontation

In meetings where there is a free expression of feelings, it might happen that feelings are directed against one or more members of the Group. The immediate difficulty is to know when to intervene. The facilitator should not have the role of rescuer, diving in to protect any member who is in danger, as this can take away Group responsibility. On the other hand, failure to intervene will be unhelpful to both the member and the Group, and in extreme cases it becomes impossible for the sparring members to get back to their former relationship. This may result in one or both leaving the Group.

What the facilitator has to do is to turn the situation so that the Group may benefit. This can be done by putting the situation back to the whole Group, by getting members to look at their own feelings.

'Sorry to interrupt but I am beginning to feel a bit uncomfortable. I wonder if other members of the Group are feeling as I do?'

After feedback, the facilitator can then have some idea of how to proceed. The emphasis is to depersonalise the situation and so make it applicable to all Group members.

'It struck me that feelings were running high and I suspect that most of us have been in similar situations. I have for sure. While not wishing to go over old ground, I would like to ask in general how we resolve difficulties when they arise.'

Once the Group temperature has been reduced, then the topic of expressing views without being subjected to personal attacks can be discussed. It should be noted that too directive a style of facilitation is likely to increase Group tension and thus provoke confrontation, so the facilitator has a role in setting the atmosphere to increase expression of feelings but lessen personal confrontation.

Scapegoating

In the Group meeting there are likely to be a variety of pressures and stresses on members, many of which have been brought in from outside. There is an accompanying need for individual members to offload and this might be done on to one particular Group member. If a Group member is seen as somehow blameworthy, then members feel justified in continuing to blame him or her. There may also be an unconscious desire to project feelings on to the selected victim (Scheidlinger, 1982). The whole concerted dumping action produces a false cohesiveness, and this makes the rest of the Group feel better. However, such cohesiveness is false because there is guilt associated with the scapegoating, though it is often unexpressed until later.

The facilitator is present not only to stop scapegoating but also to help members examine what is going on, the different feelings and thoughts that are around and the Group's reactions to what is taking place. In this way members can be helped to understand the process in the meeting and when it happens in the family.

Sometimes scapegoating is viewed purely as a Group reaction, unconnected with the individual concerned. This is rarely the case. Usually there are reasons why a particular individual has been selected and it is worthwhile if the facilitator gently helps the Group to look at those reasons. Some of the commonest tend to be when a member:

(a) does not enter into things, self-isolates from the rest of the Group;

(b) monopolises the Group and is insensitive to the needs of others;

(c) abuses the privacy of others, cross-examines or is prying;

(d) is physically or verbally abusive;

(e) abuses the rights or property of others in the group; or

(f) intrudes into a member's private space, makes inappropriate contact or touching.

These causes (Pearson, 1990), or others, need to be identified. The facilitator is the best person to do so, to tactfully get the whole Group to examine what is happening, to see what effects the individual is having on the other members, and the effects the rest of the Group have on the particular member.

Facilitation and over-control

Facilitation is a process in a Group setting which can produce its own difficulties. No person is perfect, and facilitators can and do get things wrong. Indeed, so much of facilitation is a matter of judgement that it would be unrealistic to expect it to be error-free. Training and experience will reduce errors, but cannot eliminate them entirely.

Possibly the most common misjudgement by facilitators is that of over-control. When starting facilitation with a new Group, there is likely to be a degree of anxiety in both the members and the facilitator. This can be one factor that leads to over-control and the use of too directive an approach. Such anxiety tends to fall away quite quickly once facilitation has begun, but there are other factors which can maintain facilitator anxiety.

One which tends to characterise novice facilitators is a search for perfection. Wanting to get everything right is seen as possible only if the facilitator takes control in the meeting. Anxiety about perfection is thus transposed into concern about keeping control of the meeting.

Another cause of anxiety which results in over-control is that of facilitator fantasies, such as imagining that without them in the meetings, the Group would simply collapse. Alternatively, facilitators think that without their presence, the Group would run out of control. Only by having a strong structure to the meetings can the Group survive in the long term. However, these needs and fantasies are no basis for action, and facilitators have to come to terms with them, not enshrine them in the Group.

All of these factors point to the need for facilitators to have support and supervision for themselves to reduce the chance of errors and personal factors interfering in the work.

FACILITATION REVIEWS

Introduction

The arrangements concerning facilitation should cover the reviewing of the Group and its facilitation. Usually the facilitator must suggest the idea, as members are unlikely to think of it. Reviewing, say, after six months and then at yearly intervals, should not be seen as separate from but part of the total facilitation process.

The reviews can be made formal to the extent of typed sheets being given out at the end of a meeting. These are to be filled in at home and returned the next time the Group meets. The sheets can cover a variety of questions regarding the Support Group:

1. What were the member's initial expectations?

2. How useful was the information given before coming to the Group?

3. What has the member found useful about the Group?

4. What was difficult for the member about being in the Group and at the meetings?

5. How does the member feel the rest of the Group relates to the facilitator?

6. How does the member relate to the facilitator?

7. Is the facilitator too controlling?

8. Does the facilitator help the member to understand matters better?

9. Does the facilitator help the Group to function well?

10. In what ways could the facilitator improve Group functioning?

The question sheets completed by all members are given to an outside person who can give a written report back to the Group for discussion. This might seem a bit intimidating and Groups may want to use another method. However, this process can be liberating for the Group and improve cohesion – provided the whole review is handled well. Alternatively, reviewing of facilitation can be incorporated into overall Group reviews, as will be explained later.

Facilitation timespan

The yearly reviews are helpful as facilitation tends to be time-limited. Facilitators are likely to want to do different work after two or three years, but there is a more important aspect to be considered.

It takes some time for the facilitator and the Group to get to know each other well, so the facilitator becomes really good after a year or so. Thereafter, there is likely to be a growing expertise and efficiency which reaches a peak at two to three years. Then there will probably be a slow decline in the standard of facilitation. Having reviews can identify this decline and decelerate the decline in work practice. Reviews raise the question of the possible termination of the current facilitation and ensure that the facilitator does not feel locked into the task.

It should be added that facilitators may not be conscious of the decline in the standard of their work. What they may notice is that they are beginning to feel irritated in Group meetings or that members are becoming more 'difficult'. They might also feel that facilitation is a chore. For this reason, at reviews the facilitator should consider the following questions:

- Do I look forward to facilitating, or is it becoming a burden?

- Are there times when I am simply not concentrating fully in the meetings?

- Do I feel that the Group is getting out of control or taking the wrong direction, and feel annoyed as a result?

- Do I find myself getting irritated in Group meetings for no real reason?

- Am I finding it increasingly difficult to 'switch off' from events at Group meetings?

- Do I find the meetings run-of-the-mill and uneventful?

Affirmatives to these questions indicate that the facilitator is probably getting less out of the work, and might want to plan terminating facilitation within the year.

In time, it is not just the facilitator who will change. The Group in turn may be affected and find it more difficult to see other points of view; it may increasingly question, if indirectly, the facilitation. There is always the underlying question of whether the facilitator is using the Group to satisfy personal needs. Knowing when to bring the work to an end is a professional requirement.

If the termination of facilitation is well planned, it can be a useful rather than a purely negative experience. Consideration should be given to ensuring a planned changeover, with the new facilitator being introduced to the Group. All of this underlines the fact that facilitation requires planning over time. Support is also needed to carry through such planning and to ensure that facilitators are positive about their leaving; they should realise that their leaving is a loss experience for them, as well as for the Group (Goodyear, 1981).

FACILITATOR SUPPORT

Introduction

Support for facilitators is essential because of the nature of facilitation, and not just because those engaged in it feel under stress or are unsure how to deal with problems that arise. The role of facilitator is a unique role in the Group and a lonely role, open to stress and resultant work impairment.

Pressure comes through facilitators constantly coming into contact with the raw feelings of members, yet having no opportunity to express how they feel during the meeting. Of course, as facilitators do not have drug users in their families there would seem to be little reason for them to get very upset. But constantly coming into contact with Group feelings and having to see the world from the members' perspective is painful. Indeed, to experience a mother's pain, a sister's anguish, a father's despair or a partner's anger can be overwhelming, unless the facilitator prevents this becoming so. The balance of allowing oneself to experience such feelings and having to control the experience is stressful.

Facilitators are ultimately responsible for ensuring members who experience strong feelings and confusing thoughts are not damaged by what takes place in the meetings. This means there has to be total concentration in the meetings by facilitators, who have to exert a great deal of self-control. They should not be directive but self-directive; they order only themselves. However, there may be a temptation to be directive at times, and then having to deal both with the desire to be directive and with one's consciousness of wanting not to be directive. All of this becomes even more difficult when we realise that there is not likely to be much positive feedback for facilitators.

Nature of support

The solution is twofold. Facilitators should learn to be self-supporting, to look after themselves. This includes taking time out to relax, to keep in good physical condition and to keep strict boundaries in their work so that it does not begin to take over their life. Also facilitators should ensure that they get regular support for themselves by going to individual counsellors or getting help from a facilitators' network.

There are five interlocking areas of supportive help.

1. The facilitator requires someone on whom feelings can be offloaded, feelings evoked by the Group meetings. The point is that if feelings are not discharged, then they might be expressed in unproductive or even damaging ways, either in the facilitator's everyday behaviour or in the meetings themselves.

2. Support might be needed to deal with feelings that arise between facilitators and individual group members. They might be a result of a direct reaction between individuals or they may arise through facilitator countertransference, where certain Group members trigger off feelings about other people in the facilitator, feelings which can interfere with ongoing work.

3. The role of facilitator can be stressful and this can be aggravated in that facilitators may receive little positive reinforcement in the Group meetings. This can cause facilitators to think they are not doing a very good job and they can feel irrelevant, even powerless. What starts off as slight detachment in the meetings can become self-perceived isolation. To such feelings are added the stress of remaining even-handed in the Group, although the facilitator may relate better to some members than to others.

4. There can be Group feelings of sadness or anger that can exert a powerful effect and can threaten to swamp everyone, including the facilitator. Such feelings have to be resisted – not always easy when the facilitator has to do so many different tasks. There is a great need for the facilitator to discuss feelings in order to be able to work efficiently. There is also a need to talk through more cognitive aspects of the work, such as the stage of Group development, interactions between members, difficulties in the

Group, problems arising from shared content, and how facilitation can be further improved. To talk through the work is supportive in itself.

5. Facilitators can fall into routine ways of working and fail to be creative. Often this comes from habit, from tried ways of thinking and working, rather than being prepared to experiment with ideas, and being ready to make mistakes and seem foolish (Zinker, 1978). Support is required to help maintain the standard of facilitation, to ensure each Group session is treated with freshness and innovation.

Co-facilitation

Usually there is a minimum of two groupworkers in a group, as this provides mutual support and a better quality of work. However, in Support Groups two facilitators would be too powerful an alliance. Apart from the difficulty of obtaining two facilitators for a Support Group, it should be added that for them to work efficiently together, they will have to relate well both as people and as co-workers (McMahon and Link, 1984). Special consideration has to be given if there are minority persons in the Group, and consideration given to the ethnicity of the facilitators (Hodge, 1985). It should not be assumed that co-working is necessarily an advantage (Bowers and Gauron, 1981), but, if well prepared and carried out, it does provide advantages.

4 INITIAL WORK

INTRODUCTION

The aim of the Support Group is to deliver mutual support to all its members, and this requires structure and planning. Simply getting people together and expecting that this by itself will lead to improvements in members' lives is unrealistic. In fact, such an approach can lead to negative feedback and a worsening of their situations (Vaux, 1983).

However, the Group members are not involved in formal groupwork, directed specifically to problem-solving, therapy or task accomplishment; they are gathered to support each other. This means not only the content but also the methods and style of work in the Group should be influenced by this aim. They should be supportive, even when difficult matters are being tackled. To achieve this, Support Groups are facilitated, not led. Also members have to take as much responsibility for themselves as possible, and all members should attend to every other person in the Group.

Much of the support consists of listening to and discussing the accounts of members, what has happened to them since the last meeting. This is taken in a relaxed manner, the Group ensuring everyone has a chance to speak. The members take whatever comes, and are prepared to accept any thought and feeling, so there has to be flexibility to take the unexpected. However, in the long term there is the danger that meetings can become routine; the energy, learning and enjoyment in the Group begins to dip. For this reason, other forms of work can be programmed into the meetings every so often, perhaps every six or nine months. The various ideas to be presented later – themes, family work, work on co-dependency, roles, problem-solving and coping – are all relevant to the aim of support. If one of these is introduced every six months, then a three-year skeleton programme can be devised – provided this is relevant to members and they agree.

Nature of work

What happens in any Group meeting can be viewed as taking place in several interconnected areas: what is happening in the Group between members; what the Group members want to achieve or are achieving; and how the Group as a whole is going. As a result it is not always obvious how best to proceed. Perhaps the easiest approach at this initial stage is to look at what might occur at the early meetings. Once some general structure is in place, then preliminary ideas of the support work can be thought out and the work planned.

INITIAL MEETINGS

Initial considerations

The initial meetings are likely to be important as they set the tone for what comes later. If the Group starts off on the wrong foot, it can take some time before matters can be righted. So the following points might be of relevance to those facilitating Groups in their early stages.

Attendance

There may be a variable number at Group meetings, so the importance of attendance has to be stressed to every new member. The emphasis is not just on the personal benefit, but also that attendance will be a help to other members of the Group. Indeed, the Group can only function if members come on a regular basis.

Founding meetings

At first only the founder members, possibly just two people, might turn up to the Group meetings, and this situation may continue for some time, leaving those members unsure whether anyone else will turn up. The temptation is to end the meeting early and get off home. Yet, despite how members feel, they have to turn up and they have to stay, even though this can be a lonely and frustrating business. If a new member does come to the meeting and there is no one present, then that person might well not return to the Group. In addition, once knowledge of what happened is known locally, other potential new members may decide not to come.

Introductions

Groups do not necessarily work well, so some initial structuring is introduced to short-circuit a lot of unnecessary time and energy. For example, at the very beginning of the meeting a formal start is announced. The facilitator introduces himself or herself and then briefly outlines the facilitation role. Then the basic idea of the Group can be explained with reference to its aim and objectives.

Support is described as coming mainly through members talking about their thoughts, feelings and actions, and listening to the experiences of the other members. Simple as this may seem, it begins to make those present feel better. Frequently, Group members will reinforce this point and describe how coming to the Group helped them to face the world in a more positive manner.

When members begin to feel better, they are able to participate more fully in the Group and discover their own ways of dealing with their personal difficulties. As facilitator, I like to add that help comes through Group discussions rather than the giving of advice. Members will have been given similar information on referral, but they often fail to take it in because of their high level of anxiety. Just as in individual counselling, the model of counselling is explained (Egan, 1986), so there should be some explanation of how support is delivered. However, as the nature of work in Support Groups is complex, any explanation must be limited to a mention of the expression of feelings, reduced anxiety, detachment, reflection, sharing, comparison and looking at personal options. In practice, explanation over time may prove more easy for members to take in.

Facilitator as a model

At this early stage, the facilitator is likely to do a fair amount of modelling what is appropriate member behaviour. With a limited knowledge of what is expected and what happens, members can be confused, they feel unsupported, and their distress is increased rather than decreased. If this situation is allowed to continue, new members can become angry, especially with the facilitator from whom they expect a lead.

For instance, at the start of a meeting, the facilitator might thank a member for his or her contribution, even if it was just that of listening. However, it is best if this comes from other members. The facilitator must not become the 'thanker-in-chief', so one task is to get the Group to increase feelings of reciprocity by listening and showing their interest in what has been said. However, sometimes members are so distressed they feel unable to help each other; when a member speaks there is very little response or feedback. In such cases, the facilitator should ensure that a member's effort is not overlooked and the speaker is thanked. The important point is to ensure that members feel they have been heard, listened to, and acknowledged. This increases self-esteem and reinforces that person's ability to act positively and constructively.

Thus thanking and acknowledging are picked up as the right way of doing things in the Group. In time, this will be accomplished in other ways, so members do not have to be appreciated in so public a manner. After several months together, just having others obviously listen will be sufficient. So facilitators do not follow a set of rules of how a Group should be helped, but have to judge how best this can be accomplished. This demands constant attention and ongoing assessment of the Group, its dynamics and functioning.

Further steps

At this early stage, the basic Group rules should be mentioned, and it is useful to have a discussion about confidentiality. This is often a rather vague concept for many members, and one that Groups are not always keen to tackle (Roback et al., 1992). It is also important that members are allowed time to get to know each other, and the facilitator has to ensure that this process happens. Members should say their names and briefly say why they have come to the Group. Names are used continually in these early sessions. Nothing is more embarrassing than not knowing a member's name and having to ask it at later meetings. We should also remember that people do feel good if their name is used, and their presence and individuality are acknowledged.

Talking about reasons for coming to the meeting is an essential part of the process of trust building and the sharing of personal information, and enough time should be allowed to do this adequately. Sometimes members want to start work immediately and ignore initial introductions and trust building. However, this usually works to the long-term detriment of the Group.

The facilitator may say a fair amount at the very beginning of the Group's programme of meetings, and set the facilitator role. This also fits in with the needs of members, who are too uncertain to lead the Group for themselves. Yet as soon as possible, the facilitator should work to avoid a high profile in the Group and any leadership role. It may help if the facilitator states that he or she intends to say a lot initially, but to take much more of a back seat later.

Initial anxiety

The facilitator should be aware that new members are likely to be very anxious. Often members say that they spent the first session wondering to what degree they should open up to the Group, and if they did so would they lose control and make a fool of themselves. If the Group has been running for some time when they first come, new members are likely to experience these feelings to an even greater extent. They see the other members as experienced, as people in control of themselves, unlike how the new members feel.

'I have to admit that I did not enjoy the first meeting. I was scared. I never said a word, just listened to everyone else and the kind of things they were saying. Afterwards I wondered whether to come back to the Group as I did not enjoy it, but I also remembered what others had said when talking about what had happened to them. I was glad I did come back and by the end of the second meeting began to feel a bit easier.'

These first meetings are likely to be critical, and sometimes a member might not return. This may be no reflection on the Group, but an indication of the stage that particular person has reached in coping with difficult situations. However, members have to be sensitive to a new member's general anxiety and be as welcoming as possible.

Absences

Attendance at Support Groups should be purely voluntary: members attend because they want to do so. Equally, if they do not come to the Group, then one reason might be that they do not want to come.

This might mean the member found the meeting unsatisfactory, or that the Group had given the member all that the member needed. It should also be remembered that absences are more common with larger groups, where members often feel that they will not be missed if they do not come.

However, absences are a concern to those members who are left wondering what could have happened to the absent member. There are concerns that something serious might have happened, or the person has fallen ill. But there are also underlying worries.

In a Drug Family Support Group the subject of loss is usually a very live issue, and the apparent loss of a member from the Group can be very unsettling. Indeed, sometimes the unexplained absence can have a snowball effect and result in other members failing to appear at the meetings. So contacting absent members is important, if only to ensure that they are all right. The information is relayed back to the Group, and anxiety is reduced. Also, if the member is ill or has been involved in some form of accident, then knowing that the others care is supportive.

Finally, it should be remembered that sometimes those who come to the Group may not be ready for the experience and have to work towards being able to use the meetings. They may miss meetings but return at a later date.

'I remember that first meeting and wanted to come back, but there was a lot going on and I felt I could only deal with so much. I could only deal with my situation and could not help anyone else. Now I feel stronger and perhaps I could help.'

Sometimes members do not come to the meetings as they want a break from the Group, or upsets in the family divert them from attending. However, this may be the very time when the member wants support. Keeping up some form of contact is useful, as some members will find it difficult to return after a break.

Member: 'I was going to contact you earlier; I meant to get back to you.'

Me: 'It's really good to hear your voice again.'

Member: 'I've been selfish, wanting to do things for me, rather than come to meetings.'

Me: 'That doesn't sound selfish to me. It sounds like good sense.'

Member: 'I was in a bit of a mess and I wanted to get myself better before coming back to the Group.'

Me: 'They would love to see you again.'
Member: 'It would be nice to see everyone again.'

Members almost need an excuse to come back, and approaches from someone in the Group can provide a hook allowing them to return. This might be needed as the idea of coming back can seem intimidating. Members can feel guilty for being away and anxious about their reception, though such fears are likely to prove groundless on return.

'I was glad to come back. Everyone treated me if I had never been away and they even remembered my daughter's name. It was good to be back.'

The question arises as to who should contact the absent person. This can be decided in the Group. However, in cases of unexplained continued absence, the facilitator might have a role to play. In the case of one absence, the member had been beaten up by her drug user husband and as facilitator, I was asked to visit rather than a Group member.

Although members' partners are invited to come along, they do not always do so. Their support is still appreciated. However, it can happen that partners begin to feel unhappy with members coming to a Group and exert pressure for non-attendance. It is not the Group role to interfere between partners, merely to let the other members know the reason for any absences.

In general, facilitators and the Group have to come to some understanding about final absences. Sometimes they can be positive in that members leave having obtained what they want, and this can be a very positive move. On the other hand, absence can reflect an inadequacy in the Group and its functioning, and the member can leave dissatisfied. Groups are not always helpful, but it is the role of the facilitators to make them so (Rogers and McMellin, 1989).

New members

Over time there will be a slow decline of numbers in the Group, so new members have to be introduced. Their arrival is usually warmly received by the older hands, but facilitators need to be aware that matters may not be so simple. New members can threaten the stability of the Group, and the role and status of existing members. Signs of this may be seen in the ambiguous reactions to these new entrants. The old hands appear welcoming, yet they make repeated references to past happenings or experiences of which the new members will be ignorant. Such subconscious behaviour may represent moves to establish new members in their position in the Group hierarchy, impressing on them that they are new members. By such means, new members define themselves, and are defined by the rest of the Group, as newcomers. They take on the identity and role of newcomers, and tend to talk and agree with each other. In time, newcomers become integrated into the Group and relate to everyone (Morland, 1985). Facilitators should be aware of this integration and act against any impediment to that process.

Subgroups

The formation of subgroups within the Support Group is a natural development. The most common aspect is that of pairing, where a couple link up through their mutual compatibilities and give each other support. With such support, they feel able to talk more openly, express their own views and suggest plans of action. Apart from pairing, larger subgroups can form and it is helpful to have a view on them, for the sake of good facilitation.

Subgroups are not necessarily permanent but may form and dissolve, and new subgroups arise. Any difficulties come when subgroups are relatively long lived.

Pairing tends to produce little or no problem, as each pair is only a small fraction of the total Group number and so has relatively little power. Also, there can be several pairings in a Group, which tends to lessen the influence of any one pair.

Difficulties come with the formation of cliques, subgroups to which some members are not admitted. Even so, there can be two main types of cliques. First are those that arise through circumstances such as members sharing the same car to come to the meeting, or members going to the pub for a drink after the meeting. What can happen is that small informal meetings can occur outside the main meeting. These cliques can be unsettling to the other members.

More unsettling are those where members are intentionally excluded. These cliques are hostile power groupings which are often aimed against the person seen as Group leader (Yalom, 1985), who might be the facilitator. These cliques are associated with an increased drop-out rate of members from the Group.

Generally, it is not so much the subgroups and cliques which are destructive to the Group, but the silence that surrounds their existence. By asking in meetings whether anyone else has noticed how certain members seem to get on well together and form their own little group, the facilitator can open up the subject for general discussion.

Subgroups can act for or against the Group as a whole. They may represent a minority of members who have common views, and if these views are shared strongly enough, the subgroup can go on to affect the whole Group (Moscovici, 1980). How they are judged by the facilitator depends on how they affect the Group aim of giving mutual support to all members.

More examples of subgroups

Couples constitute potential cliques. Partners tend to talk mostly to each other, know each other's non-verbal signals well and make private references which mean nothing to the rest of the group. This is not inevitable, as I have known couples go to Group meetings and speak very little to each other. The facilitator has the responsibility of highlighting the situation and making known the Group's feelings about it. Sometimes in discussion couples are surprised that the rest of the Group sees them as being closely aligned, as they see themselves arguing and very dissimilar in outlook! The facilitator can help in the process of changing private perceptions into a shared reality.

Another example of a subgroup formation is that of the emergence of core members. These are the Group 'faithfuls' who can be relied upon to turn up, as opposed to those who occasionally turn up or those who have not been coming to meetings for long. After a time the core members link together and this can make newcomers to the Group feel like outsiders. The result in extreme cases can be that newcomers do not stay long in the Group, reinforcing the cliquish nature of core members.

Further time in the Group

We should remember that all members are individuals and there is no simple formula as to how they will react or behave. Some take a long time to participate openly in the Group, but this is not time lost if it is used in listening and in being supportive to those speaking in the meeting. At this stage there is a balance between the new member wanting time and space, and the others wanting him or her to participate.

'I could not speak for weeks and weeks. Even so, I was listening to what people were saying and I didn't feel alone. Also, it gave me an idea of how things would go.'

It is often worthwhile to check out with new members how they feel at the end of the session. Discover whether they feel under strain, whether they will be returning to future meetings and how members can make things easier. Just being able to speak of their fear about being in the Group can prove helpful. Other members have their own experiences of first coming to the Group, and sharing them can diminish the newcomer's anxiety. It can be useful if the other members demonstrate that talking about being in the Group is quite permissible, and anxiety and feelings are a normal part of the Group experience. This also partially sets the working style for the new members.

New members will require time to pick up the informal rules and the kind of things that members talk about, and this means they need time to listen. However, though new members may not speak, it is best to acknowledge their presence. They have to know that they are of value to the Group and their presence makes a difference. Often members will come to meetings with very low self-esteem and merely to be named can stop them from feeling totally insignificant or invisible. The following reply might be helpful; it does not press the new member to talk about herself but does allow her the chance to contribute.

'Well, June, this is your first time at the meeting. How are you feeling right now?'

This should be sufficient to give the new member the chance to contribute, to say something. It might be quite minimal, yet be enough. I find this is also useful for the rest of the Group who may be unsure whether a new member should be encouraged to contribute or allowed to stay silent.

At crisis point

We should remember that members come to Groups very often because they feel they are at some personal crisis point. Accordingly, they bring their crisis and disruption to the meeting, sub-merging it with strong and even threatening feelings. As a result, the member may dominate the meeting, requiring the facilitator to intervene gently and ensure the others also get their time. This intervention has to be balanced against the task of helping the particular member.

The crisis need not be mainly about family drug use. The difficulties can be about almost anything, and the drug use may be no more than a way of getting help. Whatever the reasons for coming to the Group, they should not be dismissed. Facilitators and members have to be flexible enough to respond to a variety of expressed needs and wants, and not be confined merely to drug matters. In one Support Group, issues that arose included the risks of HIV infection, social isolation, past physical abuse, alcohol use and personal relationships. A member's crisis may be a stated problem. This is often only part of the story, as the crisis may be embedded in other difficulties. As a result it would be wrong to imagine that solving the stated problem would be the only work to be done. So the crisis may have no easy solution or have no solution at all. Those involved often feel unable to cope with the situation and whatever is done seems to lead to insurmountable difficulties or a dead end.

'Some folk were after Ronnie and came to the door threatening that they would get me as well as him. I told the police but they said nothing could be done until an offence was committed. I couldn't take them on as they had whole families behind them and I've just got Ronnie.'

Such situations seem difficult to deal with and anyone might well wonder what could be done. However, it is important to take a constructive attitude. Often difficulties are in the mind of the person concerned: there only appears to be no way out. In fact, in the example given the mother faced up to the crowd who were quickly cowed. It is important to see that some situations are difficult solely because there seems to be no solution: for example, the common problem of deciding whether the family drug user should be put out of the house.

'I can't bear her coming in under the influence; I just get scared. Yet if she's not at home then I worry about her, whether some day the police aren't going to come and say they have found her dead in some gutter.'

A crisis is a construct, something built out of feelings and cog-
nitions. As such it can be deconstructed, broken down into its
elements. The presence of other Group members can assist in
the process and diminish the hopelessness through helping the
member to see the separate elements. Feelings are not diminished, thoughts are not dismissed, nor belief systems changed.
For new members, their crises are real crises that need to be
understood, through their elements and through the help of
other members. Most crises are not just private constructs but
are socially manufactured, and are best analysed out with Group
assistance.

PLANNING THE WORK

Overview

Support, as mentioned earlier, requires the acceptance of what
cannot be changed, at least by those who come for support. This
acceptance requires several different forms of work being brought
in to play.

1. Members of the Group have to be allowed to rid themselves of
   impeding feelings which will stop them from thinking ration-
   ally about what they want to do.

2. Members have to be able to look at themselves and those past
   experiences which may be interfering with the process of acceptance of their situations.

3. Members might have to deal with defences that they have
   erected to protect themseves from their high anxiety resulting
   from their situations.

4. Members have to be able to see their situations from a variety
   of angles, to take different views and so be able to adjust their
   beliefs to what they see as being applicable to them, to their
   situation, to their reality.

5. Members have to be able to make the most of their situations
   and have to be helped to overcome any difficulties that are
   surmountable.

Modes of work

These objectives are initially to be achieved by four principal modes of support undertaken by the Group members: ventilation, worry reduction, sharing and self-disclosure. The specific support modes are not aligned with specific work objectives but taken together, taken as an interrelated foursome. If carried out properly, they should cover all the objectives.

As well as the members' work, there are three aspects of work in the Group that the facilitator or Group members should assess and act to improve as they reinforce the four support modes. These aspects are structuring, being positive and self-esteem.

Role of support modes

Much happens in Support Group meetings, so it would be wrong to suggest that support modes are the sole forms of activity or all the work that is necessary. However, for support to begin to be effective, they are the basic forms of work in the Group meetings. Other work modes increase the effectiveness of such work.

NATURE OF THE WORK

Introduction

Every Group is different, which is the joy of working in Groups and also the challenge. There is no set approach, so what is given here as support work should be seen as no more than suggestions. Above all, the human quality of the nature of support work should never be forgotten, and steps should be taken to retain that quality.

Getting the atmosphere right, having a democratic and equi-potent value system, having a facilitator that works to make himself or herself virtually redundant as the Group progresses, are important. Also the Group should adhere to the overall aim of support, while being aware of other distinct and different aims such as therapeutic outlooks, community intervention and political action, which come under other remits. The road that any particular Group takes is its own choice, but to make relevant decisions requires self-monitoring and understanding of the Group and individual needs.

Matters that arise

It should be appreciated that there has to be a balance between work and what might be seen as more extraneous matters. The atmosphere has to be kept such that members remain interested and meetings do not become too serious or too heavy, so members take in what is being said and what is happening.

Most of what is said in Support Group meetings centres around members' accounts of what has taken place since the previous meeting. For work purposes this is seen through the four work modes of ventilation, worry reduction, sharing and self-disclosure. Other aspects of working may also be used: that of emergent themes; specific aspects such as family functioning, roles and skills. These forms of working should be used with discretion and not be allowed to swamp the routine feedback from members about their lives. Consideration must always be given to the members and not to specific forms of work which the facilitator thinks should be done. Forms of work emerge from the meetings; they do not have to be imposed on it.

The role of the facilitator is to balance what is happening in the Group and be aware of when members are not getting the most out of it. This does not mean facilitators know better, as they are merely assessing the situation in the Group. Ways of working must always be discussed with the members as their say is the important factor, not what the facilitator thinks.

TELLING THEIR STORIES

Introduction

The initial and main part of the support work comes from members telling their stories, recounting what has happened to them. This takes place with the received attention and encouragement of the other members. New members might need more time to tell their stories compared with other members recounting what has taken place since the last meeting. Whatever the situation, the facilitator has the role of ensuring that the account is related to the here-and-now, that there are feelings still connected to the events and that they are not repressed. Usually members' accounts can be given without the need for any intervention. The only thing that might have to be said by the facilitator is 'Yes', 'Right', or

'Take your time!' New members must be given space to tell their story as they want. They should feel they can say whatever they want. It should be remembered that they might have tried to tell it before to partners in denial, to professionals who tried to pigeon-hole them, and to neighbours who took a very judgemental view. It can be quite a new experience for members to say how they see things and how they feel.

Benefits of telling their stories

Members who tell their stories will discover that the process has many benefits. It ends feelings of isolation, reduces debilitating self-blame, and lessens self-doubt about what has happened in their life. These are all benefits that apply generally to such account-giving in groups (Gold-Steinberg and Buttenheim, 1993). There are also secondary benefits: for example, the breaking of self-isolation can relieve feelings of hopelessness (McIntosh and Zirpoli, 1982). The process is also therapeutic in itself because the action of telling is liberating; a positive action which makes the speaker feel better (White and Epston, 1990). This does not mean that what is taking place is therapy. It is however a reflec-tion of the fact that talking about one's life carries so much more than the mere content, more than just what is told. It can affect the whole thinking process (Fuller, 1982), and enable the person to feel more in control.

What is recounted is more than a perception of a member's world: it is his other world. What members try to do is to see themselves and significant others in relation to their world. To do this demands their understanding of what is happening to themselves, to others, and to themselves in relation to others. This may be difficult. Sometimes members are in shock and can hardly believe what is going on in the family. Telling their stories is an important task which helps members to begin to get more control of their situation by starting to deal with themselves and their realities. The repetition of the same story, as often happens after a sudden shock or crisis, is not for others but for themselves. It shows members trying to make sense of their worlds and this lays the ground for starting to come to terms with the situation (Andersen, 1991).

All of this means that members should be allowed to tell their stories in full and in their own way, to accept the diversions, to allow for false starts, for what may seem to be exaggerations or fantasies, contradictions or omissions. New members might not present a very coherent account of their difficulties, but this is not nearly as important as the fact that they have been able to talk. However, the benefit of telling one's story can diminish over time. To get the most out of the experience of giving one's account, further work needs to be done. To this end, the facilitator should be aware of the four support modes.

VENTILATION

Initial thoughts

The first task of the Group is to attend to the feelings of those present. This is part of the overall programme of empowering members, who may well be at crisis point and overwhelmed by their feelings. Their immediate need is to give expression to those feelings, to get things off their chests, to unburden themselves of things they might never have said to anyone before. They should be encouraged to do so, to ventilate their feelings, even if they find this upsetting at first and others in the Group find it discomforting.

It is usually assumed that the rest of the Group will be supportive to a member expressing strong feelings, but facilitators should be aware that sometimes members can be ambivalent to this ventilation. The Group will want to help the member, be part of the process of expressing pent-up feelings, yet feel uncomfortable about contact with those feelings. There may even be a quick rush to comfort the member and be sympathetic. The following example from a Group meeting shows what can happen.

'I'm sorry, I'm sorry, I can't stop myself from crying.'
'That's all right, that's what it's all about. We have all had a wee greet here from time to time. I felt better for it.'

This is a very natural reaction, yet it cuts off the ventilation process and does not help the member under stress. Such actions usually result from other members getting caught up in the account, getting upset, and so cutting off further distress for themselves, rather than allowing the speaker to work through his or her distress (Lehman et al., 1986).

The role of the facilitator is at times that of getting Group members to stay with their strong and even distressing feelings. The simple act of ridding oneself of contained emotions, worries and anxieties is the first step whereby a member feels better, and this may require members having to hold on to and work with their feelings.

Ventilation and personal defences

It should be remembered that most members will have tried to deal with their difficulties for some time. They will have built their own defences, such as denial or emotionally distancing themselves from the situation. Part of the use of ventilation is to allow members to relax those defences and be realistic about their difficulties.

Sometimes minor rephrasing can be suggested by the facilitator to help the identification of such defences and how they might be changed. It is important that such work on personal defences does not interfere with the overall support aim. Any work done on defences has to be carried out very carefully; whether it is done at all depends on the judgement of the facilitator, who senses the relationships in the Group and where the particular defensive member stands in relation to them. Whereas wrong judgement in ordinary groupwork can easily be recovered, in Support Groups any such wrong judgement can seriously interfere with the general atmosphere of support and prove quite counterproductive.

Nevertheless, some work on personal defences can prove to be of use.

'It's very annoying when you see your son under the influence in public.'

'Sorry to butt in, it's just that I'm slightly confused. Is what you said a general statement or does it concern you? You see I am wondering if you get very annoyed with Duncan, with your son.'

'I suppose I do.'

'I brought up the subject only because I think it will help you to say you get very annoyed with Duncan when he ...'

'To say I get annoyed with Duncan when he is mumbling and stumbling around so everyone can see him? Yes, I do get embarrassed and then he laughs at me. But I have to face the neighbours.'

'So it is not just the embarrassment but Duncan's reactions and lack of consideration.'

'That's it! He has no consideration, acts entirely selfish.'

As we can see, the overcoming of some of the defences is done to enable the member to progress and is done, it is hoped, in a supportive manner. There is little justification for breaching a person's defences if nothing is done to substitute adequately for them.

When dealing with ventilation in the Group, the facilitator has to be aware what distancing can occur and its various forms. For instance, feelings can be placed in the past as if they no longer affect the member. The facilitator can either ask how the member feels about things now, link what has been consigned to the past with feelings at that very moment, or emphasise the point that the past still affects us all. What members mention, even if it refers to the past, is still likely to have significance for them in the present, or it would not have been mentioned.

'I felt very guilty when I heard James was on drugs. I wondered if me and my huband had not split up, things would have been different.'

'Can I ask you Jeannie, do you still feel guilty?'

'How do you mean?'

'Do you feel guilty about James being on drugs? At this very moment, do you feel guilty about it?'

'I try to think what happened did not affect him, but really I know it did.'

'So what I am picking up is that you do feel guilty.'

'It is difficult not to wonder.'

'You know what a dreadful bully I am, Jeannie. I want you to say whether you feel guilty or not.'

'You're right, of course! I do feel guilty.'

'And how do others feel about this?'

How much the facilitator can press members is always a matter of judgement, and an ongoing judgement. A new question is asked only after monitoring the effect of the last, how comfortable or not the member seems. Some members find it helpful to be pressured in such a way, others would react badly or become inhibited. For this reason, it is often worthwhile when summarising at the end of the session to ask how members felt when one of them – Jeannie in this case – was being helped to express how she felt.

A rather different form of distancing is that of shifting interest on to the drug user or someone other than the Group member. This is not always an obvious action, and it can also spread in the Group, so everyone gives accounts of difficulties they have experienced with drug users in their families. This is fine as long as the original speaker is not lost in the process.

Concentrating on the drug user also opens up the possibility of blame, either of the drug user or others, including members themselves. Blaming is essentially obstructive, leads nowhere and is very undermining, despite the fact that at first it can make members feel better. The facilitator does not have to stop blame if it is part of the ventilation process. As feelings subside, however, the whole question of blame can then be examined. For this reason, though ventilation can seem no more than letting off steam, it does provide material to use in the Group. The fewer restraints members feel, the more useful that material can be. This has to be set against whether the Group can take and usefully work with what has been said.

Acceptance

Some aspects of support have to be carried out only after the basics have been put in place. If we return to Group ventilation, then this is the first step in the process of acceptance, of feeling able to actively manage a previously unmanageable situation.

'I wouldn't miss these meetings as it gives me the chance to dump all my worries. I come, talk about what's happened during the last two weeks and then, that's it. I am ready for the next two weeks, and anything that happens I store up for the next meeting.'

How individual members behave depends partly on the Group culture. There are unwritten understandings and rules requiring members to act in a certain way. With regard to ventilation, members often feel they should get things off their chest in a fairly dramatic way. This confuses the character of Support Groups with that of other helping agencies such as Alcoholics Anonymous, where personal confession is part of the treatment process. But Group members do not come for treatment, they come for support and so we have to make known the accepted nature of ventilation.

Facilitation and ventilation

All Group members are individuals and are different to some extent and in varying ways, so how they express their feelings is likely to be peculiar to each one of them. One of the jobs of the facilitator is to judge the quality of the ventilation. For example, what might appear to be a very modest act of ventilation of feelings might actually be

very significant for that person. The facilitator has to be aware, as
indeed do all the Group members, of how far any member can go
with a degree of safety. Members should not be pressurised to say
more, if to do so would be distressing and unhelpful to them.

Ventilation may seem to be just one person's behaviour, but that
person is likely to be affected by others in the Group; ventilation is
rarely just an individual process. Indeed, if it were, the member
could get the same benefit from speaking to a brick wall. So the
facilitator has to monitor ventilation with regard to the individual
speaker and to the rest of the Group.

Inhibitions of members

Sometimes members, especially those new to the Group, are reluctant to express their feelings. This might reflect their family
upbringing, their parents having impressed on them the need for
emotional restraint or even repression. Men can be reluctant to
show emotions because of their cultural background. So there is
no point in saying that they should let go, promising that they will
feel better if they do so, when they have difficulty with this
process and letting go makes them feel worse. Members have to
decide for themselves how much of their feelings they can release.
They make a judgement based partly on how others in the Group
behave, but generally they are quite capable of deciding for themselves their own level of self-exposure.

Facilitators should pay attention to each member as an individual
and not make simplistic assumptions about them, such as women
are much more at ease when dealing with their emotions than men
are. Women may also be chary of being open about how they feel,
believing they should be 'strong' for the family. And obviously all
women, like all members, are different. Also we should be aware
that members' willingness to ventilate can vary over time. For example, one member decided not to come to a meeting after her son
became ill, sensing she would break down if she began to talk about
her feelings, and not wanting to do so at the time.

Specific inhibitions regarding ventilation

Group members may feel inhibited about saying precisely how
they feel. This might arise through not knowing how they feel.
They experience a mixture of emotions and are confused as to

how they really feel. Members might at first appear to show little emotion, and give a factual account of situations without letting go, as in this account by a mother describing finding her son:

'I found him blue and cold. I threw water on him but he didn't come round. He didn't come round for twenty minutes. I thought this time the overdose has killed him.'

The mixture of feelings confuses the member who does not know how to react privately, and has even less idea of how to behave publicly. What is required is that the facilitator and other members help the member to distinguish and identify the various feelings experienced. Time is needed to reflect on what has been felt, and then to name the separate and various feelings. This public naming is important as it moves the member to accept fully that personal feelings are involved, and then to own those feelings.

Ventilation and a multiplicity of feelings

The many feelings together can produce a sensation of personal chaos, so that those affected feel they are going mad. This chaos is reduced or even eliminated by those affected separating and identifying their various feelings, but this might only be possible after the prime task of admitting to the sensation of chaos and then being reassured. It is often worth explaining that experiencing more than one feeling at a time, feelings that are often contrary – love and hate, sadness and pleasure, pleasure and guilt – pulls the person in different directions at the same time. The result is total internal confusion, but a confusion that can be cleared up. This legitimisation of a member not knowing how he or she feels, allows that person to look closely at what is happening.

Even if the member is not blocked due to a multiplicity of feelings, it is still a good idea to see whether other feelings are being experienced. This usually requires a question such as, 'Do you have other feelings right now?' The point might have to be pushed a bit and the question phrased more specifically: 'Did you feel guilt as well as anger?', or, 'Were you relieved as well as feeling sad?' These secondary feelings are important as they tend to turn straight forward situations into problematic ones. It may be comparatively easy to deal with feelings such as anger, but if members have to deal with a combination of anger and guilt, then they experience considerable difficulty.

Thoughts around the acceptance of feelings

Another stumbling block is that members imagine that their feelings expressed in the meeting have to be acceptable. What they see as acceptable might be showing themselves to be worried or anxious, rather than letting the others know they feel glad or angry. This might arise through a general belief that people should not only react in certain ways but also feel in certain ways. It is not always easy to express the actual emotions experienced, so part of the solution is identifying what might be expressed in different situations.

'There are times when I wanted him dead for all the hurt and pain he had brought to the family. Then I find myself defending him when people outside the family criticise him – in spite of it all.'

A member might have to be helped to express underlying feelings. Simply saying 'you must have felt angry', or other appropriate statements helps to legitimise how a person feels and the expression of those feelings. Another approach is to ask the rest of the Group if they have ever been in a similar situation and encourage them to say how they felt. Though this might interrupt the member's flow, it can provide sufficient support for that member to proceed further.

All this requires the rest of the Group to empathise closely with the member, to be able to tell when someone is blocked or holding back. Any action taken must be done tentatively to begin with, as the Group or the facilitator might have misjudged the situation. No one should imagine they know for sure how another Group member feels.

Difficulties in acceptance

New members often assume that difficulties in accepting what they have said comes from its harrowing nature, causing negative feelings in others. In my experience, a lack of acceptance tends to come from different causes, such as the fact that they are new members. A lack of acceptance can also be personal. We should realise that not everyone in the Group will necessarily like each other, and this can lead to a lack of acceptance. However this is not necessarily the case, as not liking each other does not preclude acceptance. In the case of difficulties of acceptance, it can be helpful if the facilitator is publicly supportive to the individual member.

'I would like to thank you Wendy for telling us that, especially as it was obviously not an easy job for you. I don't know what the others here think, but it seemed to me that it took some guts for Wendy to talk to the Group.'

Other difficulties in acceptance of new members can come from monopolising the Group, not allowing anyone else to talk, or interrupting when others are talking. The facilitator has to be aware that what can seem slightly irritating can become very annoying to other members if it happens repeatedly, so some form of action should be taken, otherwise acceptance becomes even harder to achieve.

Starting to work on feelings

Ventilation is not the mere dumping of feelings, an emotional offloading on to others in the Group. Admittedly, this might not seem the case initially, as members follow their natural desire to get rid of pent up feelings as quickly as possible. And once the process has begun, a torrent of feelings can be discharged. This should be accepted; the Group listens attentively, showing the member that it is all right to talk emotively, to display feelings openly, to shout, to cry and to laugh. New members have to know that the world does not end because they are behaving emotionally, and have to know that other people are capable of accepting such feelings in a quiet and helpful manner.

On the other hand, if the release of feelings continues for a long time without work being done on them, then what takes place is no more than emotional dumping. There is the danger that such intended ventilation might be a way of eliciting sympathy rather than empathy. The member might be playing the game of being a victim with no desire to do more, no wish to try to improve the situation. The ventilation of feelings is merely making the person feel well enough to continue the process the next time, to continue in the same victim role.

Members have to do more than let go of their feelings to get the maximum benefit from the Group experience; they have to deal with the emotional aspect of their difficulties (Folkman and Lazarus, 1980). Members have to stay with their feelings, to really experience them again. Sometimes this means they have to be asked to repeat key emotional phrases and expand on their feelings. Questions such as, 'How does that make you feel right now?' or, 'What would you like to say to him if he was here this moment?' or, 'That must make you very angry.' What tends to be unhelpful is if feelings are diminished, explained away, rationalised or made the subject of apologies. Members should be steered away from such tactics.

Reliving old feelings is insufficient if there is no reflection on them by the member and the Group as a whole. The facilitator, after the initial rush of feelings and anxiety, should be prepared to intervene in the slackened emotional flow and ask everyone to begin to look at particular aspects of what the member has said.

Strong feelings

Turning members' attention to reflecting about the expressed feelings of a member may not be easy. Attention should be given to the release of particular emotions, above all those feelings that are strong and suppressed. In the security of the Group it is acceptable to let go of even extreme feelings and acknowledge them. Once such feelings have been acknowledged, it then becomes easier to work with them.

What might be noted is that the sharing of these feelings is their public acknowledgement as well as their open expression. The member does not merely express feelings but learns how to express them, and learns to say precisely what is bothering him or her. This might require assistance from the other members or the facilitator, in order to make a moment available to reflect on the process of expressing feelings. Sometimes it can be helpful if everyone takes a minute out to consider how they feel, and relate this to physical sensations, identifying what parts of their bodies they are aware of, where they feel tension and what feelings are related to particular bodily sensations. Then they can be acknoweledged.

If the Group is working well, members will sense the accepting atmosphere and this enables them to open up, even when strong underlying feelings are involved. We have to realise that members can feel very strongly about drug use in the family. Even events in the past can force their way into the present, their accompanying feelings can be immediate and almost overwhelming as the past comes vividly to life.

'I locked the garage door and hit him with a stick. I was so mad, I picked up a drill and wanted to drill holes in his kneecaps ... '

This quote came from a quiet housewife pushed to the edge of endurance. Yet this is often how strongly members feel, and it should be pointed out that all feelings are valid. We cannot control how we feel, though we can control how we behave. Members should be reassured about this as they sometimes equate the two, and then fear that how they feel will be translated into action. The role of control is overlooked, which, on reflection, is surprising as what members tend to show is high control over their behaviour.

What is useful is to stress that ventilation is a controlled release of feelings, which can be used outside the Group – provided there is going to be a helpful audience. Ventilation allows people to move to more rational views and decisions and to rid themselves of interfering, blocking or repressive feelings that distort logical thought. The process has to be seen as constructive, and members should not feel guilty about their feelings.

One difficulty that can occur is with the egocentric or self-absorbed member, whose ventilation seems to lead nowhere because there is no end to it. The person operates by constantly and unrealistically expressing feelings, feelings that can be very shallow or part of a very defensive way of dealing with the world. This fact may not be immediately obvious, as such Group members seem very eager and willing to ventilate, and they appear very honest and self-disclosing. Only later does it become apparent that such egocentric members are not interested in the Group except as an audience to their personal dramas. This can be counterproductive once the other members sense they are being used. The facilitator might have to intervene and help the member stop, and then look at what is happening. Ventilation is not just for the benefit of the individual but for all of the Group, and a balance has to be maintained.

The role of other members

The useful ventilation of feelings, like all useful actions of individual members, depends on a good response from the Group. Just as immediate blocking or diminution of the expression of feelings is unhelpful, so no reaction at all is equally unhelpful. However, there is no simple formula to determine the most appropriate response, but the Group being a place of security and learning, any unhelpful reply can be remedied. Helpfulness generally comes with honesty, so an unthinking response is, paradoxically, often better than a measured reply.

Group response

A good response comes from how the other members react, not just to the ventilation but to individual members and their personal situations. The facilitator has the role of ensuring that the response is appropriate, that feelings are accepted and not dismissed. Sometimes this requires certain statements to be highlighted, by the facilitator repeating them or asking the member to enlarge on them. However, care must be taken that feelings are experienced and not just talked about, that they are felt in the Group and not kept at arm's length.

Further aspects of working with feelings

The ventilation of feelings is only the first step in working with feelings. Indeed, to release feelings constantly and then not to progress can leave members feeling frustrated in the long run. The end result can be a disinclination to take the process of ventilation seriously.

So work with feelings has to continue with an examination of what their meanings and implications are for that individual. For instance, parents might have strong feelings but they also have to conform to what they see as acceptable behaviour; they then begin to sense that it might be wrong to feel how they feel.

As one mother said:

'There are times when you want to murder them. You think if they were dead, then you would have some peace of mind. But then you come to your senses.'

Sometimes members believe they have to keep an internal rein on their feelings, and this can be a strain. This is even more the case if there happen to be other stresses such as there being more than one drug user in the family. Parents may feel they have to repress feelings such as anger, fearing not only how others may react to open expressions of feelings, but also how they will be able to deal with it themselves.

'I get so wound up that if he came to the door I would strangle him. In fact, if anyone came to the door I would feel like doing that.'

Though feelings are internal to the person, there is the concern that they will not remain so. This constitutes yet another anxiety.

Further reaction

Members may go beyond this stage. They see that they have certain feelings and as a result they are behaving in a particular way. They then react to that behaviour. As an example, the following is a father commenting on his anger:

'Yes, I used to feel angry with Jenny and everything that was happening. Then I was afraid of what it was turning me into. I was angry at my reactions.'

So the act of releasing feelings is one stage of the helping process but it should be linked with other work, such as that of identifying feelings, and legitimising those feelings through the process of sharing. However, for some members, legitimisation of feelings depends on their being normalised.

Normalisation

Normalisation comes when members realise that what they are feeling and doing is normal. By allowing themselves to express feelings about matters which are not that important, they can build up confidence to express feelings about situations which are more difficult, and more highly charged with emotions. For some individuals, only by going through the lesser expression of feelings can more sensitive subjects be uncovered.

'She was so ill that they gave up all hope, took out the drip and said she would soon die. She was unconscious, not being fed and not getting any treatment. And then she recovered. I thought she would have changed, that it would have given her a fright. It didn't. She went back to jagging up and I found myself hating her for it. I thought it would have been better if she had died in the hospital.'

By checking out whether others have felt the same or understand how a member feels, the process of normalisation can be begun. What should be understood is that members coming to the Group often feel bad about themselves, and this makes their perception of how they feel subject to negative influences. Normalisation is one approach to helping members see their perceptions as being at variance with how other people react to a member's expressed feelings. Members can spot the false perceptions of others, even if they fail to identify their own misperceptions.

Reflection on the process

It is often worthwhile for the Group to take time out to look at the work that has been done. Working with feelings produces relief in itself and this fact can usefully be acknowledged and celebrated. This might seem strange at first, but for those coming to the meeting for support, it really gives the sense that something is being achieved. This not only makes the Group feel better – an important advance – but lays the basis for further work. It is always important to reflect on the work done; not merely to absorb what has been done and to better it, but to be able to move on to another level of working.

General ventilation

One avenue to further progress is to encourage the ventilation of all feelings brought to the Group, and not just those feelings caused by family drug use. Members may well be carrying such feelings because they have had a bad day, they are caught up in financial worries, or they may be thinking about what their partners said to them the previous day. Getting rid of these feelings is useful, as they can interfere with support work. General ventilation can also relieve feelings that build up as a result of being part of the Group, from the pressures and frustrations that arise through being a member (Bales, 1953). Letting go can assist the Group's functioning.

General ventilation may be required from time to time and this can be done by all members thinking of a particular frustration, anxiety or annoyance, and then everyone speaking at once, saying what they want to say. The idea is that by everyone talking at the same time, no one feels the centre of attention and so becomes inhibited. The process can cause a good deal of laughter, which is no bad thing. However, this action is best done by Groups whose members have known each other for some time and agree to try it out.

Incidently, some Groups start off meetings with a relaxation exercise but this does not seem very helpful to me. Feelings have to be expressed, not further contained or eliminated.

Behaviour outside the Group

The ability to express feelings should become part of the members' normal behaviour. For very self-controlled people this can be difficult, but it is still better in the long term to release rather than to store up feelings. By giving permission to ventilate, the Group reinforces the normality of expressing feelings.

It should be said that helping members to achieve self-expression is a learning process, an indirect process, and one that should not be rushed. It is best to avoid forcing matters by questions or statements which begin:

'If I were you ...'
'Don't you ever feel like ...?'
'Why don't you ...?'

These are rarely helpful, and can even seem threatening to members and make them even more self-controlling.

What is more helpful is to hear how members have managed to deal with their feelings outside the Group, and for members to react to such accounts.

'I was out in the street and lost control, effing and blinding at the three of them. Then I had to go back into the Centre as I had left my bag there. I apologised to Peter, who works there. He told me I had said what he always had wanted to say but his job didn't allow. He also thought that they had been passing drugs.'

'You were quite right. I would have done exactly the same.'

'Linda didn't say a word, she knew better. That boy, selling pills. If they have an addiction then I feel a bit sorry for them, but that thing doesn't use at all, he just sells drugs.'

'Yes, I hate those who do that.'

Members of the Group can support and normalise behaviour that is an expression of feelings. This is important, for as long as a member is choked up with strong feelings, as long as energy is caught up in repression, then it is harder to get help for oneself.

ANXIETY REDUCTION

Introduction

Ventilation is a 'letting go' or expression of feelings, usually arising from an ongoing situation or events that have happened in the past. However, there is also the future to consider, the possibility of some difficulty or disaster happening. Those affected by drug use are likely to worry or to be anxious about possible death, separation, violence, and family breakup. Anxiety can inhibit members from participating fully in the Group and lessen the benefit of their attending.

Anxiety is a product of how members feel and how they inter-pret those feelings, a product of the affective and the cognitive (Folkman et al., 1979). In the meeting, members begin to feel better through ventilation, sharing with others and releasing their feelings. This process can be sufficient to dissipate anxiety or at least to keep it under control. However there may be times when members suffer from anxiety which they are unable to eradicate. This may reflect their high degree of personal anxiety, or that other members in the meeting are in a similar state and unable to help. Under such circumstances, the facilitator might have to act to get the member or the whole Group to face their worries.

Worry work

The first step in helping is to encourage members to declare as precisely as possible what is worrying them. Precision is impor-tant. Often the worries are vague, and this vagueness makes them seem more threatening and less easy to fight.

'I worry, worry all the time what's going to happen, become of Colin.'
'Yes?'
'It just seems to go on and on.'
'What exactly are you worried about? What do you think will happen to him?'
'God knows ... taking drugs.'
'Are you concerned that one day he will die through taking drugs?'
'Yes ...'
'You don't know that.'

'But he's taking that smack.'

'My Garry been taking it off and on for years, and he's still here.'

'Right. Now does Colin inject heroin?'

'No, his doctor prescribes methadone and he won't use needles.'

'So we know the chances of him getting HIV by needle use has been dealt with. Also if he is not using the needle then the chance of overdosing is very small.'

'But if he goes back to the smack ...?'

'Aye, they often do. That's up to them. You can't tell them what to do, they just please themselves.'

'I don't know whether to tell him.'

'What are you going to tell him? "Don't take smack, Colin"? They don't bloody listen, and you're wasting your time.'

'If Colin was taking smack and is now on methadone, then he has decided himself to change. Talking about him using heroin when he has changed to methadone might just annoy him. Why not tell him how pleased you are that he is on methadone?'

'But methadone, that's still drugs.'

'Come on, we all take drugs in some form! No, Paul's right, Colin is making the effort to look after himself. He might be coming off in time, you never know. It would give him a boost to know you were behind him.'

'So you think I should be in favour of the methadone?'

'Takes some of them years to get to that stage. Better than jagging and spending all his money on drugs.'

'Yes.'

There are several points which come out of the above quote. Worry or anxiety can become a habit, members can be caught up in it and find it very difficult to escape. It may need considerable time for members to change, so pacing is important – as is having realistic expectations.

It is not possible to take away all worry, but it can be made more manageable. Having a drug user in the family is always going to be a source of anxiety, so the aim is to be able to live with that worry.

Time was taken to try to specify the cause of the worry. It seemed at first that it was the use of heroin, but then we discovered that Colin was not actually taking it. This is quite common, members worry about what is not the case, about what might happen. It is important to find out exactly what the worry is, as first answers might be misleading.

Giving information can be helpful, it does assist members in being specific and bringing in reality. However, information is rarely enough, and giving someone the facts might well fail to end personal anxiety.

Attention should be given to the person, as well as their particular worries. Time spent trying to argue the person out of the worries usually fails as the problem is how he or she feels and this affects how matters are seen. Helping requires making the person feel better, more positive, less trapped by worry. Only then can specific worries be tackled.

Garry's mother was trying to help and this points to the role of the facilitator not just being directed to the anxious mother but to the whole Group. In this case, although she wanted to help, her attitude was initially tinged with irritation. So part of the facilitation consisted in trying to ensure that real help was given, and this included lessening Garry's mother's irritation. Account must be taken of the fact that all Group members have their own feelings, and these are not irrelevant.

Some members may continue to worry for no good reason, simply because they have irrational beliefs which sustain their anxiety. This is often expressed as the 'what if ...' syndrome, where the person just expects the worst (Vasey and Borkovec, 1992). This can be so ingrained in some people that individual help might be required, as high anxiety can affect the whole of the Group.

Irrational beliefs

Worry is based on feelings which can produce distorted or irrational beliefs. These beliefs must be confronted in order to deal properly with the worry. There are many such beliefs, and some of them may be found in the list below.

1. What I do has to be approved by everyone.

2. I have always to be competent.

3. If things do not go right, then the result is catastrophe.

4. If I think about things going wrong, then they will go wrong.

5. There are right answers and perfect solutions.

6. Whatever happens, individuals, families and organisations have to be kept going and intact.

7. I need someone stronger than me to rely or depend on.

8. What will happen to me is determined by my past.

These beliefs set impossible aims and standards, which cannot be achieved. They also put the members into a double-bind as they seem to indicate that whatever is done cannot improve the situation. The effect of irrational beliefs can often be seen when members say they have to do something, but what then follows is a list of reasons for not acting: they do not know what is the right thing to do, they wonder if something better could be thought of, they fear others will obstruct any change, and they think any change will lead to failure – and they are paralysed, stuck between action and inaction.

Work on irrational beliefs

Sometimes it is necessary to take time out from the usual business of the meeting to look at members' irrational beliefs and deal with them.

The first point to make is that although the beliefs may be irrational, they are personal beliefs and as such they may be dear or important to the Group member. Any work on irrational beliefs has to be done very gently. Too direct an approach with members may be interpreted as a personal attack and cause a counterproductive reaction.

So it is not helpful for the facilitator or Group members to contradict, disparage or attempt to refute members' irrational beliefs. Members are unlikely to be argued out of their beliefs: instead, they have to see them and themselves as mistaken.

For example, suppose a member adheres to the belief that she is the prisoner of her past. She has a totally fatalistic view of her life. Then one approach might be as follows:

'I agree it sometimes seems that way, that we cannot really do anything. I have felt like that. However there have also been times that, despite such feelings, I was able to have influence and was able to bring about a measure of change. I wonder whether others in the Group have had these negative feelings. Have you found you were able to cause things to change despite how you felt?'

This approach in the meeting does contain some useful points.

- Show that you appreciate how the member feels. This brings the member into the discussion.

- Reinforce the appreciation by sharing, saying that you have felt the same. This limits the member's feeling of isolation.

- The word 'seems' is useful as the facilitator can agree with the feelings but does not have to agree with the thinking that arises from those feelings.

- Any disagreement can be modified by not making it complete. Phrases like 'there have been times' always leave a person with room to manoeuvre, so the member is not wrong. It is better to avoid right and wrong, and move toward constructing a picture of what is the case – where interpretations differ.

- The other members are brought in before the anxious member has a chance to reply and the Group gets stuck on one specific worry or on one worried person. All members are likely to have suffered considerable anxiety, so the problem should not be confined to one person.

Sometimes the anxiety will continue and there is little to be gained by going on and on in an attempt to help. However, such members usually do improve over a few meetings and this can be reinforced by commenting on the fact, even if the improvement seems quite small.

Information collection

As has been noted, part of the process of lessening irrational beliefs hinges on the twin aspects of eliminating such specific beliefs and by replacing them with beliefs founded on more realistic perceptions and solid information. In fact, the whole process of gathering and sharing information is usually seen as one of the principal benefits of belonging to a Support Group, a way to personal empowerment. The difficulty is knowing how to gather information, and what information is reliable and what is unreliable.

Sources of information

Information about drugs is obtained from many different sources, but these can be placed into five main categories. These are:

1. The media.
2. Community and neighbourhood sources.
3. Drug education programmes.
4. The medical profession.
5. The law.

These sources influence each other but they also have their own characteristics, often giving their own perception of illegal drug use.

The media and drug information

Perhaps the best analysis of media and drug information is actually from the US, where there have been many reviews and evaluations of drug programmes. Research into drug education and newspaper reporting highlighted the following five aspects (Bomboy, 1974), which seem equally applicable to the popular British newspapers.

(a) information given is often based on ignorance, fear or false perceptions;

(b) newspapers are more interested in a story that sells papers than in the truth;

(c) myths are reported as fact due to excessive reliance on local sources, usually the local police;

(d) reporters seldom cross-check with street sources; and

(e) newspapers are generally unwilling to go beyond Government provided propaganda.

Television generally tends to be the same, partly because many television reporters have had newspaper reporting experience. Support Group members are often rather cynical about the media, yet still appear to absorb information from them.

Neighbourhood and community information

Community information is useful as it tends to be relevant for Group members, though it is also likely to be biased. Local opinion tends to be unsympathetic to illegal drug use and there is usually much anxiety, especially with regard to the dangers to children. The emphasis is on prevention, enforcement and exclusion with regard to drug use, with concerns about local housing, businesses and facilities. Neighbours tend to reinforce local information, which can be well informed, but the accompanying understanding might be more limited.

Drug education and information provision

Most drug education, under the aegis of health education, has been school-based, and started in the US to prevent young people getting involved with illegal drugs by frightening them, a tactic which proved ineffective (Wald and Abrams, 1972). 'Scare tactics' were used later by the British Government in its 'Heroin screws you up' campaign in the 1980s, which was also ineffective (*BMJ*, 1985). Unfortunately, although young people might not have taken on board the scare messages, the parents of drug users had their anxiety reinforced.

Drug education did then attempt to give schoolchildren the 'facts', so they could decide for themselves. This was a definite advance, though it was hampered by the fact that many older children were fairly well informed themselves and able to spot inconsistencies in attitudes to drugs and the selection of facts. Little is said about the criminalisation and decriminalisation of drugs, and the enjoyment factor in taking drugs. The dangers of tobacco and alcohol are appreciated, but the dangers of prescribed drugs are usually left unsaid.

There have been doubts expressed about whether drug education achieves the aims of its remit (Schaps et al., 1981; De Haes, 1988), so its role in not highlighting some aspects of drug use is of concern. Although drug education was originally aimed at children, it has been extended to parents of schoolchildren as an optional resource. Also, drug education views are given to local community groups and are becoming increasingly important. This links up with the fact that drug education has been increasingly politicised (Stimson, 1987), as have the Health Education Authorities.

Doctors

The medical profession uses drugs and is thus regarded as being the best source of information about illegal drug use, even though doctors receive little training about it at medical school (Glass, 1989). Their knowledge of relevant drug matters can be quite low (Pekkanen, 1976), and most doctors have a low involvement in helping drug users (*AIDS and Drug Misuse*, 1989).

The remit of General Practitioners is to treat patients, and this is what is done, giving patients as little information as possible. As a result, doctors are not good communicators (Cartwright and O'Brien, 1976) in their jobs. Part of this reflects the fact that doctors have little time to give to each consultation, and so do not welcome patients' questions (Waitzkin and Stoekle, 1972). Even where there is open doctor–patient communication, doctors are not always very good at giving helpful explanations (Cartwright and Anderson, 1981), and patients frequently do not understand or do not remember what they are told (Ley and Spelman, 1967).

It is assumed that doctors will give patients and others the 'facts'. In reality, they are just as likely as anyone else to stereotype patients (Hooper et al., 1982) and label those who do not conform to their wishes (Browne and Freeling, 1967); and doctors are markedly disinclined to become involved with those persons who have been stigmatised as deviant (McKinlay, 1979).

All of this means that doctors have a certain view of drug use and drug users, their facts moulded by the medical view of life.

The law

The law is important because people tend to see drug problems in very much the way that the law defines them (National Commission on Marihuana and Drug Abuse, 1973). In Britain there would seem to be a clear link with the medical profession as it dominates the Advisory Council, created under Section 1 of the Misuse of Drugs Act, 1971. Not only does the Council advise the Government, but under Section 31(3) of the Act, the Secretary of State shall not make any regulations under the Act except after consultation with the Advisory Council. In fact, the suggestions made are often not taken up, and drugs policy has increasingly become politicised, linking in with media and public pressure, which is frequently poorly informed.

Problems with information

As can be gathered, information about drugs and drug use is partly determined by source. If more than one source is used, then there can be resultant confusion which only adds to Group members' anxiety. Some members will react to the different views by declaring that no one knows the answers. This further increases negative feelings, leaving parents and partners wondering where accurate information can be obtained. In the absence of such information, personal beliefs, personal guilt and anger, opinion and prejudice may all be used to construct a 'rational' explanation of what is happening (Brown, 1974).

There is no perfect answer. All of us have to live with a degree of uncertainty. What is required, besides information, is an appreciation that other people will see drug use in different ways.

Information work

Despite difficulties in gathering and using information, it is important that Group members feel they have adequate knowledge about drugs, and to work at the problem with the different answers they might get about drugs.

The first move is to find out what knowledge already exists in the Group. It does help if the facilitator is well informed about drugs and drug use, not as a source of information but to act as a balance to any member who decides to be the Group expert. What is important is for everyone to grasp that they do not have to possess a lot of medical knowledge and they do not have to know how things happen, only those things which are likely to affect them.

'I have to be careful when she comes to the house, careful about hanging up her leather jacket as she often keeps a syringe in the bottom lining.'

'She used to get really snappy, and said it was the time of the month. But it seemed always to be the time of the month! I began to realise when she was withdrawing; that that was the way she'd be, and it was best to leave her alone. It became like a code, whenever she would withdraw then she said it was the time of the month, and she knew that I knew what was going on. Of course, now she's prescribed and it's different. She said to me last week that she was having her period and I asked her if she had run out of methadone. She asked me if I was off my head. This time it really was her time of the month.'

'Ronald looks terrible, his face is all clapped in, and he's that thin. It's no use giving him a good meal as he says he can't face it. But he will eat sweet things, so I leave them in the fridge and never mention them. He goes straight in there and eats them. Mind it still doesn't stop him moaning, saying he's off drugs and there's nothing to eat in the house.'

The amount of information might seem quite small in the quotes given, but the advantage is that, in my experience, they are usually better remembered than more academic explanations.

As facilitator, I like to make a note of such remarks, partly to get the Group to expand on them, but also to link up with more direct information such as the risks of HIV and hepatitis, the nature of withdrawals, and drugs and weight loss.

What is being built up is the Group's own knowledge store, and after a time it can be helpful to have the gathered information written up and given back to the members. They are likely to be surprised at how much knowledge they have accumulated. Once the Group begins to feel more confident about their ability to know what is happening, other sources of information may be introduced.

More than one source can be used – Health Education personnel, drugs workers, doctors, Drugs Squad officers – but members should first take time to draft some questions they want answered. This not only helps any visiting speaker but also gives the Group more control. Control is essential for the Group, as information alone will not diminish anxiety. Members have to be confident about that information, they have to be empowered through the very process of gaining knowldge about drugs and drug use. Time should be given to talking about how members feel after having had a speaker to the Group or having visited a drugs agency. The different information and views of the separate speakers should be highlighted and the Group should work towards an acceptance of those differences, along with an understanding of why they exist.

Work on information is a long-term process, and it is best if the Group does not to attempt too much too soon. It should also be remembered that the process of gaining knowledge is as important as the knowledge itself.

SHARING IN THE GROUP

Sharing with others

Ventilation, to be fully effective, has to be aligned with other aspects of support work, such as members sharing their personal experiences. By sharing, members find they are not alone; what they have experienced has been experienced by others.

'On the scheme where we all live, it is all bought houses and you don't speak to anyone, don't let anyone know that your son is on drugs. And you're scared in case they do find out. Coming here allowed me to talk to people outside the house for the first time.'

Discovering that a family member is on drugs can be painful and distressing. The rest of the family will be upset, frightened, angry and shocked. And there may be no one they can talk to, no way they can let go of their feelings. As a result the family can feel isolated, fearing the reaction of outsiders, who might be unsympathetic and unhelpful. To some extent, families or partners are treated as being contaminated by the drug use, and this increases feelings of being different and apart.

'We have always been a respectable family and looked up to the police. Not now! Ever since Alan got involved in drugs they have been at the door and treated us as if we encouraged him or something. The way they have behaved has made us lose respect for them.'

Breaking personal isolation can lead to further benefits, as isolation can result in a degree of detachment from reality. It engenders fantasy, and acts as a repository for unresolved feelings. The lack of meaningful social interaction can cause an amplification of pain and distress, usually worsened by the accompanying sense of unreality. All of this is reduced by sharing in the Group.

For example, guilt is a common characteristic of families where drug use occurs. Sharing relevant experiences in the Group is a good method of diminishing guilt, making it easier for members to express their feelings.

'I thought it was me, that no one else in the world had a son on drugs. You know others must be in the same boat, but you still think you are the only one. And then you wonder – why me?'

As may be seen, sharing is merely part of a total process of coming to terms with drug related difficulties.

The nature of sharing

Sharing experiences can be liberating, though there can be some difficulties along the way. To be effective, it has to be a giving of information, thoughts and feelings, accompanied by an acceptance shown in attentive listening. This does not always happen if Group members are caught up in their own situations, and the facilitator might have to intervene to ensure feedback.

When sharing in the Group, members bring to the meetings their own pasts, their present and future hopes and expectations, and a wide range of experiences which relate not just to drug issues. The Group has to be open to new information, ideas and feelings from its members. It is often surprising how they shed light on present concerns, even if indirectly.

'I wish we had been told when my Dad was ill with cancer. At least at the time we would have understood why he had become so bad tempered towards us.'

'Yes, Alec is very ill now, and he's moody. As you say, it is not pleasant but you understand the situation.'

The original observation linked up with ideas about severe HIV infection in the family, and helped members not to see issues in too narrow a way, to see their difficulties as not just being specific to illegal drug use but to life in general. Sharing in the Group is not an end in itself, but a way to help members deal with their situations. It is useful to hear how others have acted, and whether it proved to be of use.

One advantage of describing actual situations is that it can be appreciated that there is no right or wrong, merely people dealing with life in their own way. In the long term it helps to know there is no right answer, and members do not have to search for perfection. Using the experiences of others in the Group, members become more understanding and understand more. This comes from really listening to the other members, as this sister of a drug user did:

'To let you know, Spencer has been staying with me. After a time you get to know their ways. You can see the moves coming and I just tell him – no way! I don't believe him when he "has lost his script", I know he won't pay any money back. Don't get me wrong, I'll help him all I can but I have to tell Mum, "Don't let him con you!"'

The essence of sharing is to involve the Group as much as possible. The facilitator can help by keeping quiet and letting the members have their say, encouraging the rest as well as the main speaker. After a time, it becomes unnecessary to do so, sharing quickly becomes the norm.

'When Terry was taking that stuff, it was as if everything depended on him, and the world had to stop for him. He would not come home on time, even though he knew a meal had been cooked for him. We would have to sit about, wondering if he was going to turn up.'

'That's it! Ray is exactly the same. You don't know where you are. I wonder if he breaks promises on purpose or whether he simply forgets.'

'Sometimes they are in no position to remember – out of their heads.'

'It makes you think they do it on purpose, get that way as an excuse.'

'Ray is good at that. Excuses, excuses.'

'And how does that make you feel?'

'Angry, as he thinks I'm going to swallow everything he says.'

'Yes, Terry can't even think up good excuses. They are always the same.'

'And they get so annoyed if you don't believe them – at least Ray does. Looks me straight in the eye and says, "Don't you believe me, Mum?" They play on your feelings.'

Comparison

Like all helping processes, sharing has its potential drawbacks. Members may come to the Group and hear of problems far worse than their own. The facilitator has to ensure that this fact does not hold them back from speaking, that they do not regard their situations as being insignificant in comparison, and consequently not worth mentioning. Members come to the meeting with feelings of pain and distress. These feelings are real and should not be discounted, whatever the particular situation may be.

In fact, what comes out in Group meetings can act either positively or negatively, and to some extent this depends on the members' perceptions of the emergent material and how it is handled. For example, painful material might reinforce negative feelings or it may have a positive effect. Part of the art of facilitation is to ensure that pain and distress are faced and that ultimately the experience proves positive and helpful. This applies equally to aspects of the work such as sharing and comparison.

'I came to the Group and saw that there were others who were worse off than me and they were coping. It gave me that wee bit of hope. And I realised that Fiona's laddie was further on than mine, and perhaps she was coping with things I would have to deal with in time.'

Comparison is helpful as it allows members to form a baseline of experience. What is taking place is normal for families where there is drug use. Interpretation of what is happening is difficult in isolation, but becomes much easier in the context of a homogeneous group where it is possible to compare different experiences (Festinger, 1954). We should also be alert to the opposite, that the level of functioning of more experienced Group members can be intimidating to newer members or those with low self-esteem. The Group in the next example had been discussing HIV infection.

'When I heard how Susan copes with things, I thought I could never do that. Goodness knows how I will deal with things when my daughter gets that ill.'

It is at times like these that the presence of other members is useful. Those who have experienced so much are the real force in the helping process. What perhaps would be inappropriate when coming from a facilitator is more acceptable when coming from members, as they have gone through similar experiences.

'You will cope with things. I was like you, I never thought I could face what was going to happen, but you get the strength. I don't know where it comes from, but you will get it as well.'

Again, the facilitator is responsible for ensuring that what is happening in the meeting is used to the members' advantage. This ability of the Group to change perceptions, to see situations from a different and more positive point of view, is of importance to all.

Sharing and Group reactions

When sharing experiences, the Group has to learn how to react usefully to a person's disclosure, in particular to identify with and publicly acknowledge a member's experience. Failure to identify with personal disclosure diminishes what the member has said, and so diminishes the person. The facilitator has to watch for negativity, such as members' replies which might begin with 'I never do that'; 'I would never have said that'; 'I have never felt that' or, 'I've not been in any situation like that.' These remarks close down the discussion and do not help the particular Group member.

Sharing and differences

Sharing can help the rest of the Group as they are exposed to accounts of different lives, expanding their perspectives and understanding. This may be necessary for those members who are slightly depressed and have a rigid outlook, members who have a certain poverty in thought, commonly seen by the extensive use of cliches and repetition (Beck et al., 1979). This reflects a disinclination to allow the outside to intrude on their private worlds. Unfortunately, the walls they build to protect themselves from the outside also keep them prisoner. Sharing helps the whole Group to accept differences, not just in people's lives but in associated perspectives, beliefs, needs and desires. Accepting differences in others can help some members to begin to think and feel differently.

Thinking in new ways also comes with seeing that others have their problems too, they are not so competent in their actions, nor so pure in their motives, and there is no perfection in human affairs. Once members can move away from idealised images of the world, then they can begin to connect more firmly with reality, both outside and inside themselves.

SELF-DISCLOSURE

Nature of self-disclosure

The sharing of experiences by Group members usually involves a degree of self-disclosure, talking about themselves in an honest manner. The nature of self-disclosure should be appreciated. It is not confession, it is not simply the dumping of thoughts and feeling on others. It is talking about themselves for their own benefit and for the benefit of the Group. Self-disclosure is only helpful if work is done on what has been said. There is no point in disclosing private material needlessly, and the idea that getting it off your chest is necessarily beneficial is incorrect. So work on self-disclosure has to be followed through, and the facilitator can ensure that this is done.

Members, when they first come to the meetings, tend to talk about other people, particularly the drug user. But in time self-disclosure increases, building up trust and the ability of the Group to deal with more intimate and painful matters. For self-disclosers, the process can be an affirmation of personal worth, provided that it is a positive Group event. Even the mere act of being able to talk to others, to move experiences from the private world of individual memory to the outside world, indicates a measure of growing self-control.

The actual content of what is laid before the Group might be factual and relate to items such as experiences when young, relationships, identity, sexuality and illegal behaviour. These will relate primarily to members themselves. Besides factual material, self-disclosure should cover feelings, desires, expectations, dreams and fantasies. Any such disclosure is not merely the recounting of personal history, it also covers talking about themselves with the expression of all attendant feelings. The need for emotional content is essential as otherwise the self-disclosure has no real impact on the rest of the Group; it can even sound boring. It is through feelings that the rest of the Group is engaged and gets caught up with the member's account, and can then respond productively, with acceptance and respect.

Aspects of self-disclosure

Self-disclosure works most effectively when it is related to the present. However, initially many disclosures appear to relate only to the past, and the task is to ensure they are linked to the present. Sometimes members will say that they are little affected now by these incidents. This may be true, though the facilitator should not simply accept this declaration. And if a member comes up with the same disclosure on several occasions, then the facilitator might well suspect a situation that is very much unfinished. Nevertheless, we should not assume members necessarily want such unfinished situations to be resolved, so sensitivity is required.

Self-disclosure might also represent a member's ploy to maintain status and position in the Group, especially if there is a tendency for one member to top another's account by even more painful and harrowing revelations. This can amount to using the Group rather than being part of it. If the facilitator senses this is happening, then intervention might be required.

The facilitator also has to ensure that the Group as a whole is helpful, and this requires continuous attention. In one example, a mother talked about herself in relation to her husband. This progressed to slighting references to him and eventually the Group moved to a moaning session about men in general, before being called back by myself as facilitator to examine what was going on. By avoiding reference to self, the discussion was becoming quite negative, merely reinforcing the idea that nothing could be done about male partners.

Degree of disclosure

Members are entitled to disclose as much or as little as they feel able. There should be no pressure to self-disclose, and it is up to the facilitator to sense if this is happening. Members should be allowed to keep their privacy if they so wish, as self-disclosure can be threatening and painful.

Differences in the desire to self-disclose should be remembered and acknowledged. For some members, early childhood experiences, especially interactions with parents, can produce fears about intimate relationships and stifle desires to self-disclose (Hazan and Shaver, 1987). As everyone has different childhood experiences, we might expect variations in the degree of self-disclosure at Group meetings. Furthermore, poor relationships can further blunt a person's keenness to talk about intimate matters. However, this does not inhibit members from talking, merely lessens the eagerness to talk about themselves. Even when members do talk about themselves, many things may not be disclosed. Members might decide that the Group is important but not supremely so, and there is no reason why they should reveal all. Also, too close a relationship with others in the Group may be thought to be not only inappropriate but also threatening.

It can take time for newer members to become accustomed to the culture of appropriate self-disclosure, to trust the Group sufficiently, and to realise that the world will not end as a result of private revelations. On the other hand we should be aware of what eventual failure to self-disclose entails. It reflects on the particular member, on the Group itself, and on any facilitator. In fact self-disclosure almost always occurs, in varying degrees.

Risks of disclosure

Facilitators might worry about members self-disclosing more than they really intend, getting caught up in the Group dynamics and being carried further than they want. However, this fails to give due recognition to the abilities of those at the meetings. As self-disclosure does involve a degree of risk, members usually disclose in stages, a bit at a time, and wait to see the reaction of the others; whether they are going to be supportive, and whether they in turn are going to self-disclose.

Members can and do take care to protect themselves. They will risk self-disclosure and then retreat to safer subjects, returning to factual descriptions before again self-disclosing. Facilitators and members should not interfere with the process, as members are not just testing the Group; they are testing themselves. At times they might tell only part of the story: they tell the truth, but not the whole truth. This seems quite legitimate as it shows the stage of trust and honesty felt by themselves and the rest of the Group. Often, weeks later, members will return to the same subject or situation and be more self-disclosing. The facilitator can help here by praising the greater degree of revelation, and thanking the member for taking the risk and trusting the Group.

Difficulties in disclosure

For some people, self-disclosure is difficult as they are in a highly chaotic state. They fear a lack of control over themselves, their thoughts and feelings. To counteract this, they become more rigid, self-controlling and defensive, and this can prevent them from talking intimately about themselves. Other members see self-disclosure resulting in greater intimacy in the Group, and this can worry them, especially if they have experienced few satisfactory relationships in their lives.

However, for most members self-disclosure is something that they would like to do. Frequently they are carrying thoughts and feelings they would like to get rid of, but previously felt unable to do so. Self-disclosure can be liberating, and increase personal energy while diminishing anxiety.

Reflections on self-disclosure and its nature

Everyone in the Group has the opportunity to contribute to and help in self-disclosure. This should be contrasted with other self-disclosing situations, whether with priests, psychiatrists, doctors or social workers. In such disclosures we are not expected to play a very active or decisive role, other than to take advice or follow orders. This means that such disclosures result in full control for the professional, not for the disclosee, lessening the likelihood of personal responsibility being assumed and the person being able to grow.

Moreover, this drawback is reinforced by the professional labelling process that ensues. People may be labelled as 'sinful' by the priest, 'mad' by the psychiatrist, 'ill' by the doctor, 'not coping' by the social worker; and the danger is that such labelling is taken on by the person rather than being ascribed to behaviour. People can end up believing that there is something wrong with them, which gives them a reason to see themselves as incapable of change and not needing to take responsibility for their actions.

It is only by means of the cooperative working through of self-disclosure by the Group that such labelling can be avoided. Everyone is in the same situation but there is hope, acceptance and change. It is partly through self-disclosure that members rediscover themselves, and move towards who they want to be.

Pressure to self-disclose

There is the feeling that everyone should self-disclose. In part this is because self-disclosure is seen as being good for individual members and for the Group as a whole. But there is another reason. To self-disclose is to take a risk, to make oneself vulnerable in front of others. This can represent a potential loss of personal power and status, unless there is positive acceptance. In the Group that risk is taken because others also go through the same process, so there has to be reciprocity for self-disclosure to work well.

The facilitator has to use judgement to ensure that there is a balance between those members getting irritated with others for not self-disclosing and those who are reluctant to talk about themselves. Furthermore, premature self-disclosure is likely to be unhelpful in that it can be inhibiting and stop further disclosures. In extreme cases, the result can be a withdrawal from the Group, the member possibly feeling too much has been revealed. Premature self-disclosure can also make the Group see the member in a stereotypical way. For instance, once the Group has an early image of a member as a drinker or as an over-protective mother rather than as a person in their own right, then it can be difficult to change this initial picture. This in turn may make it more difficult to relate to the person as a person, and for that member in consequence to relate to the Group.

Lack of self-disclosure

If members reveal very little about themselves, then they will get only partial support from the Group and make the other members less prepared to do the same. So members should be very gently encouraged to self-disclose, without being pressurised.

Occasionally, a member has requested to talk to me outside the Group, to discuss a particularly difficult subject. Normally, I prefer members to share with the Group: after all, that is its purpose. Nevertheless, the facilitator has to be sensitive to the person and have a feel for the situation. So I did speak to the member, and in later meetings she was able to talk about the subject – her feelings about her grandaughter, who had been fostered out and then adopted. This was followed by her talking in the meeting and this helped her to make plans, and eventually she met the adoptive mother.

Facilitator's role in disclosure

The facilitator should ensure that the Group can take the self-disclosure and use it. Self-disclosure can reactivate painful memories both for the member and for the rest of the Group, which might need attention. Also account has to be taken of the fact that self-disclosure can be an emotional effort for all concerned, requiring considerable energy.

Once members have talked intimately about themselves, the facilitator makes the process productive by acknowledging the risk the member has taken in the self-disclosure, and this can be done by referring to the affective part of what has been said. 'That sounded as if you had to go through a really upsetting and sad experience' or, 'What you have said makes me feel extremely angry myself' might be ways of acknowledging what has been said.

The process can be continued by asking members how they feel, what it is like to be able to talk about themselves in the Group, and whether they feel better or worse after their self-disclosure. Likewise the Group can be asked how they feel, and what they would like to say to individual members. What should be avoided is the Group probing disclosing members, pressurising them to reveal more, and detracting from the fact that all members take risks in saying what they do.

Finally, the content of the disclosure can be broadened. The facilitator can ask the Group if what was said rings any bells with them, touches any particular nerve – if they have not already mentioned similar experiences themselves.

Facilitators and self-disclosure

One point that might arise is whether facilitators should self-disclose. My own feeling is that the Group is for its members and it is not appropriate for the facilitator to self-disclose, unless specifically asked to do so by the Group. Alternatively, it might be done if the self-disclosure is likely to be of help to the Group, and there has been no similar self-disclosure from the members. Facilitators should not expect members to self-disclose if they are not prepared to enter into the process themselves. And facilitators might have to self-disclose if their failure to do so impedes the support work.

STRUCTURING

Recognition of chaos

The first of the work modes that the facilitator should consider is that of structuring – helping members to bring greater structure into their lives. Those who are at a time of crisis or are under extreme stress are likely to see the world as chaotic, because they feel chaotic internally. From this feeling, members imagine that nothing useful can be done and that life is simply too much of a mess to be righted. And because this is a feeling, it will not be eliminated by rational argument alone. In such cases, the help of others in bringing a sense of order is helpful and brings relief. Members at sixes and sevens suddenly realise that they are not the only ones to feel as they do. By sharing experiences, they see that all the difficulties do not rest with them, that they are not going mad, and that the world does not rule their actions.

Sometimes this is not enough, and help has to be given to build up personal structure. This can be done by the Group reflecting back to the chaotic member how they see him or her. As ever, honesty is far more important that being nice or pretending the person is really all right. Comments such as, 'You seem all over the place!' might not at first seem very supportive, but are a part of the helping process. Such honest comments are useful as they confirm how the member is likely to see herself and feel. If someone is in a mess, then to have others openly saying so comes as a relief. It confirms the member's self-perception as accurate, and this establishes a baseline from which further work can begin.

Legitimising chaos

The next step is to legitimise personal chaos, to say that it is all right to be in a mess in very difficult situations. Everyone in the Group has to be able to understand and sense that chaos, and be encouraged to indicate they have empathised with the person. Remarks such as, 'When I heard my son had started to take heroin, I was the same. I felt my world had gone to pieces', can be of assistance. It is not just that it is permissible to be in chaos; to be otherwise would be even more worrying. The real enemy is not feelings but indifference, not reality but fantasy. By seeing the situation in a more detached manner and by acknowledging it, those principally affected are ready to put structure into their lives. Members define their limits and boundaries, and say how they see themselves in relation to the drug user, their partner and family.

It is useful in chaotic situations to label, where possible, what is happening as normal behaviour such as grief reactions or actions resulting from high anxiety. Sharing the experiences in the Group allows members to find meaning in their own worlds, and to build up their own personal structure rather than have a structure imposed upon them.

POSITIVE ATTITUDES

Need for positivity

Another aspect which helps Group functioning is that of members' positive attitudes and behaviour, something the facilitator should endeavour to maintain – though always within realistic bounds. Unfounded optimism quickly degenerates into disbelief and cynicism, both counterproductive to personal progress.

Positive attitudes and behaviour can be increased by reinforcement, by members telling others how well they have done to achieve their personal objectives or carry out useful actions. This may seem unimportant, yet so many people fail to have their actions acknowledged, and consequently they feel unappreciated themselves and are unable to appreciate others.

Perhaps it is worth remarking that giving positive reinforcement almost goes against British cultural and work norms, and should thus be used with discretion at first. Also, seeing the positive in a situation does not require members to have a false view of reality. A glass of water can be half full or half empty; only the perspective differs. If members feel better they are more likely to take a more positive view of the situation, and this leads to a greater willingness to do something about it.

Dealing with the negative

Being positive seems fine until members discover that their actions are unsuccessful. This appears to prove that they were being unrealistic. Yet failure is just a label fixed to parts of a person's life. It is preferable to view failure as a first attempt at achieving a goal, a trial run before eventual success. And having actually tried, having risked taking action, is itself a success. This may seem to be unduly optimistic, but undue optimism occurs only where goals are unrealistic.

Being positive also covers dealing with negative perspectives. These include a fatalistic view that whatever will be, will be: the individual can change nothing. These views have to be challenged, not only for the individual member's sake, but also because they can cause negative attitudes to spread throughout the Group. All of the members have to realise that they can do their bit. When facilitating I have occasionally given personal instances of being able to change or modify a situation, and this usually encourages other members to give their own examples.

Increasing positivity can come through identifying personal strengths. Abilities to listen, to empathise with others, to make suggestions, and to be self-disclosing are indications of personal strengths, and should be acknowledged by reflecting back to members that they do have such strengths. For many members this can be one of the steps in rediscovering their own power and their ability to control situations for themselves.

The Group can be positive if it uses the knowledge and skills that are within. The resultant positive actions are likely to induce positive reactions, first in the attitudes of others, and then in their behaviour (Stuart, 1980).

Dual messages

It may seem that giving constant positive messages could result in an unrealistic atmosphere. Yet the advantage of such messages is that they allow increased realism by making it easier to express negative feelings. Negative feelings on their own are likely to be taken personally and prove unhelpful, but dual messages – a combination of positive and negative – are usually quite acceptable (Kassorla, 1984). Negative feelings may have to be dealt with, and persistent negative feelings should be shared (Rogers, 1973) so they may be worked on.

SELF-ESTEEM

Nature of self-esteem

Often members have low self-esteem when they first come to the Group. The fact that they have difficulties and feel unable to cope can make them feel bad, and results in them having a poor opinion of themselves. They are likely to lack confidence, making effective action harder to contemplate and carry out. Raising members' self-esteem gives them confidence to act more decisively.

Work on self-esteem depends on having a clear idea of its nature, of how people value themselves in the context of their lives; in relation to past experiences, to present circumstances and future hopes and expectations.

Some origins of low self-esteem

General public attitudes can cause illegal drug users to be seen negatively and in stereotypical ways. Drug users are seen as bad, out of control, violent, or unfortunate at the very least. What tends to be forgotten is that each drug user is somebody's child, often somebody's partner and possibly somebody's parent. They are seen purely as individuals and not as belonging to families. However, when the families are considered, then they too may be viewed negatively, and labelled as unhelpful, problematic or bad, not only by the police but also by doctors and social workers.

Other forms of low self-esteem

Low self-esteem may pre-date family drug use, being the outcome of earlier events in members' lives. In Groups facilitated by myself, some members had been the victims of physical abuse, usually as a result of their partners' heavy drinking. The past abuse was still fresh in their minds, causing them to feel bad about themselves and making it hard to change as they were very bound up with what others might think of them. Being so outwardly dependent means members have high hopes of other people, have high expectations and yet they also have great fears that they will be let down, disappointed or rejected. The Support Group with its warm and friendly atmosphere may be seen as a haven, a place where they may be accepted.

Yet members do not suddenly gain more self-esteem, they still have fears about the Group not being the answer to whatever they are searching for. These fears are likely to be partially realised in that the actions of members might well be interpreted as being forms of rejection – and there will be times when members behave in ways that are not fully supportive. Those situations may be retrieved to some extent by the facilitator, preventing the member from becoming locked into low self-esteem.

The situation may be complicated by the fact that members may put on a false front and pretend to be more competent than they actually feel they are. Also there may be more than one member in the Group who has low self-esteem, not wanting others to know how bad they feel about themselves. So the Group may have members feeling bad, but putting up a good front. They see others, who might be doing exactly the same. Members might be expecting a lot from each other, and fail to get from the Group what they want: in some unspecified way they feel disappointed, and this can give rise to anger or depressive feelings.

So, although low self-esteem might be an individual characteristic, it can affect the whole Group, which becomes suffused with negative thoughts. So coming to the Group does not necessarily counteract negative perceptions. However well run the Group is, it might never measure up to the expectations of some members. Thus a proactive stance is required. The Group has to take steps to increase members' self-esteem, as only this will ensure that members have a positive perception of what the Group is achieving and therefore of what they can achieve themselves.

Work on self-esteem

Although members of the Support Group might have low self-esteem, its cause is of less concern than its raising. The process may be divided into the reinforcement of positive self-esteem and the diminution of the negative feelings.

Positive self-esteem can be increased through the appreciation of self. This entails the acknowledgement by members of what they have achieved as people, how they seem to others, how they think they seem to others, and how they feel about themselves. All these often have to be accompanied by the reframing of perceptions, and this means taking a more positive yet realistic view of life, and in particular a more positive view of their own lives.

Hearing of the achievements of others in the group can sustain hope, and even non-achievement can be helpful, demonstrating that other people have difficulties as well. The role of the facilitator may be required in these discussions to ensure that the Group is kept both positive and realistic in attitude. The facilitator may also ensure that the goals achieved by members, however small they may seem, are highlighted and appreciated for their worth.

Work on the negative

To feel good about oneself, work may have to be done on negative self-perceptions. This can take a considerable amount of time as such views are often rooted in the past and have virtually become part of a person's identity. How people see themselves is largely influenced by how others see them and how much influence those others can exert on the person. The influences may be as diverse as parents, home life, education, work, religion, local community, social class and culture. The members alone know the various factors that have gone to shape them, and once the process of identifying such factors has begun, individual members start to lessen the criticism of themselves, though criticism of aspects of society might well increase.

It can be useful, in addition, for members to identify in what way they have a poor regard for themselves. They might see themselves as weak, as obsessively perfectionist, as overly self-critical, or as failures, as lacking in abilities, as the victims of circumstances. Members have to be challenged about these tunnellings of perceptions and Group members have to help each other to be more realistic.

The problem of poor self-esteem is that facing continual adverse public perceptions eventually leads to an internalisation of the attendant negativity. From personal behaviour being regarded negatively, comes the progression to seeing people negatively, and then to the people seeing themselves negatively. This final stage is often accompanied by a rationalisation of the self-perception. People will describe themselves as 'unlucky', as 'victims of fate', or say 'life is against me'. Such comments may be symptoms of very low self-esteem. Work on the problem can take some time, as rationalising can be extensive, and negatively perceived past experiences are used to 'prove' that the person is right.

Facilitation and an example of work on low self-esteem

When facilitating, so much can be happening in the Group that low self-esteem may go unrecognised. This leads to difficulties. In groupwork, the worker can decide to look at the whole topic of self-esteem, whereas in facilitated support work, there has to be a reaction in keeping with the meeting. The facilitator might intervene gently when members are self-deprecating or self-blaming, and then allow matters to proceed. In time, such interventions do affect the general atmosphere in the Group, and other members will take the lead and watch for signs of negative self-perceptions.

The subject of cognitive distortions does not have to be explained to the Group, but what can be shown usefully is the way certain attitudes, often to be recognised by key words or phrases, may be noticed and commented upon. Such clues to low self-esteem may be seen in the following three ways (McKay and Fanning, 1987). First, making over-generalisations, which are often introduced by words such as 'never', 'everyone', 'always', 'impossible', and 'no one'. Members might say, 'When he is like that, I never know what to do' or, 'Everyone says when your daughter ...'

Members might talk this way because they feel powerless, frustrated or overcome by feelings. What is necessary is for them to distance themselves from those feelings, and then decide whether they really believe what they have said. If they fail to do this, in time they will come to believe their own statements, especially if no one challenges them. Facilitators do not have to labour the point; a small intervention might be enough as the following example shows.

Member: 'The only time I ever see him is when he's wanting money..'
Me: 'The only time...'
Member: 'Well ..., he's often spent his giro by the weekend so he comes saying he needs money for food. For food! That'll be right! ...'

By over-generalising, members are distorting the reality of what is taking place and preventing others from helping. It is difficult to reply constructively to statements containing words like 'impossible' or 'never'. As may be seen from the example, once the over-generalisation has been challenged, then space is made for comment and support.

Second, members may imagine that low self-esteem must be readily apparent as a lack of confidence, diffidence and giving in to the views of others.

This may be the case, but low self-esteem may be well concealed. Members might seem very confident, though such confidence is likely in time to prove to be a shell that is easily broken. What often characterises these seemingly confident people is their rigidity in thinking that is strictly defensive in nature, covering up self-doubts. The signs of rigidity in thought include an insistence on seeing the world in 'either ... or' terms, as being either black or white, good or bad, right or wrong. This may be revealed in words such as, 'either ... or', 'if ... then', or in over-generalisation words such as 'all', 'none' or 'never'. Another form of rigidity comes with words implying necessity such as 'must', 'have to' and the negative 'cannot'. Repetition of these words might signal low self-esteem and a need for intervention.

Finally, another result of being very defensive is that people can turn in on themselves – they become the centre of their universe, but it is a universe that is often ranged against them.

What we see is that everything becomes personalised and has to relate to them, but is declared to be beyond their control. This way of thinking may not be obvious initially, but may be seen in debates or discussions, when matters are taken personally. Others are seen as 'having a go at them'. Trying to convince these members that the world is not against them is unlikely to succeed. What may be needed is a different approach, for example that of paradoxical intervention.

Member: 'I never seem to get a chance in life. Everything is against me. That's the way life is.'

Me: 'You're right, the world is against you. There's no point is doing anything under the circumstances. In fact ...'

Member: 'OK, OK! But it's still not easy.'

Me: 'And that's why the Group wants to help. So can you say precisely what the difficulties are?'

In this way, what takes place in the meeting is used in passing to increase members' self-esteem.

5 CONTINUING THE WORK

GROUP FUNCTIONING

Introduction

Having started the support work, then the Group begins to operate as a unit, members acting and interacting to achieve the overall Group aim. Initially, worry reduction, ventilating and sharing suffice. They lay the foundations for support, but they are not enough. The Group needs to be aware of how groups in general function, so that the development pains and difficulties do not interfere with the support work. Also, deeper work is required to ensure that the support offered will at least be adequate.

Group model

The following model of Group functioning is based on that of Tuckman and Jensen (1977), and is used here because it mirrors my own experience of working with Groups. However, experience has shown me that the characteristics of Groups that are led, as opposed to those which are facilitated, are much more marked and their stages in development easier to identify. The aim of mutual support can largely suppress the signs of Group strain and cover up the underlying Group dynamics. This means that relevant signs have to be picked up from what members say informally in an individual capacity, or what is said before and after the meetings when members' guards are lowered.

Seeking a way forward

The immediate question is why it is necessary to know about Groups? The initial meetings almost always go very well. Members are quickly relieved of much of their anxiety about coming to the Group, even before any work has been done on worry reduction. They soon discover that far from being frightening, being in the company of the other members is enjoyable. They have a place to get rid of their feelings and that makes them feel better. They can not only talk openly about having a drug user in the family, but can also be heard by people who really listen to them, people who know what it is like.

The support modes of ventilating, sharing and anxiety reduction, with some self-disclosure, are then used and found to be helpful. Only after this initial stage does momentum seem to decrease. The members' anxiety has been lowered, some of their immediate concerns have been met, the rush of ventilation has decreased and even the process of sharing experiences has lessened. The Group appears to lose direction. So members search for an answer, for some way of retrieving the early good feelings that marked the initial meetings.

Group development

The change in the meetings might be put down to the members having got to know each other better and the fact that their needs have altered slightly. But this still does not explain what is taking place. After initial meetings, the Group becomes more hesitant and there are silences. There is the expectation that someone in the Group will take a lead. This is a critical point. The control taken by the Group leader comes almost by default; there is a vacuum and someone fills it: someone to take care of business and thereby give a feeling of security. What is happening is not connected to the content of the meetings as such, but is related to their development.

False Group cohesion

With this leadership, the Group is less anxious and appears to be functioning extremely well. Members can be quite animated and talk about their experiences, find incidents and feelings in common. The strangeness of being in a Group has gone and there is a feeling of acceptance, with the emphasis on mutual agreement. Members tend to concentrate on what they have in common, and this includes what they agree on. All of this is liberating for members who previously felt isolated and helpless. But members have other feelings. They begin to sense a togetherness and a unity in the Group.

However, this feeling is partly a product of members putting emotional investment in the Group, wanting it to succeed, and therefore not endangering its existence by disagreements. Members tend to say what they think should be said. There is little risk-taking, and there tends to be a total acceptance of members' accounts, so learning from each other is limited.

Storming

A Group which has this cohesion works well for some time; indeed for many meetings. Then another change takes place. The Group seems to lose some of its togetherness. Members who got along with each other well begin to be less easy in their interactions. Discussions now seem to verge on arguments, and members begin to gossip about each other. Members might even wonder aloud whether the Group is working well, whether everyone is really benefiting from it. There might be attacks, usually indirect, on the competency of the facilitator. All this can occur despite there being no reason for the level of trust to have decreased. Nevertheless, strains become noticeable and the Group unity appears slowly to be dissolving.

Reasons for lack of cohesion

The apparent unity or false cohesion is a product of members feeling they have to behave in a certain way. Indeed, they are afraid to act differently, afraid of rejection by the others or of the Group coming to an end. Thus false cohesion was in part a product of Group myths, which helped initially. But in the long term their unreality tells against them. The unreality was exposed by the members' growing trust and mutual acceptance, which allowed members to express themselves more openly in the Group, and this included disagreeing with other members.

The growing strains and disagreements can be likened to adolescent behaviour, a necessary stage of maturation. So it is unhelpful for the Group to try to get back to the previous state of false coherence, even if in retrospect it seemed a calmer and easier time. Such a backward step would merely block Group progress. It should be understood by the members that it is the build up of trust that allows them to feel confident and secure enough to disagree. Disagreements represent an advance over false cohesion. Because members can disagree, they find out more about each other, discover that some needs and some experiences are common but some are not.

It is a time when members begin really to notice differences.

Members may come from different social classes, have had a different education, different forms of employment, and hold their own particular expectations. Their life experiences are their own. Once this has been appreciated, then members sense themselves as part of the Group, but they also see individuality. By identifying their individuality, members are likely to sense a growing self-esteem and self-confidence, necessary precursors of successful personal action.

Results of cohesion loss

It is useful to remember that security allows members to feel strong enough to express their feelings, including hostility. This hostility may be towards anyone in the Group, including the facilitator. So members might question the need for facilitation, question how well the facilitator is performing his role, and query the fact that he or she does not have a drug user in the family.

Facilitators should not reject such statements. Instead, they should use them to comment on what is happening in the Group, how good it is that members are able to express their feelings. And facilitators also have to consider whether the statements might be accurate in themselves and their implications. It would be wrong to see criticism simply as a product of Group development, a stage that members are going through.

Another aspect of this stormy stage is that the facilitator, being non-directive, allows possible struggles for Group leadership. Instead of the facilitator being indirectly attacked, some members will push themselves forward to be leader. This process can be quite subtle, consisting of gentle putdowns, or becoming the Group expert and analysing situations. Other methods might include eliciting the support of the facilitator, or any other approach that will advance the individual member.

The effect of contesting the leadership is that the energy of the Group is not directed towards mutual support. The facilitator has to gauge this point, and intervene to diminish the wasted efforts. This can be done indirectly, such as by supporting the least powerful member of the Group, or more directly by assessing how the members are feeling and whether their efforts can be redirected.

'Norming'

After this stormy phase, there comes a period when the Group settles down, and there is a greater cohesion, a greater feeling of belonging to and identifying with the Group. A real sense of togetherness and personal warmth appears. All this results in greater trust and members getting on better together. The former difficulties are overcome and part of this comes with the establishment of norms, of roles and status in the Group. Having cleared the air, the members take up more established positions.

Performing

With the new informal structuring of the Group meetings, the members can get down to work. The quality of work, with the increased Group cohesion, will be raised. One slight drawback is that the Group can become inward looking, and this can make liaison with outside bodies more difficult. Also, there can be an idealisation of the Group and the role of the faciliator has to be to maintain realism.

Group cohesion is the medium in which the best support work can be done. This demands a balance, for if the Group cohesion becomes overwhelming, then it again becomes more difficult to express dissent.

Work around Group development

The facilitator being aware of the different stages of Group development means little if this is not shared with the members by doing work around the theme of such development. This can be done by:

1. Asking members to reflect on what it was like before they heard about the possibility of receiving any help or support, what it was like having to live with family drug use. This could take a very long time, so it helps if the facilitator identifies a few aspects and quickly summarises them; a single word can be enough – 'anger', 'stealing', 'secrecy', 'confusion', for example.

2. The next step is to talk about the time when members heard of the Group and the meetings, and for members to list their hopes and expectations. Again, the single word summarising can be used.

3. Then the facilitator can ask members to say how they experienced the first few meetings: how they felt, how they saw other members and ask them to describe the Group as a whole.

4. Finally, members should say how they feel they have changed since coming to the meetings, and how they see the Group as having changed. It is advisable to emphasise the need for support in these observations. There is no intention to criticise members, and the facilitator needs to ensure that this does not happen.

5. The intention is to be able to introduce the idea of the previously outlined model of Group development. This might well require the facilitator to ask Group members to discuss how they experience the Group, looking particularly at aspects such as friendliness, togetherness, trust, discussions and arguments, and help and security in the Group.

6. Further work comes with an introduction of the forming–storming–norming–performing model, and the identification of the various stages. This model is a suggestion, one possible idea of Group development, and has to be given as such. Because the Group aim of support tends to mask the different stages of development, there is not likely to be total acceptance of the model.

7. The final stage is to look at the possible changes that have happened in the Group meetings and see whether some of these can be accounted for by what happened. Though this seems an academic exercise, what is really happening is that members suddenly feel a degree of freedom and are more inclined to speak about the Group and its meetings, to mention matters they have thought, sensed or observed and yet have never previously talked about.

The overall aim is to improve the quality of support in the Group by making members more aware of what might be going on, and for them to feel less inhibited about speaking their minds. Awareness of the Group enables what is said and done to have a Group as well as an individual dimension, making possible remarks directed to everyone rather than just the intended individual in the meeting. This makes it more difficult for anyone to take things purely personally.

Networking

Although interest may be in the Group and its development, attention should also be given to member contact outside the Group. Networking, or members keeping in touch with each other by phone or by meeting between the Group sessions, can be helpful as it diminishes the power of the facilitator and places power and responsibility back with the members. Networking moves members out of possible Group dependence to functioning on their own, and eases the application of what is learned in the Group to their families.

Almost from the very beginning, members should be made aware that networking is a possibility within the self-help set up; a way of breaking down the social isolation of some members. Time should be given to the discussion of any networking in the meetings and time given to talking over any networking that has taken place. Networking that is covert and is not discussed can lead to the formation of unhelpful subgroupings

Endings

Awareness of what is happening in the Group and what is happening outside needs to be supplemented by a view of the situation of a member ending with the Group, otherwise the whole topic of members leaving remains undiscussed. Similarly, members do not think about stopping their attendance at the Group, although many will leave in time.

Members who leave the Group may do so for several reasons. They may find the Group too threatening or discover that they have not reached the stage where they can benefit from it. They may still be at the stage where they need cover-ups, dissembling and unreality to be able to cope; the pain and difficulty of facing reality being too much at the time. Sometimes members simply do not get on with each other and this can become an important factor in making a person seek alternative help and support. Other members might find that their families, especially their partners, are not keen for them to attend the meetings.

'I won't be able to come to the Group any longer; we are moving away. Actually, it is my husband, he's not keen on my coming back. He expects me to stay in every evening.'

On other occasions it is the drug user who is concerned about the Group, although part of this rests with the anxiety that the member may learn too much about drugs and drug users and become a threat to the drug user's domination of the family. There can also be misapprehensions about the aim and objectives of the Group, which can lead to members being pressurised into non-attendance.

'Rachel calls it a grassing-shop, thinks we spend the whole time talking about her or others on drugs. I tried explaining it was for the likes of me, parents and the like, not for her.'

Finally, there can be positive outcomes in that some members will attend for a time and then leave. They feel that they have received and given as much as they want, and that it is time to move on.

Feelings about endings

When a member leaves the Group there is always a degree of upset, feelings of loss and other possible feelings such as guilt. The others wonder if they were the cause of the member leaving, or whether the Group is not as helpful as they believed. Everyone feels something when personal relationships come to an end, even if those relationships are of short standing.

Feelings are split because there is regret that anyone leaves the Group, yet this has to be set against the fact that attendance is completely voluntary. No impediments should be placed in the path of those wishing to go, no attempts made to persuade them to stay. Everyone is responsible for their own decisions and has to stand by them. However, it is preferable that any leaving is made as positive an experience as possible, both for the member about to leave and for the rest of the Group.

Work on endings

The first step that may be taken by the facilitator is that of looking at the feelings and reasons the member has about leaving. This is not always possible because members might leave suddenly and not be contactable. However, wherever possible, it is best if the facilitator or someone from the Group does try to make contact, to find out whether there is unfinished business on the member's part; whether there are matters the Group should know about. The facilitator is best positioned to undertake this task, being less likely to take what is said personally, if negative things are said by the departing member. Whatever the feelings and reasons, they should be accepted. It is not the facilitator's role at this juncture to argue the member into staying with the Group.

Of course, it helps if the member can suggest any way the functioning of the Group can be improved. This provides an opportunity for the leaver to indicate indirectly any concern felt. Usually, it should be added, there are no bad feelings and so feedback to the rest of the Group is positive.

'It was good being at the Group and I enjoyed it. How are the others getting on?'

Such feedback is not trivial. It goes towards completing the leaving for the rest of the Group, and ensures there is as little disruption as possible. Any negative comments have to be dealt with carefully, and personal criticism seen as rarely helpful. What can be fed back are comments about Group functioning in the context of future improvement.

DEEPER WORK IN THE GROUP

Introduction

The Group, after the initial meetings, may require deeper work. This is not merely a result of the early meetings having set the conditions for such work, but members' expectations will have been raised. The question is, how should this be done; what should the Group do?

The normal practice, almost routine, at the meetings is for members to talk about what has happened since the previous meeting, mention some of the new difficulties that have arisen and what has been achieved. This is fine, except that for some members little will have happened. From one meeting to the next, there seems to be little to say about their situation, although they can listen to the others and participate in discussions. Also, after a few meetings, simply talking about what has happened can become routine, almost a ritual. Once this is the case, feelings become blunted and the benefit for the Group is reduced.

Remedies for the routine

One answer is to attract new members. This results in new ventilation and sharing by the members. The routine is broken, the Group has had an injection of energy. No further problem. But this is likely to be a temporary expedient only, and there will be the requirement of constantly attracting new members, which can become an issue in itself and detract from the provision of Group support. Moreover, the regular influx of new members causes the Group to regress, and not get past the stage of hearing and sharing new experiences.

An alternative is to enlarge the scope of the Group, changing what is seen as support. The members might decide to be a local information resource as well as having the meetings, or to take up a campaigning or lobbying role. There is no reason why Support Groups should not choose whatever members want, whatever they think is best. However if such changes are merely a result of being unsure how to progress as a support resource, then this can be to the Group's loss.

Enlargement of the support work

Rather than avoiding the question of support, the best option might be to go into it more deeply. The facilitator can help the Group to take a more detailed view of the work by ensuring the content of the members' accounts is expanded. Such work could not be done at the very early meetings – the Group would not have been ready – but having come though the initial stages, deeper work is both possible and desirable.

Expanding meeting content

There are several ways in which the content of meetings can be deepened and expanded. Three such ways are as follows. First, by listening to members' accounts and asking them to give more detail where it seems useful. Usefulness is measured according to the extent that the members will benefit from such expansion. At a simple level, the facilitator can help the member to give more information, which is shared with the whole Group.

'I waited for Darren to phone but he didn't. Normally he phones on Sunday, well, he comes up for something to eat and I think he gets bored at the weekends anyway. Although he says he's been off drugs for the last six months, when I went down to the house I knew he had taken something. So I went in to the house ...'

'Sorry, but can you say how you knew he was back using again. What signs gave him away?'

'I can tell when he's taking drugs. He speaks with a raspy voice and then he says things like, "Honest Mum, I'm not taking anything. It's just that I didn't sleep last night, that's why I'm just about falling asleep." Well, I've heard that before! And he can't look me straight in the eye, so I know that he's not telling the truth.'

Getting such detail is useful for the Group because of its very practical nature, not the sort of information to be found in text-books. The enlargement of content can usefully be accompanied by a discussion of what has been said. The facilitator has to be alert to not letting members give their accounts one after another, but ensuring that the process is interactive. The aim should be to get several members involved, which often needs no more than the facilitator keeping silent.

'I told Louise she should go to the doctor and get on to that methadone. I told her that would help.'
'In what ways do you see methadone helping Louise or making things easier for yourself?'
'Well, she wouldn't have to buy heroin, spend all her money on it. And there would be no risk of her going shoplifting again. I reckon all the stores in town must know her by now.'
'Methadone, I don't see it is better than heroin. You get addicted to the stuff, just like you do with smack.'
'But doctors know best.'
'Know best! I doubt it ...'

Second, the facilitator should help members to discuss a wide range of subjects. Some members have a rather fixed idea of what should be talked about, sometimes mirroring conversations with doctors, social workers or psychiatrists. What they may not have realised is that such conversations are treatment orientated and are biased according to underlying theoretical medical or therapy models. This bias may be seen in the way members slant their conversation at times:

(a) there is a tendency to talk about drug users rather than them-selves;

(b) there is an emphasis on the role of parents of drug users but little on grandparents or other family members; and

(c) home life is highlighted but rarely meetings with workmates, hobbies, sports activities or clubs.

The facilitator may make enquiries about those topics which are rarely mentioned in order to produce a balanced account. Another aspect of underlying thought patterns comes with the use of certain words or phrases such as 'sick', 'inadequate', or 'out of control' as applied to drug users. Such words show certain attitudes and on occasions it is worth getting the Group to look at language and associated attitudes and ideas about drug use.

Finally, the facilitator can help members to concentrate on feelings. It is easy to mistake members' accounts as purely factual, and ignore the feelings behind them. For completeness, feelings should be disclosed, and this sometimes means that members have to be encouraged to be more fully disclosing.

'I found out that James was taking drugs about a month ago. As if it wasn't bad enough Andy being like that!'

'You must have been very upset.'

'Yes, very upset ...'

'Angry, perhaps?'

'Yes, angry. But most of all it was the shock. And the fact that I thought at least James was OK, whatever his brother was up to.'

'And how do you feel about Andy?'

'I know it's not his fault, he tried to stop James, but I can't help blaming him. That causes my husband to get on to me.'

'That cannot help.'

'I feel so helpless.'

What might be noted from the above quote is that members do not simply react to facilitation; they add to their account in their own way and begin to expand it for themselves. What seems to be no more than the facilitator getting a member to say a bit more, develops into something rather different; what the member wants to say. This depends on the member being responsive and wanting to say more – not always easy for the facilitator to assess.

Sometimes members imagine that life and their own personal situation is just a matter of facts. When they look at their lives they tend to highlight reason or logic, seeing feelings as being mere appendages; only occurring in highly charged situations. Yet feelings are always involved to a greater or lesser extent in any human context.

For instance, a member might say that since the last meeting nothing has happened and so there is nothing worthy of comment. This perspective ignores the role of feelings.

'I haven't seen Eileen in four weeks now, so I've nothing to report.'

'Does this often happen, periods of not seeing Eileen, and how do you feel. Worried?'

'From time to time. I suppose I do get worried. I mean I worry when I see her and she's taken something. But then I don't feel any better if I don't see her. I imagine her lying dead somewhere or the police coming to the door and saying she's in the cells.'

'And what do you do about those worries?'

'I want to go out and see her, but Rab says I should just leave her, and she will be fine. She always is, but that doesn't stop me from worrying.'

As may be seen, it is hardly correct to say that nothing is happening for this member. So situations can only be understood if feelings are fully brought into members' accounts.

Widening the content further

The content of meetings can be further expanded by getting away from hard facts and looking to less definite material. This material can be assigned to three categories: expectations; fantasies; and dreams.

Talk by members about personal expectations helps as it is talk about the future, turning attention away from the past, the source of much of members' negative feelings. Discussing the future can lay the basis for hope, and this can be translated into positive action. As long as hope is kept within realistic bounds, it can be made to work for the members.

Future expectations may also explain present behaviour. There is a problem here in that members are often not aware of those expectations; they are often just unquestioned and accepted beliefs. This means the facilitator might have to help in their identification and suggest certain ideas, such as:

1. The family will continue in its present form.

2. The drug user will die if she/he does not stop.

3. The other children in the family will not take drugs.

4. The drug user will not stop using.

These might or might not apply to Group members, but looking at the ideas, all of which are highly debatable, leads on to discussions about them, not just as ideas but as personalised ideas – what it means to have them as expectations. At this stage of the Group, members should not hide behind mere rational discussion; they should own their expectations and feelings.

Further widening of content

Hard facts are further left behind if the facilitator introduces the topic of fantasy. This may be started quite generally with the facilitator and members talking about their personal fantasies. This usually livens up the meeting! Then fantasies can be examined in more detail, particularly those that refer to what might happen and what is likely to happen. One reason for this investigation of fantasies is to assist members to differentiate between cold facts and their worries, fears and expectations; what is public reality and what is personal reality.

As a final suggestion, members might like to discuss their dreams. The reason for doing this is that, like free association, dreams can be revealing, but, in my opinion, only if members are asked to say what the dreams mean to them. There is no question of anyone else interpreting dreams. The idea of this particular approach is to help members 'loosen up', to get them to think differently about what might be happening. Some sense of this type of work can be gained from the following example – a member recounting her dream.

'Someone had died and the relatives were asking what they should do. He had drunk a lot of water and they were trying to burn the body. I noticed the material under the body had been lit, but only in one place, so I lit it in a couple more places. I was relieved to see the body was now quite burnt. Somehow there were two bodies, or two skulls at least. One was the burnt skull of a small child and the other a man's face which had changed to a mask of mud, showing drooping folds of flesh.'

'And did this suggest anything to you.'

'I don't know what it all means.'

'Just hold it in mind and see what thoughts come. Take your time.'

'I think the person who had died was John, but I couldn't be sure. I knew who it was and yet I didn't. Perhaps that is John, I know him and I don't. I'm afraid he will die and I wouldn't know who has died. A child in an old man's body, and the mask. It's funny how it all seems to hang together. The curious thing was I wasn't upset at all, just helping out by burning the body.'

The facilitator can enquire as to whether there was any reason for selecting that particular dream and how the member feels after explaining the dream to the rest of the Group. Whatever is in a member's mind can be worth discussing.

Facilitation and work

The facilitator has to understand that enlargement of members' accounts has to be done sensitively, and it might be that the Group is not ready for this sort of work. For this reason, the introduction of new approaches should be done tentatively. Equally, members have to be informed as to what the facilitator is doing or would like the Group to try.

The backbone of the meetings is members' own accounts, and the facilitator is only attempting to get members to enlarge those accounts by discovering, identifying and sharing new aspects. This can be done by increasing content quantitatively and qualitatively. Alternatively, members can see situations from a different angle, using unobserved thoughts and feelings. Methods such as talking about expectations, fantasies and dreams are employed only to discover and investigate those different thoughts and feelings. The aim is to return to members' accounts with a wider perspective.

There can be a real danger that methods of work take over from members simply talking, that support changes into directive groupwork, that the Group moves from the members towards the facilitator. But the Group belongs to the members and must remain so. Too little intervention is probably better than too much, and facilitators should be very careful about how they broaden members' accounts and discussions.

THEMES – POWERLESSNESS

Introduction

Over many meetings the facilitator will be aware that there are underlying issues and themes which can be found running through the discussions. My practice has been to use such themes to help the Group to look more closely and in a slightly different way at their lives. In order to do this, it is helpful to jot down notes after meetings, which soon build up to a considerable amount of material. From this material can be selected quotes and references that are likely to form a consistent theme.

Themes are a range of ideas relevant to the Group. Each theme or concept can be expanded, deepened qualitatively, or seen from different perspectives – just like a member's account. In fact, themes can be treated on one level as being a complex account given by several members. This means that the previous work done on accounts using support modes such as ventilating and sharing, can be applied to themes.

Selecting themes

There are many possible themes that can arise, so the selection depends on two main criteria. These might be:

1. Those statements with which several members agree, and which link up with statements from previous meetings. There can be common ideas which run through what members say over several meetings, and spotlighting a theme brings them out in an overt and consistent manner. An example is that of statements that reflect members' powerlessness.

2. The amount of feeling that accompanies statements made at the Group meetings; statements that move. If members feel strongly about various matters that can be gathered together under one heading, then this can act as a theme. An example is those accounts touching on death, another possible theme.

So there are the criteria, one mainly cognitive and the other mostly affective. The themes themselves should be relevant to the Group, which means they represent a major aspect of support.

When beginning this selection process, the facilitator's work notes might disclose no particular pattern and give little clue as to what the theme might be. The following is one example of a statement that was noted down after a meeting.

'How much longer is it going to go on, her taking drugs. Is she going to use drugs until she dies?'

This is only one of several quotes recorded at the time. There are various possibilities of themes that could have emerged, such as women and drug taking, death, getting help, family anxiety, or perceptions of parental roles. However, this statement was later linked with those made at subsequent meetings.

'I used to say to Judy that if she would tell me if she was using, I wouldn't mind. I just wanted to know, and perhaps I could help. But she would never tell me. She would just say, "I'm all right, Mum."'

'I asked the doctor how he was, if he was getting better. But doctors don't tell you anything, said it was confidential. I told him I was his mother, but it made no difference, I was not to be told.'

It is only with the accumulation of such quotes that the underlying theme emerges, and the facilitator begins to link up members' statements. It has to be remembered that the process seems easier that it is, as there can be a great many statements and potential themes.

'I tried to get her to stop, tried in her own eyes to bring her right down, to get her to see what she was doing to herself and others. But she did not change and it was me who was hurt at the end of it.'

With more and more quotes, the facilitator can pick out a provisional theme, and then it becomes easier to recognise further linkable quotes.

The theme introduced

From the above statements, there seemed to be an underlying issue or theme of personal powerlessness. Having identified this as a theme, the immediate task was to analyse it. It seemed to me, from what members had said during meetings, that a lack of information was one aspect of this powerlessness, and not knowing what was happening as a result of drug users' evasions or lies appeared to be a second aspect. This is not intended as a comprehensive analysis, merely a way of generating more material for the meeting. To work on the theme, the agreement of the Group is required. Asking whether they would like to discuss powerlessness is likely to seem vague and rather intimidating. But if members are asked whether they want to talk about topics such as knowing more about drugs or what they can do when the family drug user keeps lying to them, and are told that these are all aspects of personal powerlessness, so the Group will also be looking at a lack of power in the family, then the theme becomes more comprehensible and is more likely to be taken up.

Issues around drugs knowledge

The preliminary work on powerlessness consisted of examining with the Group what was lacking with regard to drugs knowledge. One point that emerged from Support Groups was that most members felt they knew practically nothing about drugs.

'When I discovered Diane was taking drugs, I was at a loss as it was a different world to me. I knew nothing about drugs. This worried me as I was scared of them and felt unable to help at all.'

When first aware of the drug use, parents or partners are likely to be in a state of shock, and find themselves incapable of doing anything. This reinforces their feelings of powerlessness, but it also raises questions about what powerlessness is. It was assumed to revolve around drugs knowledge, but, in addition, knowing about states of shock is now seen as being relevant.

This has practical implications in that members in the Group, conscious of their lack of drugs knowledge, may ask for someone from the Drugs Squad, or a drugs agency, to come to the meeting and tell them about drugs. But this does not address the actual issue which first presents, that of a shock reaction and not knowing what to do, despite all the knowledge a person might possess.

'Neither of us knew what was going on, except Phil had changed. Then someone, I forget who it was, suggested drugs, that Phil might be on drugs. We were devastated!'
'And what did you do?'
'We didn't know what to do at first, we had absolutely no idea, no idea at all.'

What we see is that at this stage knowing about states of shock might be more important than knowing about drug use. Yet even if that was known, the problem would move to that of a parent or partner not knowing what to do. This applies particularly to parents, who are assumed to know the answers to life's difficulties.

'I didn't know anything about drugs, I hadn't even heard any-thing about them. I kept thinking that he had had a drink. Even when my eldest son told me, I still did not believe that Gordon was on drugs.'

It might be that those affected by the drug use do not know about drugs, but they might also not want to know and prefer to be left in the dark. This might seem perverse, but there is a place for avoidance or denial in the short-term when faced by an over-whelming threat (Lazarus, 1983). As one mother remarked:

'I know nothing really about drugs, and I don't want to know. I suppose it's my defence. If I don't know about them and what might happen, then so much the better. I don't want to know as I don't feel I could handle it.'

So knowing about drugs has its own implications, and in a situa-tion where nothing can be done directly, where the drug use cannot be stopped by anyone but the drug user, members might find that drugs knowledge merely increases their anxiety. The overall conclusion is that Group members should not make assumptions, but always decide for themselves what they want. They might not want to have drugs information or they might require special support to deal with such information. Members also have to ask themselves why they want information about drugs and what sort of information will be of real use. Knowing facts may be of little use unless they can be incorporated into a wider synthesis, a wider understanding. Knowledge might be seen as a source of power: this can be true, but is not necessarily so.

It might seem that drugs knowledge has been presented in a very negative light, but members should appreciate the complexity of the topic and not rush to do what appears obvious. Absorbing drugs information may not be as helpful as expected, especially if its implications are not discussed. What is required is information provided by the members, processed for the use of the Group, and directed to practical ends.

For instance, knowledge of drugs allows members to recognise possible drug use. So if heroin use is suspected, the best test is to look at the person's pupils, to see if they are very small even in low lighting, and these pinpoint pupils are a sign of someone under the influence of a strong opioid drug, which might be heroin. The drawback is that doctors are allowed to stare into a patient's eyes but this can hardly be done by parents or partners, not without running the risk of causing considerable resistance. And with brown-eyed people, it is not so easy to see their pupil size – at least from normal distances. What can be helpful is for members to rely on other signs, some of which will be known and can be shared with the Group.

'I thought she might be taking something. Her voice changed, it went up an octave and she was slurring slightly.'

Empowerment has to be for Group members, not for anyone else such as the medical profession, so appropriate information is required. But as members will agree, knowing signs of drug use is seldom sufficient. Using can start during adolescence, a time of rebellion, when teenagers resent perceived parental interference, when they wear different clothes, act differently and have sudden mood swings. Under these circumstances, it is not surprising that the use of illegal drugs goes unnoticed. It is difficult to know what is normal.

But the main reason for not recognising drug use still seems to be that it is seen as happening to other families. No matter what the evidence might be, families never imagine drugs could be involved.

'I should have tippled something was up. She stayed in her bedroom and wouldn't let anyone in, except a string of friends who came to the house. They weren't the kind of people you would particularly want in your house – dirty and rude. And she was on the phone all the time and always seemed to have money.'

And even if the family did know what the situation was, this does not empower them if there seems to be nothing that can be done.

'I didn't know what was going on, I was that ignorant about drugs and everything. Then I found out what was going on and learned to recognise when he had taken something. But I couldn't do anything about it. I couldn't stop him, however much I was told about drugs.'

So what becomes apparent is that drugs knowledge is not necessarily sufficient, even though its lack is associated with feelings of powerlessness. Putting the knowledge into action may still not be enough. Sometimes parents will try to use what they know about drugs, but even this is not enough.

'I said he had had a shot as his eyes were pinned. He said I knew fuck all. He said he had taken Contact 400 for his cold, which contained atropine, so of course his pupils would be different. If I didn't believe him then the two of us could ask a doctor. I felt as if I didn't know anything.'

What might be observed from these discussions about drugs and the family is that powerlessness may be related to unfamiliarity with drugs, but it is a complicated relationship. Knowing about drugs might not end that feeling of powerlessness. Discussion highlighted some aspects of this relationship and this was useful as Group members felt happier knowing where they stood. There was agreement that there was little to be done to change the drug use. Help; acceptance; threats: none of these seemed to make any impression. So just knowing about and recognising drug use might not be so helpful.

However, there are positive aspects as well. Members said they felt better in themselves if they knew something about drugs, if they were able to understand to some extent what was going on. The fact that they could not effect any change in the drug user did not detract from the importance of such knowledge.

Working the theme

The theme can be treated as a member's account writ large. Accordingly, the facilitator can help by encouraging members to expand the theme, or by suggesting different aspects of the chosen theme.

Expansion can come quite easily with other members giving their accounts. Expansion also comes with seeing accounts from a slightly different angle. Powerlessness comes with a lack of drugs knowledge, so we might ask what sort of knowledge is required. One avenue might be to be able to recognise drug use, but to do so not through the medical effects: instead, lifestyle is the main clue.

'Rachel wouldn't get out of her bed and go to college. She used to complain of being ill, saying that she must have the flu. I never suspected anything, even when she refused to have the doctor in. Only later did she admit she had been withdrawing.'

Being able to talk through a family member's drug use from its known beginning is helpful as strange behaviour can be put into context and seen as originating from the drug user rather than the parent or partner. This in turn decreases their feelings of guilt and powerlessness.

'After Ron started to take drugs, he became moody and didn't laugh like he used to. He turned suspicious and would spend hours in his room.'

There will be similarities enough in each different account for members to realise that their experiences are not isolated cases. Each Group member is familiar to some extent with personal powerlessness.

'Judy always used to be very smart and tidy. Some of her new friends started coming to the door. Well, you wouldn't want them in your house. Dirty torn jeans and unwashed hair, and they would not speak to you. They would come in and go straight to Judy's bedroom.'

However, what is also happening with the help of the facilitator is that the separate accounts are linked with the theme. But the work goes beyond this, with members being asked whether they were aware of the link. Awareness of powerlessness can lead to power as long as members work at it. So members are asked if the telling and discussion of the different accounts makes them feel better, happier, less anxious and more confident. It is through the appreciation of such feelings and the awareness that they feel better, that members begin to see that the action of talking, listening and sharing is connected to the gaining of personal power. This power is primarily that of having a greater degree of control over themselves.

Further work on powerlessness

The facilitator can help by making suggestions, by linking to powerlessness aspects of drug related behaviour that may not be obvious. If we consider the omissions, evasions and lies that might be present in drug users' behaviour, then they reinforce the ambiguity of personal relationships. Everyone in the family is uncertain what is happening save the drug user, whose position of power in the family is increased accordingly.

'It's all the lies. You would never believe the things she would tell me. Imagine going stealing first thing in the morning! She was never like that – so many lies. I wanted to believe her but I couldn't. There were so many lies that I began to wonder who was right and whether I was going mad.'

As members agreed, people might lie occasionally and they might be evasive or not disclose information, but drug user behaviour was qualitatively different. At times quite blatant lies would be told. This is different from most families where there comes a stage when any lack of honesty is admitted. With those using drugs, concealment, dishonesty and lies can become almost reflex actions.

'What I can't understand is that he will say he hasn't had anything. But anyone can see that he's had something. Then it's, "I've been off for a week but just had something this morning, just tablets the doctor had prescribed." And I know he's lying. Then he says, "What's the matter, don't you believe me?", and of course I don't. Then he comes out with, "That's terrible, when even your own mother doesn't believe you. How can I keep off if my mother is not giving me the benefit of the doubt, if she doesn't want to help?" Finally, I end up feeling guilty, though God knows why.'

The drug users' need to maintain unreality, to keep up the pretence, is necessary in order for them to feel in control: partly in relation to the family but mainly in relation to the control of themselves. At times this need can reach almost a desperate stage, as drug users find their lives taken over by their drug use. The outcome can be the evasions and lies, just to maintain an illusion of personal control and a united identity.

'I found a bottle of tablets, DFs, and I knew what they were. He said they were antibiotics and I was mistaken. It was probably my age, I was going through the change of life, and that was why I was so crabby and suspicious. If that was the case then the change of life had been going on for the last ten years!'

It is important for some drug users that the family, or usually parents or partners, believe what has been said, this so reinforces the illusion they want to be preserved. Thus it is not just that drug users lie but that they keep up such behaviour to prolong the pretence.

'You listen to them and you know it's all a pack of lies. But they keep on trying to convince you so that in the end you wonder if you are mad or them.'

Part of the difficulty is that family members are bound together by relational bonds, they have feelings for each other. This is a disadvantage when faced with someone whose feelings are repressed by drugs and who is able to ignore such family bonds. But we also might note that the idea of the drug user wanting to dominate the family is too simple a view. Drug users might be trying to control their own lives and to do so requires control over others.

Understanding more about drug use behaviour may be expected to help the family, but there is also the question 'So what?' Knowing what is happening does not take away the pain that the family feels. Dealing with the cognitive does not ensure affective issues will be relieved, as this drug user's partner was later to admit.

'Things have been very hard, very up and down. I did think they were going to be OK this time; I had faith in him. Then he started using again, we had a row about it and it was me who overdosed. I feel I can't take any more. I still love him but I can't deal with what's happening; can't deal with it at all. It's the lies he tells. If he was straight up, then perhaps I could help him. I can't help him and I'm beginning not to care.'

The work may have appeared almost to leave behind the theme of powerlessness, but the aim of support work is to change members' views of their worlds. Themes enable members to make a different and more comprehensive picture of themselves and their families.

There are two aspects of support themes that should be noted. First, it is no drawback if the accounts go beyond what seem to be the bounds of the theme. Gathering momentum, members discover more about their situations and worlds, and if this does not always relate to the theme then no harm is done. Useful work is more important than sticking to arbitrary rules.

The second point is that accounts are taken to be related to a chosen theme, but the relationship is more complex. By working through a theme, using different members' accounts, the theme itself comes to be seen differently. This does not mean that previously it was seen wrongly, merely that it is seen not as a given concept but one that grows with the work done. In fact, the theme of powerlessness is doubly changing, as the work alters members' feelings and this in turn changes what powerlessness means to the Group.

Official help

Taking a flexible view of themes is necessary for facilitators too, if they are to help the Group to view the family and drug use differently. With such flexibility, they can make suggestions as to how themes may be expanded. For example, many members want help for the drug user and, through aspects of work on the theme, facilitators can get Group members to examine help that is offered. But the view on such help is likely to be much more comprehensive than the usual feelings simply because now there is the backing of a whole perspective. In the theme under scrutiny, official help is seen from the angle of powerlessness. This is not the only perspective, yet it gives one particular viewpoint on help and members see the situation in a way in which few have viewed it before.

So Group members who are considering help for the drug user will turn to doctors and psychiatrists, experts who know about drugs and whose job is to help. But there are drawbacks. By having experts dealing with someone in the family, power has been lost by parents and partners.

If someone is ill (and the drug user is often far from well), then the family has a role. In fact, most illnesses are treated in the home without summoning outside assistance (Turk and Kerns, 1985). Similarly, behavioural problems of adolescents, which might include drug use, are dealt with by parents without asking for expert help.

Asking for expert help seems a good solution insofar as it takes much of the immediate worry away from families. Yet it also marks the families' inability to deal with or cope with the situation. And there is no reason why families should not deal with drug use, at least on their terms. Although expert help might seem the best option, it is an option which has implications for the whole family.

'Richard agreed to go for help and the doctor prescribed methadone. I thought that was going to stop him taking drugs, but they get addicted to it as much as to heroin. He's as much a drug addict as ever before.'

This might simply be seen as family members not understanding what doctors are doing, but equally doctors may not understand the family's situation. The caring role has been largely taken away and for mothers especially this can be difficult as it is closely aligned to their identity. Medical treatment may have done no more than reinforce family powerlessness.

The powerlessness theme

If we try to summarise the idea of powerlessness as a theme, then Group members come to recognise their powerlessness in the face of the drug use itself, the lies, and the role of expert help. Having identified the theme in some of its forms, action can be planned and taken to better the situation.

But, in addition, following a theme can lead in many directions and result in different perceptions. This allows members to see drug use and themselves in a more rounded way, and this understanding itself makes them feel better.

Themes, like members' accounts, can be linked together and be mutually reinforcing, and help to build yet further understanding.

Finally, members are helped by the process of working through themes. This action itself gives members a sense of greater control over themselves and the world.

Of course, there are limitations to be found in theme work. Sometimes members look for a definite outcome and expect themes to provide some sort of answer or solution. But there are none. Themes are merely a way of working to provide support; they supplement other work modes. Also powerlessness is a mainly cognitive theme, and is best balanced by a more affective theme such as that of death.

THEMES – DEATH

Introduction

Death as a theme emerged in two different Support Groups and is now, with the advent of HIV infection, especially relevant for families. As with other themes, it may be selected by the given criteria procedure. Like other highly emotive topics, death might be mentioned in passing but not discussed in any great depth. Being a taboo subject, discussion may be avoided (Nisbet, 1984), yet members also want to deal with it. Sometimes members may even feel they are not allowed to discuss it, as the meeting is for families affected by drug use and is not a Bereavement Group, although talking about death in self-help groups is known to be helpful (Videka-Sherman, 1982).

However, one of the strengths of theme work is that it is a method of expanding the content and support of meetings. Perhaps it is only fair to add that my own views do intrude into the whole subject of death, as I believe that anyone who has not come to terms with death has not come to terms with life, and everyone should talk seriously about death at some time. Others may disagree.

Affective themes and members

Care has to be taken with all highly emotive issues and themes as they may apply to Group members. Concern about death tends to peak when people are in their fifties (Bengston et al., 1977), and some parent members are likely to be in this age range. But this general anxiety is less important than the fact that discussing death can open up intense feelings. For this reason, members should be asked if they have had a recent bereavement and whether they feel able to speak about death. It can be worthwhile if members think carefully about this. Death is thought to apply only to older people, to parents rather than partners. However, it is helpful to point out that miscarriages and stillbirths can represent a loss, and one for which there is little recognition.

Discovering who has suffered losses in order to increase Group sensitivity to their feelings may not be sufficient. Some members might have suffered loss and not have worked through their grief. So the meeting might be the place where grief is started or renewed. Expressions of grief are part of the overall work that can be carried out in the Group: the question is whether there is enough support, sufficient time and members capable of being supportive. What is unacceptable is for members to be emotionally upset at the end of the meeting and to walk away unsupported until the next meeting. Facilitators have to be very careful that work begun can be properly finished.

Another aspect that may be overlooked is whether the facilitator has suffered any loss and has any unfinished business. It is very easy for people to say that they have dealt with losses in their lives, yet most of us are liable to be affected by thoughts of those we loved, years after coming to terms with their death. Grief can be a lifetime process, so it might be misleading to think that past deaths or losses will not cause the facilitator upset, especially when dealing with death. For this reason, my method is to ask if the Group is willing for me to be self-disclosing if I feel upset. My reason for doing so is that thoughts and feelings about death might disturb my professional role as facilitator, and expressing my feelings is one way of regaining power over that role.

Starting the work

As with themes in general, the facilitator may analyse some broad aspects of the topic of death. My approach is to take death as a form of loss, and then to analyse the different forms of loss involved. The whole topic is rather more complex compared to that of powerlessness. With regard to the latter, members try to make sense of separate events in their lives, and link them together through the identified concept of powerlessness. With death, the concept is given and the task is to make sense of the concept as applied to themselves.

Continuing the analysis as applicable to drug users, death can be either sudden, as with overdoses, or a longer process resulting from HIV infection. Moreover, the death of drug users may be felt differently by parents and by partners; partly as a result of the age differences and consequent different attitudes to death, partly as a result of the different kinds of relationships.

Such very general analysis is useful in that it introduces a degree of structure into what may seem to be a chaotic subject for those participating in it. The expression of feelings can be worked on more usefully in a contained manner.

Forms of loss

There are likely to be three principal categories of loss; potential loss, ongoing loss and past loss.

Potential loss is associated with both overdoses and HIV infection, events that may happen in the future. This leads to varying degrees of anxiety according to how the drug user's behaviour is seen with regard to possible risks.

'I went to the doctor and said he would have to do something about Jo, put her on medication or something. The way she is going at the moment, she'll be dead within the year.'

The first step is that of anxiety reduction and this comes through acceptance of what is said. This has to be done, even if Group members doubt the truth or likelihood of such assertions. The point is that the assertion is not merely an alleged fact but the expression of feelings. Dismissal of the statement can be seen as dismissal of those feelings. It has to be added that the anxiety is not totally misplaced as overdoses do happen, and HIV infection is an ongoing danger for injecting drug users and those persons sexually active who do not take precautions.

The use of the support modes, such as anxiety reduction, ventilation and sharing are the usual initial approach. They have been mentioned here as often less emotive subjects are quite satisfactorily treated, yet many members react differently when dealing with death as a topic, trying to close the discussion down by being sympathetic rather than empathic. The object must be to increase discussion and Group participation.

'I used to go to his bedroom door to listen and see if he was still breathing. And if there was any sudden thump, I would dash up, thinking he had overdosed and fallen unconscious on the floor.'

By talking though such matters, paradoxically, anxiety can be brought to a more realistic level, which makes coping with the possibility of future loss easier. In addition, feelings have to be linked to present thoughts and behaviour and seen as part of an ongoing process.

'I thought about putting him out of the house as I wouldn't have to see him come in with drugs in him. Then I thought that if he was out of the house then I would just worry about him, imagine him lying dead somewhere.'
'Yes, I'm terrified if the Police come to the door as I think they are going to tell me that they have found Louise dead.'

As far as the facilitator is concerned, a balance has to be struck between allowing members ventilation to express their fears, and too long a time being spent on this part of the process, whereby anxiety is no longer reduced and might even be increased. Talking about the possibility of future losses has to be moved on, so that members reflect on present and past losses.

Ongoing loss

Anxieties about death and accompanying losses are brought to a point when actual loss has to be faced, when the drug user actually is dying, as in the later stages of HIV infection. Normally there is a reluctance to speak about such matters, and this reluctance is increased in the case of HIV infection, which is at present often seen in a prejudicial light. However, those affected by a dying family member may be keen to let go of their feelings and talk. I find the subject of loss is a useful entry point, and this general topic can be further subdivided into different forms of loss. One such loss might be that of future hopes and expectations, hopes that can be tied up with the drug user as a member of the family or as a partner.

'James was a perfect baby and he was so beautiful, and now look at him!'

'Well you know that Ralph used to be artistic, I think you've seen some of his pictures, Paul. Now that's all gone.'

'See Iain, he used to be intelligent, he used to be a junior chess champion at school and did the crosswords. Now he can't finish them.'

The hopes may be held by the drug users themselves, but often those most affected are their parents. The parents see their lives as unlikely to change; their hopes are put in their children. For parents, the most significant thing that they will leave behind is their children. This is part of the normal scheme to life, which drug use can drastically change.

'You never think you would be burying your own children. I know she is going to die. I just wish I could take her place, that it was me, not her.'

Loss can be especially difficult for women, who may have special feelings towards their children through their role as mother and all its attendant feelings. The death of children is not merely a loss of role, it represents a loss of identity. It affects not only what a mother does but who she is. This also goes with the fact that in some families the mother is very much the linchpin, the centre of the family.

'For mothers I think the worst thing is to lose one of your children. If I lost my husband it would be bad, but not as bad as losing my son. Children are a part of you; you never come to terms with their death.'

Statements such as this can lead into other aspects, such as family roles and feelings towards children, and to many other parts of members' lives.

Near death

There is always a worry that anyone who has someone close to death will not want to be reminded of the fact, yet such members hardly need reminding. On the contrary, they tend to be the ones in the Group that raise the subject. What can happen is that a game is played: the rest of the Group are sympathetic and react as they think they should, rather than as they want. The grieving person does likewise. What is *not* done is a further investigation into the topic.

In fact, it is just at this stage that discussion becomes even more necessary. When a drug user with HIV infection is close to death then there are likely to be further losses. Slowly, the person who was so well known to the family is lost, seems no longer the same son, daughter or parent. In particular, the adult drug user can seem more like a child.

'I cried when he asked me to tie his laces, then dried my eyes. After bringing up a big family you think you are finished with all that. To see him now – it's sad.'

In addition there can be further losses, like that of bodily form. This causes difficulties as people near death can seem very much altered.

'I looked at her and I said, "That's not Sharon." You see she was all bones, no flesh at all. You were scared to touch her.'

It might be hard to recognise the person, a daughter in this case, but the more worrying question is, if she is not the person I thought she was, who am I? Part of the help and support to be given is encouraging members to express feelings and articulate questions, even if they seem bizarre or are not easily understood. Alterations can be in bodily form or in the way the person behaves.

'I don't know how to handle Vince now. He's changed.'
'In what ways?'
'He's angry ... moody ...'
'Do you feel he's perhaps not the same person he was?'
'No, he's not the same person. He's changed.'

There are mixed feelings, confusion and chaos. The facilitator has to live for a time in that chaos, to know how members of the Group might be feeling. The facilitator brings structure, but this has to start with him- or herself. Real structure cannot be brought unless chaos is experienced.

Talking through the feelings around death in the Group is supportive as the meetings may provide the only occasion when such discussion is possible: it might be the case that it is difficult to have helpful sessions within the family, where feelings are running high and will over-run all rational aspects. As discussed previously, talking to friends can be difficult because of the prejudice that can exist.

'The neighbour asked me what the matter was with Sharon when the ambulance took her away. I said, "pneumonia", but felt bad having to say it. Later the woman up the stair asked and I just said, 'AIDS', and the relief of being able to say that! I thought, what the hell, fuck 'em, I was proud of my daughter.'

The death of a drug user is seen as the death of an individual, but it affects the whole family, affects the whole functioning of the family. The situation is seen at its clearest when there is more than one drug user in the family. The family can be so affected that, although able to deal with one death, it cannot cope with a second. Loss is added to loss, and the result is more than simply the combined effect.

'I visited James in the hospice up to his death and after. I don't think I could do it for Brian. It would just bring everything back again. I couldn't go through the same again.'

All of this support in the Group is only really justified if members are helped to deal with death better, especially the death of the family drug user.

Living with a death

Talking through aspects of death helps members to deal with anticipatory grief and feelings about the future loss of the drug user. It helps members to understand what is happening to them and validates the feelings they are experiencing as they begin to cut off and sense loss even before the death occurs.

'You begin to grieve for them before they die. You know what to expect and so begin to switch off a bit as they get more and more ill.'

This does not detract from the distress of the death itself, but talking about the death to come promotes a degree of acceptance which makes the passage to death easier for all (Reiss, 1990). Also, it does allow the bereaved person to recover more quickly after the death and to accept the loss in a shorter time. Members are able to exert more control in the situation, and this may be needed not just for themselves but also for the drug user. Drug users when dying are not able to exercise much control over their lives and have to rely on others to a large extent. Support assists them in gaining more control over their dying (Kelner and Bourgeault, 1993), putting limits on the degree of medication and returning power to the family (Labrecque et al., 1991).

Talking in the Group about a future family death allows the expression of all feelings, including those which seem wrong, which seem inappropriate and not to be declared in public. Yet unless those grieving can express their true feelings, the whole process is diminished. The general attitude of not speaking ill of the dead seems to extend to those about to die. Relatives are not supposed to say what they really feel and think. This is likely to be beneficial as members should be helped to ventilate and work towards some measure of acceptance of the coming death. This allows members to react more usefully with the person concerned, and for better social relationships to be established, which in turn helps the dying person by reducing the degree of their personal suffering (Achterberg et al., 1977).

The members' ventilation might show a variety of feelings, but all are acceptable provided they are true feelings.

'It may be horrible to say it but you are glad when they are dead. You miss them but finally get some peace.'

Once one member is able to talk honestly, then others are also able to do so, and this should be encouraged. Even when people have died, honesty is the best policy. What has to be remembered is that death does not take away true feelings.

'I could not feel sorry at the time when I saw him lying there. For the first time in years he seemed at peace, so I did not feel sad but happy for him.'

'It's as if they don't have to keep fighting any longer.'

'Aye, he was finally able to finish the struggle. I think it was a relief for him.'

Sudden death

Death might have been unexpected, as with an overdose, and with little or no anticipatory grief. The shock is likely to be overwhelming and there is often a great desire to know whether the act was intentional or accidental. As the latter is seldom known for sure, the grieving might never be satisfactorily finished. Attention has to be given to accounts of death, their precise circumstances, as every death is a different death and is the death of an individual.

Continuing after the death

The death of someone close to a member affects the whole Group; every member will be grieving to some extent for the drug user. For this reason, when a death does take place, the facilitator should take account of its Group as well as its individual effects, and make the Group aware that all of them can be affected. Group action such as attendance at the funeral is supportive for the bereaved and helpful for the other members (McNeill-Taylor, 1983).

Back in the Group meeting, talking about a death can be upsetting, yet it can also be useful because people do not always get the opportunity to do this (Parkes and Weiss, 1983). Often, the bereaved might be given special consideration for a few weeks, and then there is a general expectation that they should return to normality. Accordingly, less attention is given to them, and outsiders feel that they have done their duty. In addition, parents might have little option other than to return to their normal roles as quickly as possible; they are still expected to take care of and support the rest of the family. The time for grieving is greatly foreshortened.

'We are all actresses, we have our parts to play. We have to carry on. There's nothing else to be done.'

In fact, talking through does help the bereaved, and the more highly stressed that person is, the greater the relief (Vachon, et al., 1980).

So the facilitator should encourage bereavement talk, even though members might be highly anxious at times, and the Group intimidated by the intense feelings, preferring to ignore them. This is not helpful. The bereaved can be in a state of shock, their world seems totally chaotic, and talking can restore some feeling of normality, whereas pretending that the death never took place only reinforces that chaos. This can be aggravated by the actual experiences that occur in times of grief.

'See, when the doorbell rang then I used to shout out, "Come in Louise", and then remembered she was dead. Sometimes I would wake up in the night, and then I would think about the family and could not get back to sleep.'

Such upsets are often seen as happening close to the time of death, whereas they can occur at any time. Stimuli like anniversaries, reminders such as significant sights, sounds or smells, can set off bouts of grieving.

'I'm all right until some little thing happens. See, one of my grandaughters said, "Why don't you and Jimmy and me put on our coats, and we can go to heaven and see Sharon?"'

Work and the Group

The Group can help simply by listening to what the grieving member has to say and accepting whatever is said.

'I found it good that I could talk and everyone would listen. I wasn't looking for answers, I didn't even take in what was said, but after a while I felt better.'

This talking-out process may be repeated several times, often using the very same words. This is more than repetition, it is part of the person's method of coping with the death, and there should be no inhibition about using this method. Remarks like, 'Yes, I remember you saying that last time', can stop what is an important process.

The process is helped if the facilitator can share some greater understanding with the Group about the stages of grief. The first stage is shock, when the person cannot take in what has happened. By asking members if they have ever been in shock and how they felt, the Group comes to understand the state and remember it as a stage of grief. Exactly the same can be done with the other stages of grief: denial, blame, depression and finally acceptance.

The importance of this work is that what seems abnormal might be normal for those grieving. They are not going mad and are not out of control. The second point is that members see there is some sort of end to the process; that there are various stages the bereaved will experience but they will not be everlasting and in time matters will improve. It should be added that the stages of grief are not neat and tidy, and the process of grief does not move from one stage to the next. Part of the nature of grief is its chaotic nature, and this fact should be a matter of attention. Acceptance of grief reactions and identifying them as such can legitimise the feeling of personal chaos. Members have a right to feel as they do, so attention is paid to what members feel about their feelings.

Grief is not just an individual reaction as it characterises whole families – parents, brothers, sisters and children. Particular concern was shown by members as to how young children – members' grand-children – might react to a parent's death. This is an occasion when the giving of information can be helpful. It can be helpful if members are aware that children of two years or less have a concept of loss, but not one of death. Up the age of four, children will talk of death, though they have no idea of it as an irreversible process. To them death is like sleep, a temporary state (Nagy, 1948). It is only above the age of five that children begin to have a real idea of what death means (Lansdown and Benjamin, 1985).

The reactions of young children to death can differ from those of adults, a fact that adults do not always appreciate. They do worry about their parents possible death, but very much as it affects them.

'Young Roy, he asked what would happen if his Mummy died. Who was going to look after him and cook him burgers?'

In general, chidren tend to be much less inhibited in their reactions and thus are much more likely to show anger and less likely to internalise their feelings. What should also be remembered is that children can react badly to the death of a brother or sister (Pollock, 1989) and the effects may be worse than in the case of parents.

Death and the family

The emphasis has been on individuals rather than the family as a whole and how grieving affects it. The reactions may be the same, such as denial, blame or self-blame, except that it is the whole family, all members, who react in the same way (Lieberman and Black, 1982; Bowlby-West, 1983). However, these are different in that they might arise through all members being in denial, all of them blaming or self-blaming, or it might only appear so. Thus everyone can be reacting in a certain way because that is how they think they should react in the family. Moreover, if one person in the family reacts honestly, then the rest of the family might also do so – because they realise that that person is being honest and there is a lack of honesty about.

What talking honestly in the Group can do is to carry honesty and understanding into members' families so that families can deal more easily with the death; good communication is a major factor in the avoidance of pathological functioning in the family (Bowen, 1976). Also, members can understand the secondary effects of a death, such as the stress it can lead to in marital relationships. The mother and father might react differently and have difficulty in accepting their differences (Dyregrov, 1990). Also, it can happen that one member of the family, often the mother, may be left to carry the feelings for the rest of the family (Large, 1989).

Reflections on the theme of death

What started as a matter that arose in a Group meeting, an allusion to death, has lead to matters that seem to have little connection with drugs or drug use. This underlines the fact that the Group is for support, and the search for support may take the members in different directions, according to their needs and desires. Rather than trying to narrow the scope of discussion, the facilitator should enlarge it to such areas that may be relevant and helpful to the Group. It should not be forgotten that support is important and helpful in the grieving process (Maddison and Raphael, 1973).

Death has been treated as a form of loss, and it should be understood that it is merely one example. There are likely to be many other kinds of loss that have been or will be encountered by the members: loss of relationships, loss of children from the home, loss of ignorance and loss of some individual freedom. The grief reactions to such losses can be identified, and the behaviour of members themselves or other family members better understood. In fact, all major changes in life result in the loss of old forms of behaviour, so loss is one of the most important aspects of human life.

Understanding loss leads to greater control for those who have been bereaved (Bahr and Harvey, 1980) and for those who have the role of supporters, and to the greater ability of members to take decisions and be themselves. Greater understanding can lead to members being aware of possible difficulties and dangers, such as the possible dependence of parents on their children (Rosenthal, 1980). However, it should be noted that the theme was initially discussed because the Group expressed a need to do so. Forcing the issue, talking about death because it should be done or because it would be helpful, runs the risk of turning out to be a premature intervention in a natural grieving process (Williams and Polak, 1979).

Themes in general

Themes have their own specific uses, such as discovering more about power and death, or any other theme that is chosen. They are also a way of enlarging the perspectives and understanding of members beyond the narrow confines of family drug use. This is very necessary in the long term, as a total absorption in the family and drug use locks Group members into a world dominated by drugs. What many members want is some detachment, to be able to live their own lives and for the family to function as usefully as possible, and not to be dominated by drugs.

Themes themselves can differ considerably, so facilitators have to work out how they might best be tackled. As may have been noted, a major task in working with the theme of powerlessness is that of identification, whereas that of death is not identification but working through. This points to the question of the role of the facilitator, and how themes can be worked upon in a non-directive manner. The art of facilitation is for work to be done, with members being virtually unaware of the fact and, similarly, they should hardly notice the facilitator's role.

With the work on themes comes a progression from the Group occupying itself with individual facts or isolated events, to a greater interest in situations and processes. This is helpful in itself, as understanding families rests on being able to grasp processes and overall situations.

6 SPECIFIC WORK AREAS

FAMILY ASPECTS

Introduction

Drug use is usually seen as an individual form of behaviour. It is the drug user who takes the illegal substances; no one forces him or her to do so. However, such behaviour does affect other members of the family, who in turn interact with one another and the drug user. In fact, as the family is a group tied by feelings towards each other, there will be multiple interactions and the family as a whole will be affected.

It has been noted that family members try to accommodate the drug related behaviour within the family and try to cope with the resultant difficulties (Wiseman, 1980). The outcome of such accommodation is that those affected by the drug use will exhibit changed and varying behaviour.

'Her father doesn't say or do anything. He tries to kid himself that she gets drunk and doesn't want to admit that Marion is using drugs.'
'And how does that make you feel?'
'It annoys me. I tell him that he should do something, but he says the children are my responsibility and so it's up to me. I tell him he's not pulling his weight, but he just ignores me.'

What might be noticed is that a crisis like drug use puts a strain on everyone concerned, a strain on the family. Everyone reacts differently, some deny what is taking place and are under-involved. This denial often happens with fathers, partly because many fathers of drug users tend to be peripheral to the family, (Stanton and Todd, 1982; Kokkevi and Stephanis, 1988), though this is not invariably the case, as evidenced by this father:

'I've seen myself driving along the roads at two or three in the morning trying to find her. I've been up to her flat and thrown out all the people I found there, I've helped her do up where she stayed. In the end, none of it did any good.'

Mothers, on the other hand, tend to get over-involved.

'I can't see my daughter suffer, see her withdraw and end up shivering, shaking and crying out for someone to help. At times she has been so bad that I had to go up to the flats myself to buy drugs so she would feel better. People say I'm a fool to myself, but they're not her mother.'

Of course, all families are different. Other families may differ completely from the two examples given. Nevertheless, one of the tasks of Support Groups is to look at the differing degrees of involvement by family members and the result on the family.

Nature of work with families

Another approach to family and drug use is to identify the various strains and stresses that can result from drug using behaviour. This can be done by asking the Group to give examples of such behaviour.

'If Hale comes to stay then we have to lock up the cupboards in case he steals from them. And you can't leave him alone in the house or the telly would probably walk.'

'My sister was taking Susan's jeans for a wash and came back to say she had found a syringe in the back pocket. I faced Susan with it, but she said she was just holding it for a friend, said she did not inject drugs and hadn't done so for two years. What was I meant to believe?'

Again, everyone tends to react differently, but it is noticeable that denial is a reaction more common with fathers. What can be picked out at this stage is that the examples given in Group meetings might not just be individual instances; they can mirror a certain theoretical perspective. Because what has been recounted in Group meetings links up largely with the findings of researchers and workers with drug families and their explanations; this points to those explanations having a certain validity. This being the case, theories about the family might be something to be shared in the Group. This has certainly been my view, and I feel that members could profitably be introduced to various ideas or theories about family functioning and drug use. The extent of this process depends very much on the

Group reaction. An indifferent or negative reaction demands an end to the process, otherwise family support is liable to turn into misplaced family orientated groupwork.

Beginning an investigation of family functioning

Members are under stress from family drug use and possibly from other difficulties. They come to the meetings for support and are entitled to expect that support. The idea of looking at how families function as opposed to talking about the effects of drug use can seem threatening and hardly supportive. For this reason, any work on family functioning has to be carefully introduced and the Group has to be encouraged to say how they feel about the idea. If there are negative feelings, then the members can agree not to proceed further; alternatively, the facilitator might suggest that they look into those negative feelings and that members be allowed to talk through them.

'I thought the meetings were going to be about drug use ...'
'Support when there is drug use in the family.'
'OK, support, but not about family matters not concerned with the drug use.'
'But if that drug use is connected in some way with the family or getting support we should know more about families ...'

Apart from leading to a decision about whether or not to take up work about family functioning, it also lays the basis for the next stage.

Family homeostasis

Drug use behaviour in the home causes reactions and accommodations. Once the family has adjusted to or compensated for the drug user's behaviour, there is a tendency to try and keep on an even keel. Members of the family try to maintain the status quo, and this may include keeping the drug user as a drug user (Stanton and Todd, 1982). This paradoxical effect is not obvious, as the family will roundly declare they want the drug use to end. Their problems stem from the drug use, so why would they want it to continue? Nevertheless, their actions are such as to incline the user to continue to take drugs. Having someone in the family on drugs may be a convenient way of diverting attention from other problems, often the state of the parental relationship. This action of the family, seeing all problems as a result of the drug use and so blaming the drug user, leads to confrontation. Blame may be welcome to the drug user who sees it as unjust, proof that the situation is parentally based (Seldin, 1972).

The idea that families might maintain their members as drug users is not one that is easily accepted. For this reason, it may best be suggested only to a Group where members are likely to be receptive to the idea, where there is low anxiety and members feel reasonably in control of their lives. However if an example of homeostasis does arise, then the idea can be forwarded.

'I used to be an alcoholic and I found my husband didn't help. He would even leave a bottle of whisky out, putting temptation in front of me. Why did he do that?'

'You tell us.'

'I think he wanted me to be an alcoholic, to have something over me.'

'And do you think this might apply to Peter? Do you want him to stay a drug user?'

'How do you mean?'

'Well, if Peter stopped being a drug user, how would you feel and how would you react?'

'I'm not sure. I must admit you may have a point. So much of my life is wrapped up in Peter.'

There is a further difficulty in that members can see the idea of homeostasis as a way of moving blame for the drug use from the drug user on to the family, and on to parents in particular. For instance, drug use is linked with individual and family pathology, individuals and families not functioning correctly (Newcomb and Bentler, 1989). This fails to distinguish between families that have always been dysfunctional and those which have become dysfunctional through the drug use. It should be appreciated that calling families dysfunctional can be one way of blaming families, an unhelpful action.

It is more worthwhile to discuss families. For instance, parents may try to control the behaviour of younger drug users, yet they seldom help to prepare them to take steps toward independence (Alexander and Dibb, 1975). As a result, these drug users may find it harder to take responsibility for themselves and more difficult to end their drug using behaviour.

Family separation

One event that disrupts homeostasis is children leaving home, as this tends to alter the family dynamics. This separation is not usually a sudden action but an expected and desirable movement, linked with the children's individuation. However, when families are under pressure, for whatever reason, this adolescent maturation process can be interrupted or made more difficult.

As a result there can be two possible problems. First, the family, and this usually means the parents, put pressure on the adolescent when his or her independence threatens family stability. This increases dependence on the family. The second action is to encourage premature independence, with the outcome that the adolescent returns to the family home and resumes dependency (Solomon, 1973).

The final outcome of these separation difficulties is that, years later, family members may still be emotionally home based and over-involved with their family of origin. This may be assessed in how members view their families, bearing in mind that concepts such as under-involvement and over-involvement are very much a matter of degree and personal perception.

The type of family work employed

Apart from the work already indicated, any further work engaged in by the Group may be very indirect. Originally, my intention was to base the discussions between members on the six important aspects of family functioning as laid out in the McMaster Model (Epstein et al., 1978). These aspects are:

1. Communication.
2. Roles.
3. Affective responsiveness.
4. Affective involvement.
5. Problem solving.
6. Boundaries and their enforcement.

However, these six seemed too many, and to examine them verged on some form of indirect therapy rather than support. For this reason, discussion about families was seen through just two perspectives: communication and disengagement. Communication, both cognitive and affective, is important in all family setups. Disengagement – helping parents and others retreat from over-involvement – is a task that is very applicable to those close to drug users. In practice, these two categories of work tend to cover most of the six McMaster aspects of family functioning.

COMMUNICATION

Talking and listening

The family is a most important unit for all of us, very much making us who we are. It has its own history and culture, and its own development and change over the years. And everything is held together by communication; it is the very fabric of families.

The Group meeting provides a similar service. As one member spontaneously remarked:

'The advantage of the Group is that you have someone to talk to.'

Communication is the essence of our humanity, and reaffirms it. Good communication – talking, listening, reacting and interacting – is necessary for satisfactory family functioning. This is even more true if the family is to cope with the difficulties it is experiencing (Olson and McCubbin, 1983). However, useful communication may not be easy where members are enmeshed in a situation like drug use.

'I've got no one to talk to. Well, there's my husband but he's in the same situation as me. We can't speak to anyone else.'

It is imperative that members feel able to speak freely in the Group meetings, so that they find the experience useful. Speaking easily in the Group aids good communication at home.

Communication is important in that it can tell us about the structure and functioning of families, but this is only the case if Group members are able to give an accurate description of their families – and this means they have to be able to communicate in a satisfactory manner and give a relatively impartial and detached picture of how their families operate. For this reason, members are helped to look at their own communication.

Talking in Groups

At the risk of stating the obvious, communication should be owned, everyone should take responsibility for what they say. It should be direct, precise, and unambiguous – just like the facilitator's communication should be. However, such suggestions are not very helpful if no attention is given to members' situations, so the first step might be for members to describe their feelings about communication in the Group.

'I find it difficult to talk in the Group at times. I feel easier just speaking person to person, less embarrassed.'
'And how about at home? Do you talk to your husband and Aileen separately or together?'
'I suppose it is easier to talk to them individually. Together and they, all of us, end up arguing. Mind, we tend to argue anyway about who said what.'

This shows a very common characteristic: it is easier to talk to individuals than to a Group. By getting members more accustomed to talking together, it becomes easier to talk to the family. This is important as drug users may use the device of 'divide and rule' – play one family member off against another – and this depends on one-to-one communication, ensuring family members are unsure who said what to whom. In families under stress, the chaos will continue unless there is honest talk and active listening.

Looking at what is said

The next step is for members to understand the need to reflect at times on what has been said, and to reflect in a cool and detached manner. Sometimes this can be illustrated by taping a Group meeting and then taking a short extract at a later session to examine in detail. The following is just such an extract:

'Jim comes up to me and asks if he can stay the night. I always tell him that I'll have to check it out with his Dad, but the answer is likely to be "No". Jim said Harry had already agreed, and if I didn't believe him I should phone him at his work. Well, to cut a long story short, Jim stayed the night. I could tell Harry wasn't happy, not happy at all. Later he got on to me and wanted to know why I had insisted Jim stay. I never! I told him I thought it was all his idea.'

On one level, this is merely an account of a drug user conning his parents into letting him stay the night. But when it is examined more closely, there are other aspects that are of interest.

1. 'Jim comes up to me'; what does that phrase suggest to the Group?

2. 'Jim asks if he can stay the night'; to what extent is Jim's asking really a request, or is it something else?

3. 'I always tell him I'll have to check it out'; The speaker said 'always', but does the Group think this means always?

4. 'The answer was likely to be "No"'; what is going on here, what is the balance of power in the family?

5. 'Jim said ... if I didn't believe him I should phone him (Harry) at his work'; to what extent could the mother really phone her husband at work?

The Group gave their opinions, and then the speaker said how she saw matters. The Group found this enjoyable, and the process does underline how much information is conveyed – sometimes directly, sometimes indirectly. All of this emphasises the importance not just of talking but also of careful listening.

Listening

We tend to mention talking to people but seldom mention listening, yet the first is dependent on the second to be meaningful. Listening has to be active listening, the ability to really listen and not get caught up in one's own personal agendas. When there is drug use, talking within the family may have limited value. No one is able to stand back, detach themselves and look coolly at the pressing issues.

Members have to be encouraged to listen and be listened to in the meetings, and then transfer the skill to their family life. My approach is not to criticise inattention but to take a positive stance and commend those members who have been actively listening. This action highlights the listening. This gives the Group the opportunity to appreciate being listened to, listening to others, and to understand the importance of both actions.

More about listening

Active listening requires more than two ears: it requires the use of the eyes. In families, much of the communication is non-verbal, everyone knows each other so well that at times communication hardly requires speech. However, we tend to concentrate more on what is said, and arguments will often have phrases such as, 'But you said ...' It is more difficult to say, 'You pursed your lips, so I knew ...' Nevertheless, getting members to think about how they can communicate in the Group, sometimes just by glancing at each other, leaning forward or slightly moving their hands, starts the process of their being able to identify non-verbal signals in their families.

The skill of listening is only really possible when there are no interfering agendas and no severe anxiety which results in an inability to concentrate on what is happening and what is being said.

'I try to listen to what Jack says, but at times he gets me so wound up. He says I never listen to what he has to say.'

'It sounds as well as if he knows what buttons to push to get you going.'

'That's for sure. He gets me going and then makes out it's my fault. I suppose it would help if, as you say, I was able to stand back, to stop myself and calm down. I've had enough of the arguments as they lead nowhere.'

Challenging

The Support Group provides an arena where members can improve the quality of their communication, made easier in the supportive atmosphere.

One aspect that members might want to look at is that of arguments. It might be noted that arguments as such are rare in the Group, even though there can be debates and discussions, and members can hold differing perspectives and opinions. So the emphasis is not so much on arguing, but on challenging.

The counselling concept of challenging may be unfamiliar to Group members, so it may be necessary to explain it. Challenging is not an attempt to convince someone of another view or belief, nor does it involve arguing. It is merely a way of seeking clarification of a statement put forward by another person. Needless to say, it is dependent initially on good listening.

Challenging is used when people contradict themselves, when they make promises that are not fulfilled, or when there is a clash between what is said and what is indicated non-verbally. Any argument is not between people but is by the speaker with him- or herself.

There are likely to be opportunities for challenging in the Group, and sometimes they should be taken. Members may resort to evasion or denial, and in the safety of the Group these can be used as objects of learning. However, it is essential that this is done only very occasionally, otherwise the feeling of support may quickly evaporate. Any challenge should be done very gently and should be capable of being easily withdrawn.

'I'll be asking John about him paying into the house. He keeps promising but keeps putting it off.'

'It sounds to me as if that might be quite difficult for you to do. I only say this as, if I remember rightly, you have talked about doing this on previous occasions but have not done so. It must be hard dealing with John.'

'You're right. I know I have put this off, keep putting it off. It's just that he is so short of money.'

'They can get the money if they want to! I tell Louise, "Pay me the money or get out!" Once they know you're serious then they'll find that money from somewhere.'

Challenging is only useful if the other person responds positively. If there is any form of denial or the challenge is not taken up, then the challenging person should apologise 'for getting things wrong'. Actually, the apology is sometimes quite helpful, as the challenged person might then admit that the challenger was right, and then respond positively.

Assertion

Assertion is not often required in the Group but may be needed at home by members, so discussion about it is of potential use. Assertion is the re-establishment of personal boundaries, when someone feels their emotional space has been invaded.

Again, it is important to be fully aware of the precise skill and to talk over its applicability. In discussing assertion, some of the points that arose included recognising when another person was infringing personal space, when members felt they had been pressurised, felt threatened, or were made to feel guilty. It was seen as important to act on, and not simply to accept, such behaviour. The fact that it always happened or there were excuses for its taking place did not alter the need for action. Some members felt that replying in kind was the best answer, though this could lead to a form of low-key warfare. Other members found being assertive difficult and linked it to their feelings about themselves, their low self-esteem. This pointed to their own needs in that area.

The Group is not used to teach assertion techniques, though note is taken of courses where members can learn them. However, what is useful is for the Group to talk about personal boundaries, to learn to make time for themselves, and not to take on a victim role.

Communication pairs in the Group

By using the Group, members can become more aware of some of the characteristics of communication. For example, pairing may occur in the Group either through their introduction, such as when a man and wife come to meetings, or when two members have much in common and relate closely to each other. It is helpful if members realise that pairs in the meetings can act in certain ways: for example, disclosure by one party sets up an expectation of some form of reply by the other (Petronio, 1991), causing a skewing of communication in the Group. If one member of the pair is male and the other female, then there can be further skewing in that men tend to be more sensitive to negative feelings of women pair members, whereas the women are more sensitive to a lack of supportive listening by men (Kobak and Hazan, 1991).

Pairs produce differences between themselves and the rest of the Group. However, there can also be differences internal to such pairs as well. Though this might be pointed out in the Group, the real substance lies in the differences that can arise in families, with the parents forming the communication pair. Discussion of men feeling threatened and women getting irritated with their partners 'who simply don't listen', can heighten awareness of what is taking place in families.

Communication and its grounding

There is a danger of seeing communication as a form of self-contained behaviour, instead of behaviour between people who are part of various relationships and groups. In particular, unhelpful communication in families affected by drug use can arise through paradoxical hierarchies (Madanes, 1981). Adolescents are still dependent on parents financially and for accommodation, and yet when using drugs they can dominate their parents. If we ask how these hierarchies are identified, then pathways and forms of communication are major factors. Incongruous styles of communication are a result of inappropriate hierarchies. Proper communication comes best when there are clear and appropriate hierarchies.

Communication pathways

Using the example of the Group, members might note that they tend to communicate in various ways:

1. Some members tend to address their remarks to two or three members in the Group, who also respond likewise when they speak.

2. Some members tend to speak to the facilitator or the perceived leader of the Group.

3. Members might speak to those sitting opposite them in the meeting circle or those directly on either side of them.

4. Members might talk to the Group in general.

The point is merely to get members to identify the different ways they communicate in the Group, though this is likely to lead on to further discussion.

Attention can then be given to members' families, which are more complicated – who talks to whom, and also for whom the message is intended. This leads on to:

(a) Are there members of the family who are bypassed, not given messages they might have expected to receive?

(b) Are messages passed through third parties, such as one parent using the children to relay a message to the other parent?

By noting the different communication pathways, we can get an idea of the centres of power in the families, who is highly involved and who is little involved in their management.

Work on hierarchies

Parents cannot suddenly change their children's perceptions of them, but parents can change their own behaviour, which then changes perceptions of them. This can result in the children behaving differently. Indeed, sometimes any change in the family functioning can loosen the situation and can bring about improvements (Jenkins, 1989). The best way for parents to change their behaviour is to agree between themselves what would be best. Parents have to make their own decisions and suggesting what they should do is not helpful.

In the Group, members may suggest what they would want and then define the boundaries. Because members can feel guilty, angry or trapped, maintaining those boundaries is not easy and discussion among members is one way of getting the Group to reinforce them. The idea is for parents to regain responsibility for themselves and to set boundaries in the family, to ensure equity and still to retain the family as a family. The rules have to be specific and there has to be unanimity in the family, and certainly between parents. This is often difficult to achieve as the parents can either be under-involved or over-involved with the drug user, and action needs to be taken about this fact.

DISENGAGEMENT AND OVER-INVOLVEMENT

Setting the scene

It is helpful to see which ways of family functioning are helpful and which are unhelpful. The emphasis is on a total family perspective and this can have indirect benefits, as families can play a big part in helping members to change and even to end their drug use (Eldred and Washington, 1976).

Taking an outsider's view, we note that the over-involvement of mothers with their drug using children has long been known about. It is not an inevitable characteristic, and sometimes may be related more to the domestic set ups of working-class homes than a product of family drug use (Fram and Hoffman, 1973). Nor should we imagine that fathers cannot at times similarly become too closely involved.

There are class and cultural expectations of the family role of mothers. These are reinforced by the family, who expect mothers to have high involvement. This might also have to compensate for the low paternal involvement or the absence of a father in the home. Sometimes Support Group members will see over-involvement as the result of the drugs use. On the contrary, it is more the result of different roles and the expected roles of each partner in a crisis. In cases of schizophrenia in the family (Kuipers et al., 1992), similar marked differences in parental involvement can also be seen. Thus Group members have to turn their attention away from the drug use and look more closely at their family functioning.

Behaviour in the family

The maternal role is well known when children are small, but becomes less defined as the children grow up. The role not only becomes less clear, but its purpose and rewards diminish. Mothers may think about the time when all the children will have left home, and what their role will then be. This problem may be delayed by the children not leaving home or keeping in contact with parents, and this typifies many drug use families (Madanes et al., 1980). Even when drug users have left home, home is still important to them, used as a constant reference point in their lives (Goldstein et al., 1977). It might seem that leaving the maternal role behind and mothers being themselves would be attractive, but, just as retirement and losing the work role is difficult for men, so losing the role of a mother is not easy and the search for self-identity intimidating.

The over-involvement is two-sided, reflecting the need of the drug user to be closely bound up with his or her mother. This might seem surprising at first, as there can be constant arguments and the drug user threatens never to contact home or speak to the mother. However, this actually happens rarely, reflecting not only the drug user's need for contact, but also the mutual needs of both mother and child (Coleman, 1976). Indeed, this need for involvement may characterise all the children. Thus Support Group members begin to see that the illegal drug use does not determine the family functioning: rather, the family functioning may be expressed in part through ongoing drug use behaviour.

Moving against over-involvement

One of the ways of ensuring that parents are supported is to help them to adjust their involvement with the drug user to a better functional level. Clearly, those who are over-involved will become less anxious if they are somewhat more detached. However, it might seem that the under-involved would have little to gain from becoming more involved. In fact the greater equality of involvement is likely to improve the parental relationship.

Members usually recognise over-involvement, unless it happens to apply to them. Over-involvement does sound like criticism rather than simply a description, so we should not be surprised at a strong reaction when the term is used. For this reason it helps to approach the subject gradually, commenting on how close a parent seems to the children, how they seem to rely on her, wondering whether this causes a strain and asking how the family does in the absence of that parent. This is addressed to members of the Group in general, not just to one member, so it seems less of an exercise directed against individuals.

The big advance is for Group members to entertain the possibility of over-involvement; the idea is put no more strongly than that. With treatment groups, therapists tend to be very much more definite and insist on the recognition of certain states, situations and relationships. Support Groups take a much more relaxed stance. As facilitator, I do not advance ideas unless the Group has given some indication of being likely to accept them.

Reflecting on involvement

Once there is acknowledgement by the Group that there are very close relationships in the family, then time is made to discuss what they mean to the family. Mothers might see them as very close, but how do the rest of the family see them? Through Group discussions, members can begin to look at their roles and relationships in the family, and look at them from more than just their own perspectives. The facilitator does not lead the Group in any particular direction, though it is helpful to ask the following questions – which in this case assume that it is the mother who is over-involved.

1. What is the status of the mother's relationship with the drug user in the family?

2. Is the relationship generally known or is it partially hidden? Is it different in the presence of the husband or the other children?

3. Is the relationship mentioned in the family? Is the relationship resented by the other children or by the husband?

4. Is the mother's relationship with the drug user accepted or not, does the family go along with it, oppose it, or vary in their attitudes according to the situation?

These lead up to the final question:

5. Who benefits from the mother and drug user relationship?

For instance, arranging for the drug user to live away from home might not seem to benefit the mother who can be very anxious as to what might happen, yet it is likely to help the drug user come off and stay off drugs (Zahn and Ball, 1972). Thus the crucial question is whether it is the parent or the drug user who is helped, with the further thought that helping the drug user will support the rest of the family.

Stereotyping

When dealing with over-involvement, although this usually applies to mothers, the facilitator should take care that mothers do not become stereotyped as over-involved carers. Some mothers will behave very differently, and might even begin to feel guilty about their lack of heavy involvement. Also, too much emphasis on maternal over-involvement can make caring fathers feel undervalued. Thus the whole complexity must be discussed. Sometimes both parents or even the whole family can be over-involved, sharing an enmeshed view of reality (Reiss, 1981).

Preparing for disengagement

The work of disengagement needs the discussion of relationships and over-involvement in the family. Members have to be able to recognise for themselves if they are over-involved and could benefit from a measure of disengagement. However, on occasions, mention of disengagement can lead to anxiety. Mothers might see drug users as being unable to live with any diminution of their help. What is required is an acknowledgement that there is anxiety, and to talk it through.

'When he's out of the house then I worry if he is feeding himself properly. At least when he is at home he gets something to eat. I tell him to keep in touch but he never does – until he wants something.'

What is not always obvious is that the over-involvement might favour the continuance of the drug use, so having a place where meals are provided allows drug users to maintain their behaviour. What also has to be acknowledged is that some of the anxiety comes from the mother who is afraid to let go, and is not keen to see the user leave home. For some mothers, ending the caring role may not be very welcome. A discussion in the Group and listening to their peers does reduce anxiety and helps those members who want to disengage.

Cognitive disengagement

Disengagement has to be seen as a move consisting of a series of very small steps. Mothers will have been acting in certain ways for a long time in the family, so they may not feel very positive about change. The Group has to acknowledge possible feelings against change. This can be done by noting all the relevant comments and excuses thought of by the Group members.

'The family expect me to ...'
'I always ...'
'No one else would do it, if I don't ...'
'It would only cause trouble if I didn't ...'
'Yes, but ...'

The advantage of the Group is that members realise that several of them have the same inhibitions and feel the same pressure to keep to their roles. How they feel is not peculiar to each one of them, it is common to many women in their situation, so any change would not be the outcome of an idiosyncratic decision but a decision that anyone in that particular situation would make.

Another approach is to ask the members to imagine the worst possible scenario, to work out whether it is really likely to happen, and who should be held responsible for the resultant situation. Often anxiety builds up our expectations of disaster, feelings which are reduced when reason takes over. It may seem counterproductive to look for reasons not to change, and looking for disasters seems one way of inclining members not to change. In fact, the whole process of rational assessment can be very liberating, as long as it is carried through fully and done in a positive manner.

Behavioural disengagement

Disengagement is a process and a gradual process. Too extensive or radical a change is likely to be resisted strongly. If the mother suddenly decides that putting the drug user out of the house is the best form of disengagement, then there is a strong possibility that the action will not be taken seriously by the drug user, by the rest of the family, and perhaps by the member herself. Small steps are likely to be more successful, giving time for everyone to adjust to one small change at a time.

Reaction to change

Any perceptible change is likely to cause some reaction, so the members should be prepared. There may be straightforward reactions, such as opposition to the small alterations to the accustomed family functioning. What may not be expected are indirect results such as crises with the drug user or in the family, crises which do not seemed directly related to any enacted change. However they can serve the purpose of allowing blame to be put on the change: everything was fine until that change. The least expected type of reaction is where the Group member will oppose the change she has enacted. This seems to lack rationality, until guilt is understood to be the intervening factor. The member feels guilty and is often made to feel guilty, and this continues to cause pain until the member assuages it by undoing the liberating change.

Reinforcing change

Any change can be undone, so reinforcing and supporting useful change is essential. One way of doing this is by getting members to describe and comment on any changes towards gradual disengagement they have made. In particular, attention should be given to any resultant benefits, whether to the drug user, the member or the rest of the family. All too often members try to link changes enacted directly with benefits, but in families with the complex feedback and interactions there are seldom many simple and direct paths of causation. As a result, the advantages of particular actions may be indirectly linked. It may be that a daughter is more communicative, the husband's drinking is moderated, or there are fewer family rows.

What should be understood is that change permits increased opportunities, and the member's gradual disengagement may be the excuse for the family to change, a signal that allows changes that were only potential to be enacted. Sometimes members can feel responsible, even guilty, for setting off a train of events, overlooking that the rest of the family participated and that they are responsible for their own actions.

Compensating reactions

Though the accepted rules and norms can give the family a placid appearance, it is a continually interacting group. As a result, disengagement may be followed by a compensating reaction. For instance, a husband who has shown little interest in the drug user suddenly takes a more active role. This might be seen as a positive step resulting from the member's diminished over-involvement. It might also be seen as an unsettling manoeuvre. There can be resentment that the husband is taking over some of the mother's role, annoyance that he is only now taking some interest when he should have done so long ago. However this ignores the fact that he might not have been able to do so, as his wife had taken up her involved role. Equally, the wife might have taken up such a role initially because her husband seemed to be distancing himself from the family drug use.

What has to be avoided is the sterile blaming by members of others or of themselves. Members should see that the disengagement they have initiated has resulted in useful changes and benefits for the family. Compensatory change, when examined, is seen to be helpful in that members can disengage and this allows others to react accordingly, to fill in the gap. This reduces the fear of 'What will happen if I don't ...' It must be admitted that this demands a certain leap of faith and determination, as others have relied on the member to sustain his or her role.

Disengagement of others

The disengagement of husbands is less of an issue in the Group as husbands either tend to distance themselves from difficulties in the home arising from drug use, or simply to distance themselves from Support Groups and not come to meetings. However where there is over-involvement by fathers, this is generally towards drug using daughters (Ellinwood et al., 1966), but the general approach used for mothers is equally applicable to fathers.

Special consideration should be given to single parents as the relationships between them and their children tend to be very close. As a result, parental disengagement may appear threatening to those involved, and other options might have to be taken up. The parent might use a befriender or individual counsellor, someone to talk to and to do so in confidence. A second option might be to attend a single parent group. By having outside people to talk to, it becomes easier to disengage.

Involvement of partners

It is difficult to speak of the over-involvement of partners, as the expectation is that they should be closely involved with each other.

In addition, being the partner of a drug user forces involvement, and in several different ways.

Drug use is illegal, so partners are usually aware that their drug using spouses are acting illegally. This puts them in an ambivalent position with regard to law enforcers such as the police. Partners are not necessarily seen as criminals, yet neither are they seen as totally law-abiding. This police view may be justified, reflecting the fact that partners at times will help drug users to score drugs, they may even act illegally to raise money for drugs. The result is that partners may be categorised together with the drug users, and they, in turn, may come to accept this categorisation. They are not merely materially closely involved with their drug user partners; they are involved because everyone tends to treat them as if they were drug users.

Further close involvement comes from partners having to take care of drug users, especially in cases of overdosing or illness. Ironically, this can make overdosing more likely, as the drug user knows there will be someone present who knows what to do should there be an overdose. This might seem a bit far-fetched, but I did come across a case of a drug user who overdosed twelve times, to be revived each time by his partner. Unfortunately, the thirteenth time his partner happened to be out of the house and he died. Again, the long-term consequences of heavy involvement have to be examined.

Partners become increasingly associated with the local drug subculture. Drug users tend to associate with other users, so increasingly the partner's circle of friends becomes restricted to those on the drugs scene. This locks the partner into the subculture and also, indirectly, into the relationship with the drug user. Partners tend to have few non-using friends and do not see themselves leaving for another person, unless that person also uses drugs.

This bonding with the local drug subculture means partners pick up the associated attitudes, beliefs and norms, so disengagement has to include disengagement from these as well. However, it should be said that many partners do have very ambivalent feelings about the drug culture.

Disengagement of partners

Partners are expected to stand by each other, so judging the extent of over-involvement – meaningful when applied to parents – has less legitimacy when applied to partners. Much more weight must be given to the desires, expectations and opinions of partners when it comes to stating whether or not there is over-involvement. This is because outsiders alone cannot set the standard for how partners should behave together.

Rather than considering general ideas of relationships, what can be more helpful are discussions of the particular, the topics mentioned previously: having to deal with drug using visitors, the reactions of the police, and the partner's role with regard to the handling of the drug user's medication. These and similar matters can lead into a general talk about involvement with one's partner or spouse. It may be noted that what is not raised is the idea of disengagement, unless it is raised by a partner in the Group.

Disengagement and boundaries

The difficulty in achieving long-term disengagement, in moving out of enmeshed relationships, is that it requires the constant maintenance of boundaries. This has to be done unilaterally as drug users often have poor boundaries, tending to be egocentric and indulged by others. Moreover, boundaries may involve more than the drug user; they can include the drug user's family as a whole. Taking the example of the over-involved mother and her drug using daughter, then we should be aware that the drug user might be a mother herself. The member will have to negotiate boundaries with respect to being a mother, a mother-in-law and a grandmother. Consideration also has to be given to the fact that there might be another set of grandparents.

All of this points to the need to discuss in the Group the roles and expectations of members. For instance, what often occurs is that the Group member, a grandmother, is concerned about the welfare of the grandchildren. This results in her looking after them 'for a short time'. However, the loss of children affects the drug user, who may use drugs more heavily, her role as a mother having been diminished. The grandmother then decides to hold on to them until the drug user has 'sorted herself out'. This causes friction and ill feeling which spills over, making the children unsettled. They play up and the grandmother has second thoughts about looking after them. She resents being left with the responsibility for the children, and so returns them to their mother. But the grandmother soon starts to worry about them again, and the whole cycle of taking then returning them starts again.

What is required is for there to be boundaries which will not be overturned by sudden feelings. Admittedly, feelings cannot be controlled, but actions related to feelings are controllable. Emphasis is placed on ensuring that such actions are preceded by decisions made by both parents or by the whole family.

Work in the Group

Long-term personal detachment through boundary setting and maintenance is helped by Group members working through what is required. First, the individual member identifies areas where boundary setting would be helpful by reviewing feelings, thoughts and behaviour caused by the drug use:

(a) What things cause the member to have strong feelings such as anger, guilt or depression?

(b) What behaviour is thought to be wrong, unfair or unhelpful?

(c) What behaviour is repetitive or has occurred more than once?

As an example, Marie talked about how her son tended to trick her into 'helping' him, and how she would feel angry at first, and then confused and guilty. She saw her own behaviour as unhelpful, though this did not prevent it being repeated.

Second, once the problem has been identified then other members may offer their perceptions and ideas of what is going on. In the case of Marie, some of the observations which were peculiar to this case included:

(a) 'Tricked you? He's conned you! Done the dirty!'

(b) 'They play on your guilt. Your guilt is used against you.'

(c) 'As a parent you have a duty to help, but are you helping?'

(d) 'Drug users, they are all selfish. They really don't care a damn. And you shouldn't feel guilty as when they complain, it's only play-acting.'

(e) 'Sometimes I just think they want to put one over you, as if it's all a game.'

The facilitator should point out that what is taking place in the Group is an example of detachment, helped by the fact that it is easier to see what is happening to others than to ourselves. This being the case, Marie should not feel bad about herself. At this point, asking the others in the Group if they had experienced the same kind of troubles helped to diminish her feeling of being in some way inferior or stupid.

Third, members might then suggest what could be done to improve matters. Among the serious ideas forwarded in Marie's case were:

(a) 'You're lost if you listen, so don't listen. Just say no and keep repeating it. He'll get the message.'

(b) 'Tell him that he's just trying to con you. Let him know you know what he's up to.'

(c) 'Get him to do something for you first. He's got to learn that no one gets nothing for nothing in this life.'

(d) 'Say this is the last time you are going to do it, but only if you are prepared to make it the last time. Otherwise it's a waste of time.'

Fourth, the member is asked if any of the proposals might be of use. Marie was not greatly enthusiastic about any of them, and she was then asked what the difficulties were. It can help if the member looks at four questions:

1. Is the difficulty yours or someone else's?

2. Has the difficulty happened before in these or similar circumstances?

3. What is the worst that can happen?

4. What is the best that can happen?

Fifth, members can be a bit negative and this can be a problem in itself. Once this is understood, then it is easier to make progress and the person can decide what to do and what she is going to say. Putting into words what she is going to tell the drug user and the rest of the family does help to clarify the plan.

Finally, the member is asked to feed back to the Group what happens. Setting a timescale should not be overlooked. This process may seem very neat and tidy, but the actual process can take some time and is far from direct work. Marie, though she did not find the

Group's ideas directly useful, did feel that she had been helped to look at herself, and decided to be more assertive. Having done so, her principal feedback was that no one in the family reacted as expected – they did not react at all! They simply accepted what she suggested. The final irony was that her drug using son told her that she should have been harder on him long ago.

FAMILY BEHAVIOUR

Introduction

Over-involvement is usually seen in individual terms. The danger with such a perspective is that it can lead to a judgemental view of the person. The over-involved mother, for example, may be seen as weak, unrealistic or gullible, and may even be treated as such. This perception of over-involvement fails to comprehend the richness of family behaviour which is a product of many different views, desires, expectations and actions which are felt in and on the family. What happens in the family must be seen in Group as well as individual terms.

Drug use is a form of behaviour that can produce very considerable strains on the individual. Members are well aware of how they are affected, but they should also look to see what effects are evident in the family. Perhaps the most important is that on the parental relationship. Even with a good relationship, family drug use can cause difficulties.

'The two of us agreed to have a talk with Robert as we were both sick of the trouble he brings into the house. He argued with me first and then he argued with my husband. The trouble was that I ended up arguing with my husband and Robert just sat there looking on.'

Where the relationship has already been subjected to severe strain in the past, the pressure may open up old wounds and aggravate existing difficulties unconnected with the drug use. It should be remembered that there might be no simple linear causality: family strains may incline a person to continue to use illegal drugs, this then aggravates those strains, locking the family member into continued drug use. Moreover, parents may be well aware of what can happen.

'I couldn't go through it all again, having her here. I found I was arguing with my husband and it got to the stage where, with her back home, I wanted to leave.'

Even when the relationship is good, there can be difficulties according to the way the family functions. The mother looks to her husband for support as this is the expected source. However, this means the husband having to be 'strong' and not getting support for himself.

'I support my wife when things are difficult but there is no one I can speak to. It all comes to me.'

The situation seems different for the drug user, who is chemically insulated from reality, who has built up mental defences against the world and is thus able to operate in an egocentric manner. This should be compared with the roles taken up by parents, who are expected to carry out their accustomed parental actions.

'Terry doesn't seem to bother himself, he doesn't seem to have a care in the world. Sometimes I think I must try some of that stuff, if that's what it does! Of course I wouldn't.'

The net result is that drug users can obtain a more powerful role in the family because they can act purely in their own interests. This dominant position in the family, along with the decreased power of parents, can at times result in the roles of parents and children being reversed (Beker, et al., 1993). The drug user becomes the dominant person in the family, and the parents feel they have to fall in with the drug user's expressed needs and desires.

Enmeshment

Another effect of drug use is that one or both parents or even the whole family can become enmeshed, so intimately concerned with the drug use that they are unable to stand back and disengage themselves from what is happening, unable to be themselves rather than a prisoner of their feelings about the drug user. This can happen imperceptibly at first, so parents are unaware of how things have changed in the family. However, even when they are aware, there seems to be no way of changing the situation. Parents see no apparent alternative to how they are behaving, because they are locked in by their feelings.

'No matter what they do, you can't change your feelings for them.'

However the perceptions of the rest of the family might be very different. They see parents acting in a quite unreasonable manner. This does not make for harmony in the home.

'I've got to look after Graeme and I tell the rest of the family that I'm his mother, no matter what. They get on at me and say I shouldn't bother with him, but I couldn't turn my back on him. And Graeme says I ignore him, pay more attention to the others. He doesn't realise that there is more than him in the family.'

Family functioning depends to some extent on all members being able to communicate with each other and to reach work-able compromises. However, this can collapse when there is drug use in the family, as the drug user may no longer enter into such functioning systems. As a result the parents find them-selves in a potentially non-working set up where there is no way even to try to satisfy everyone.

Total family involvement

Drug use affects not only the parents but also any other children in the family. The usual scenario is that the drug use is known by the other children before the parents are aware of it. This means that the children may be brought into a collusive alliance to ensure that parents do not discover what is going on. However, it is probable that parents will have an inkling that something is going on, because the children are acting in a secretive way. These sibling alliances are not likely to last long as the drug user becomes absorbed into sub-cultural norms and behaviour, and drifts away from the family.

'It's as if the two of us are strangers now. We used to talk, we used to be close, but not now. And he hardly speaks to his younger brother, yet he always used to.'

Sometimes siblings are seen as too young to be included in such an alliance, and they have to deal with the situation on their own. Younger children suddenly find that they are confronted with someone they scarcely know.

'Once Grant had said, "Do you want to know what I spend my money on? Drugs!" Later I found his younger brother Bobby crying and he said, "You die if you take drugs, don't you?"'

If brothers and sisters are older they may be sympathetic, but there are limits to their sympathy, as they also are affected by what the drug use is doing to the family as a whole. They find themselves pulled in different directions and awareness of this can add to their pain and discomfort.

'John is very bitter about Rob, refuses to talk to him, and says I should not bother with him. He helped Rob come off the drugs, but Rob went back afterwards. John says he is just a waste of space and I am stupid trying to help him, that I will end up hurt. In fact, John hardly comes to see me now.'

Sometimes it is expected by parents that their children should be helpful and sympathetic with regard to the family drug taker, but the other children also have their own battles to fight because of the drug use.

'After a time Leah found her friends were dropping her, because of her sister. They found out she was Suzanne's sister. They kept going on at Leah about her sister till finally she told them she was Leah, she wasn't her sister. She was who she was, and her sister was someone different.'

It is easy to fall into the trap of labelling the drug user as 'bad' and the non-using siblings as 'good', but families have to be aware that siblings might also take drugs at some date: they are not immune (Needle et al., 1986).

The other family members who might be involved are the drug user's grandparents. Often they are of a generation in which illegal drug use was virtually unknown, and the family might pretend that everything is fine in order to avoid causing any worry. The stress of possible revelation and the effect this could have on elderly people can be a concern.

'My parents are coming at the weekend as usual. I hope Richard does not decide to turn up as he is usually under the influence of something when he does. They are too old to understand about drugs and things, they have no idea what it is all about and would be upset if anyone mentioned drugs.'

The family perspective

Support Group members often see family drug use as being directed against them in some way. This may be aggravated by drug users themselves who secure their position of power in the family by a policy of divide and rule, by giving differing accounts to different family members. But what becomes apparent in discussing the family aspects of drug use in the Group is that the whole family is likely to be affected as a unit. Moreover, the drug user is still part of the family system and is equally affected by what is happening.

The Group may gain from seeing their family as a system in which any act indirectly affects the whole system; it affects everyone. Thus it can be worthwhile to assess this.

'If we accept for the moment that the family is a group which is affected as a whole as well as individually, then if a parent acts towards the drug using member, everyone will be indirectly affected. I wonder if any member here agrees?'

'Well, what Roger has complained about is that if I try to help his brother, he sees me as ignoring him. Then he starts to freeze, ignores me. I mentioned it to my husband, but he says, 'Well, what do you expect?''

'So do you find you have to think of the family as a whole, try to balance up things?'

'That's it exactly! You can't please everyone, so if I do something for one, I have to do something for all. But they all need or want different things, so there's no winning!'

The idea of the family acting as a unit may not be familiar to Group members and it is important for their understanding that time is taken to discuss the subject.

Members' action

What can help families is their acting together, rather than pulling in opposite directions. For a start, the parents should act as a unit, especially in the face of a drug user's possible divisive tactics. The following are remarks from a husband and wife in the Group:

'We decided that Richard should not get any more money while he was still on drugs. However he said he was broke, so I have to admit that I gave in and slipped him five pounds before he left.'

'You gave him a fiver! He told me the same story and that his mother had refused to help, so I gave him five pounds. He walked away with ten pounds in his pocket! And to think I told him not to tell his mother!'

Once the parents are working together and can set agreed and lasting boundaries, the rest of the family, including the drug user, have a better chance of behaving more appropriately. This is not easily achieved, and it is usually helpful for the members to discuss four aspects of families: the parental relationship, family communication, feelings and boundaries.

1. By helping the family to function better and attending to bettering the parental alliance, not only is the family helped but also the drug user is helped indirectly. Improved family functioning can increase the drug user's periods of abstinence (Romijn and Platt, 1992).

2. Members should examine whether communication is adequate, or whether a lot is left unsaid. Sometimes it is assumed that others in the family will automatically know what someone is feeling and thinking: misunderstandings then occur. On the other hand, people can talk without really saying anything, so the quality of talk is important.

3. It helps if the expression of all feelings is encouraged in families. This is done mainly by not inhibiting their expression. Often feelings are expressed in arguments and tend to be negative. It is more helpful if feelings are expressed at times other than those of crisis, and more positive feelings are expressed.

4. The final form of help is that of setting family boundaries. This requires enforcement of such boundaries, which should be firm without being authoritarian.

Family help and the Group

As the aim of the Group is support, not therapy, the aforementioned aspects of help do not have to be given as a package, but should be given when the Group will most benefit. This is often signalled when relevant statements about the family have been made at the meetings and those present feel the subject would benefit from further discussion.

All family work with members should be done in a positive manner. This increases the chance of its being communicated to the rest of the family. It is important that members are aware that some of the help given is not only to them but also to their family. However, the fact that members are supported and thus change their behaviour will affect the whole family.

'I find that my husband's been much better since I started to come here. Perhaps it's because I'm more relaxed. We are able to speak more to one another.'

Another positive result that is worth remarking on is that improved functioning in the family allows more options. In particular, it enables members to disengage themselves to some degree from the family system and to become more individual, to grow as persons in their own right. A balance should be kept between being part of the family and being an individual, between fulfilling family roles and establishing a more personal identity.

CO-DEPENDENCY

Introduction

Co-dependency is when non-using persons are intimately linked with chemically dependent persons or partners (Beattie, 1992). This is often an issue for the partners of drug users in the Group, and may even be extended in part to others such as highly involved mothers of users. Co-dependent partners largely take on the norms and values of the drug users – the difference is that the partner does not actually use illegal drugs.

Being a partner of a drug user, and continuing to be so, demands an intimacy with drug use if the relationship is to continue. And the nature of the relationship is usually the principal factor in co-dependency, typically one of a woman living with a male drug user, a relationship determined as a result partly of the drug use, partly of the woman's relationships to men and the drug user's relationships to women. Whereas parents have difficulty in accepting that their children might be taking drugs, the partners of drug users are much more aware of the situation and have greater difficulty in coming to terms with the drug using without taking on drug user perspectives. Indeed, their behaviour is often as dysfunctional as that of the drug user, the two constituting a relationship frequently under strain and seen as immature in outlook (Kosten et al., 1983).

Origins of co-dependency

Often co-dependent people are the children of parents who are chemically dependent, alcohol being the usual substance. This would help to explain why co-dependency has its origins early in a person's life, and a co-dependent person is attracted to dependent future partners (Koffinke, 1991). It also explains the fact that co-dependent people have difficulty in changing. Despite their negative experiences, co-dependent partners may finally leave one drug user only to take up with another. Thus, using the Support Group to try to argue partners out of their situation is not likely to be of help. In fact, they build their life around the addiction, seeing all troubles as arising from it, and are reluctant to look at themselves and how they might contribute to the drug use. Alternatively, they might make a separate life for themselves while remaining with the drug user (Taylor et al., 1966).

Work with co-dependents

It is preferable to work with those aspects of co-dependency that might be amenable to Group influence. In practice, they might include the following:

1. Low self-esteem.

2. A need to be needed.

3. A need to control others.

4. A willingness to suffer.

5. An inability to recognise their contribution to the drug use.

6. A fear of change.

7. A lack of realism about the relationship.

It is important that the work is not personalised, so that particular members do not feel they are the centre of attention or that they are under attack. Instead, the aspects can be introduced as a theme for discussion with the whole Group participating. We should remember that these themes are likely to apply to some extent to all members. Talking about the seven above mentioned themes should be chosen as relevant to members, particularly partners.

Another approach is to use a more direct method with partners, who might display differing degrees of co-dependency, and to look at four areas.

1 *Independence.* This starts off with the fact that partners have come to the Group, and they are asked how they feel about that. How

does it feel to be on their own, being able to say what they want? They should also be asked whether they want to talk about their relationships and whether they feel able to do so. Independence may arise not only from their co-dependent relationship but also from the parental relationship, so the member should know that it is not just the partnership that is of interest.

2 *Detachment.*   The need for detachment has been alluded to previously, but the detachment here is to look at the reality of the relationship. It can help if, with just an outline, Group members say how they see the relationship.

3 *Leaving the past.*   A special case of detachment is that of leaving the past behind, completing unfinished business. Most of this is probably better done in individual counselling outside the Group, but identifying work to be done and encouraging the partner to get outside help can be done by the members.

4 *Rescuing.*   Rescuing is when partners protect drug users from themselves, by covering up for them and by intervening so they do not have to face the consequences of their actions. This reflects what partners might see as their responsibilities or duties, and what members might call the partner's guilt or fear of being rejected or left alone.

Again, we have to realise that the Support Group is not designed to correct dysfunctional relationships, but coming to the Group might result in changes, which may include ending the relationship. This can result in the Group being blamed by the partner, but it has to be stressed that each person must take responsibility for their own actions.

7 FURTHER WORK WITH THE GROUP

ROLES

Introduction

Roles are repeated patterns of behaviour. They are either formal, such as that of the facilitator or the mother in a family, or informal and easily taken up or put aside, roles such as the joker in the Group or the tidy person at home. Roles can be taken up for two main reasons. They can reflect the nature of the particular person: the member who clears up at the end of the meeting might be a tidy person and so takes on the job of clearing up. The second possibility is that the role may be given or even pressed upon the person, so it is agreed that someone in the Group should be responsible for seeing that the room is left tidy.

Roles impart useful stability and reassurance to Groups and families, whose members through their distress may be chaotic and vulnerable. However, role stability can grow into rigidity and thus make change difficult, so it is important to recognise roles that are restrictive. A balance has to be struck between what is useful and what may be redundant.

Family roles

The first step is to identify the various roles in the family. The facilitator can help by suggesting various possibilities, such as:

1. The Disciplinarian – who exerts authority.

2. The Temporiser – who calms family members.

3. The Carer – who looks after others, and not just when they are ill.

4. The Planner – who plans for the family.

5. The Decision-maker – with regard to family rather than individual matters.

6. The Communicator – who talks to others about family matters.

7. The Fixer – who gets things sorted out in the family.

8. The Reflector – who questions and thinks about the family.

The roles might vary according to the situation and be taken up by different members of the family. However, the idea is that members identify themselves with one or more family roles and then consider how they feel about them. Once more, the facilitator can help by getting the Group to answer the following with respect to the roles.

(a) Do I feel trapped by the role?

(b) Am I taken for granted in this role?

(c) Would it be better if someone else took over this role for a time?

(d) Do people see me only in this role; are they unable to see me differently?

(e) Do I always want to be in this role and do others always want me to be in this role?

These questions assist members to think more deeply about their roles in the family and about themselves in relation to the family. In particular, members can distinguish between roles that arise mainly from the person and imposed roles which arise from being part of the family.

Rounding-off

Sometimes, especially with women, talking about roles can lead to feelings of discomfort and even dissatisfaction. This appears hardly to be in line with the aim of providing Group support. For this reason, sessions should be rounded off by asking members how they feel, whether they do feel a bit unsettled or annoyed. The facilitator can help by saying, for example: 'Listening to these accounts I find myself feeling knotted up inside, a bit sick and angry. I wonder if the rest of the Group would like to say how they feel right now?'

Once feelings have been identified then possible reasons for them can be advanced by members, and they can discuss whether they are acceptable, and whether they can or should be changed.

PERSONAL COPING

Introduction

Like roles, personal coping with overwhelming family situations such as illegal drug use has both individual and Group or family aspects. With regard to the individual aspects, those of interest here are the defence mechanisms of denial, blame and self-blame. The emphasis placed on these mechanisms is that they are brought into play in times of high stress (Lazarus and Launier, 1978) and they are not just rational processes but involve feelings (Slovic et al., 1976). At times they can be unconsciously employed, so members may not even be aware of them. It is only when discussing personal behaviour that members begin to realise what they have been doing, and this allows them to regain more control over their lives.

Work on personal defences

Personal defences can be helpful, they may be an automatic reaction to an overwhelming situation. The difficulty arises if these defences are no longer required, if they are impeding members' continuing development and support. For this reason it can be useful to look into personal coping, to make members more aware of their own behaviour, and for them to decide whether they want to modify that behaviour.

The steps in working on personal defences might be as follows.

Identification. Members try to identify coping mechanisms that they have used. The simplest method is to ask them to think about the three main mechanisms, and then consider these questions:

Denial:
(a) Have you ever put difficulties out of your mind?
(b) Have you pretended something was not really happening?
(c) Have you seen signs of something happening but failed to see the whole picture?
(d) Have you seen what was going on but not believed it?

Blame:

(a) Have you blamed people, only to find out later it was not their fault?
(b) Have you blamed the wrong person on occasions?
(c) Have you had the experience where the moment you were told of a situation, you thought, 'It's So-and-so's fault!'?

Self-blame:

(a) Have you known something was going to happen, but did nothing about it?
(b) Have you felt sick in your stomach, even though others said it was not your fault?
(c) Have you blamed yourself for something, although there was nothing you could do about it?
(d) Have you felt at times that if you had acted differently, somehow things would have been better?

These questions do not have to be asked, but they may be useful as a fallback resource, to be used if the Group has difficulties in identification of defences.

Type of mechanism used. At this stage, once the idea of coping mechanisms has become clearer to the Group, members might be asked about other ways they deal with situations – using other coping mechanisms that have not been mentioned, such as avoidance, fantasy and rationalisation. The facilitator can take the discussion further by encouraging members to give examples. Time can be taken by the Group to talk through their experiences and get a firmer grip on past behaviour. It is also important to see coping behaviour within its context, not just as isolated behaviour. For instance, parents may be using denial about drug use, but we might well ask the extent to which the drug user's behaviour was intentionally covert. Also denial might belong to the drug user as much as to the rest of the family. It helps if everyone in the Group talks about these experiences.

Assessment. Staying with denial as an example of one particular way of coping, it – like other coping mechanisms – can be seen as failing to be realistic. Denial may be viewed negatively, whereas it might be a temporary method of dealing with a crisis. What is important is that members do not take negative attitudes to mechanisms such as denial but take a balanced view and see the good and the bad aspects of their behaviour. By being non-judgemental, the rest of the Group assists members in looking at relevant past actions.

Working through. Members may require time to work through their behaviour and those feelings that result from an awareness of the nature and implications of their coping. For instance, guilt is a very common feeling that can characterise self-blame and might have to be addressed separately.

Feelings around ending. An important aspect of coping is what happens when the particular mechanisms are no longer used. It can be interesting to get each member to think of one example of what it was like when they stopped being in denial, stopped blaming or self-blaming, and then think of the main feeling that they experienced. The answers in one Group showed a variety of feelings:

- 'I felt stupid.'
- 'I was anxious about what was going to happen.'
- 'At first it seemed things were falling apart, including myself.'
- 'I felt good, as I didn't have to kid people.'
- 'It was no big deal. I felt nothing.'
- 'I thought things would be easier, but something else cropped up. It always does.'

As can be seen, the idea that a change of behaviour would be the solution was often far from the mark. Benefits might come in time, but there was often little sense of immediate relief and progress. Yet members found that it was helpful to acknowledge this fact.

Work in the present. The final step is to look at members' present ways of coping and whether they are using the same mechanisms, and whether they feel comfortable with what they are doing or how they are acting.

GENERAL COPING

Introduction to general coping

The aforementioned mechanisms are specific aspects of coping, applied very much to the family drug use. However, consideration can also be given to members' methods of coping with stress in general. Discussion in one Support Group gave the following forms of general de-stressing:

1. No methods were employed. Some members did not see them as necessary and would not have the time anyway.

2. Talking to partners or chosen friends.

3. Going for a walk

4. Watching television or having the radio on in the background.

5. Drinking alcohol or smoking.

6. Eating 'treats', such as chocolate.

What seemed to emerge from discussions was that some members did not think it important to lessen stress, and part of this was explicable in that they were unaware of possible medical risks, other than a general idea that 'stress is bad for you'. Time was devoted at a later meeting to the subject of stress and its medical and psychological effects. Members were inclined to take stress more seriously when matters were explained. The other comment, of members not having enough time, was redefined as members not taking time for themselves. I like to link this up with detachment, of members detaching themselves from involvement in family affairs to be able to take care of themselves.

The methods used were of variable efficiency, but each member felt comfortable with them, sometimes almost making them into a ritual. Members were supported in their attempts to de-stress, and others methods such as the use of relaxation tapes were demonstrated. However, it did not seem correct to suggest that drinking or smoking might not be the best ways to relax. As will be discussed later, sometimes members may take on such work as part of the Group's remit.

PERSONAL SITUATIONS

Relevant situations

The Support Group does not have the aim of dealing with any of its members' personal situations other than those directly relevant to the drug use. However, members are bound at some time to self-disclose, to allude to past and present personal difficulties. This leaves the question of how the facilitator or the Group should react. My belief is that what is mentioned in Group meetings is mentioned for discussion, and the discussion should be a help both to the member and to the rest of the Group.

Individual situations

If work on individual difficulties is to be taken up, then the facilitator might want to discover whether other members have undergone similar experiences. If this is the case, then any discussion is likely to help several members and attention is taken away from one individual. In Groups of which I have been a facilitator, two such situations in common were physical abuse and heavy alcohol use by partners, the two often being linked.

'I think the worst thing is when your man is violent. It's bad enough when he's verbally abusive, but when he's violent it's terrible. I don't think they ever change. If they hit you once, that's it.'
'Mine did. Mine changed.'
'I didn't know he was like that ... I thought he was quiet.'
'Oh aye, he is now but years ago, after drink, he wasn't. He's stopped. I think part of it was I stabbed him.'
'I couldn't do anything like that. I used to throw things then run out of the house. I've had stitches in the back of my head. I was feared when I fought back.'
'I was as well. Mind when I stabbed him in the leg I was more worried about his trousers as they were new, all wool, and you couldn't mend them.'

The discussion of personal situations should be of use to the whole Group, even members who have not had these particular experiences should be encouraged to participate. Sometimes these discussions suffice, or are all the members want. However there may be occasions when more is required.

PROBLEM SOLVING

Introduction

Support Group members are likely to experience many difficulties having a drug user in the family, and part of the support offered is to help members to accept what cannot be changed, and also to alter what the members can and want to alter.

Group members have to work out whether they actually want help, whether they want a problem solved, and whether they are prepared to give time to the required work. Members are often in a state of anxiety and as long as they are in this condition, the likelihood of them doing useful work is low. So the immediate task is to deal with that anxiety.

Initial steps with regard to anxiety

Anxiety is best controlled through the modification of personal behaviour, rather than by chemical methods. The expression of anxiety-related feelings in the Group is the easiest way to lower personal anxiety, allowing members to begin the process of work on themselves and giving them the space and time to analyse their overall situations.

Clarification

Personal problems may be brought under personal control surprisingly quickly if their nature is carefully described, both affectively and cognitively. Sometimes members see a way of solving their own difficulties by this process of clarification in the Group. This should be positively reinforced. Wherever possible, members should solve their own problems.

If a member still has difficulties then the facilitator can assist by asking the member to say whose problem it is. Because of their low self-esteem and usual family role, some members are inclined to take on guilt or someone else's responsibility, and see problem situations as belonging to them. Such feelings are relieved through discussion with the rest of the Group. Indeed, only those who have had similar experiences are likely to be of help to some members.

Focusing

Sometimes members have a host of difficulties, and insist that the main problem cannot be solved without the simultaneous solving of other interlocking problems. It is easy for would-be helpers to get caught up in this mesh of difficulties: to break the chain, the facilitator might ask which problem causes the most pain. Note the form of the question is 'What hurts you the most?', rather than 'What is your most serious problem?', because members find the former easier to determine. Then the member agrees whether or not to work on the problem.

Different perceptions

The Group members can help by contributing their own individual perceptions of the problematic situation. This helps because everyone can get involved in looking at difficulties in one way, and not see them from other angles. Apart from a general discussion of a member's problem, the member and the rest of the Group can widen perceptions in at least three different ways.

1. The situation is described for the Group, then the member describes it again but from the perspective of another major participant in the problem. The others listen and comment on the differences they noted between the two versions, and say what conclusions they draw.

2. The situation is described and members of the Group are assigned the personas of the principal participants in the problem. They then describe how they see the situation. These versions might strike the member as unlikely or inaccurate, but they are likely to be different and so go towards enlarging the picture.

3. The facts of the situation are outlined by the member, then the rest of the Group suggest thoughts and feelings they think the member might have. The idea is for the member to be able to be flexible in how he or she sees the problem.

Different options

With the new perceptions, the member should be encouraged to look to different options as to what can be done. This process is accompanied by different perceptions and taking a positive view of things. The whole process can take some time, but discovering options will having a liberating effect, as the member no longer feels a victim of circumstances. This in turn raises self-esteem and increases the chance of fully carrying through any contemplated future action.

Action

The member with a problem should be encouraged to act, to decide on one particular option, and discuss how it should be carried out. The following points might usefully be borne in mind.

1. Inaction can be worse than action. Members may worry about any proposed action going wrong. They tend to forget that things can go awry through the absence of action.

2. Many plans tend to break down because the goals are too large. It is much better to achieve small, limited goals than to aim high and not succeed.

3. The member has to have come to terms with the relevant past. In particular, a former inability to manage a situation does not have to extend to the present.

4. Action has to be planned and fallback positions considered. Often things do not go as expected and members should take this into account.

5. The proposed action should be discussed in the Group and the member should declare what action will be taken. This public declaration helps with the resolve to carry through the intended action.

6. Another consideration is to try and keep any immediate goals or actions consistent with an overall plan. The achievement of inconsistent goals will tend to fail to produce any real progress.

Feedback

The last stage after action has been taken is that of the member coming back to the Group to relate what has happened. This should cover not only how well the planned action has gone, but any new perceptions, as action can lead to new outlooks. Also, how the person feels after the action is shared with the others. This can lead to a growth of positive attitudes within the Group, promoting a greater belief in self.

HOMEWORK

Introduction

The work done during the meetings can be increased and supplemented if some work is done between meetings. This must be a voluntary option and no pressure should be put on members to do it. The advantage is that work done in the Group meetings can be extended into the world outside (Mullender and Ward, 1991). However, if such work is done then time should be set aside for any feedback, to share the results with the Group.

Reflection on the meetings

Instead of homework, members can benefit if they think about the meeting for a few minutes during the week. To help the process, members are given a small card with the next meeting date and one line of questions to consider. The questions could be:

1. What did I give and what did I receive at the meeting?

2. What did I say that was not the whole truth and why?

3. What significant feelings do I remember from the meeting?

4. Is there anything I wished I had said or done at the meeting?

Members might limit the reflection to just one question if this increases the likelihood of useful work being done at home.

OTHER FORMS OF HELPING

Introduction

Although the Support Group has support as its aim, this can be achieved better by the lessening of anxiety and the lifting of depressive feelings. Some of the latter comes with action taken by members between meetings. Generally such action is correlated with taking responsibility for oneself, part of the overall support aim (Goldfried and Robins, 1982), but also part of the overall Group remit. Thus the Group might suggest what could be done and this might be done as a Group.

Physical exercise

Regular gentle exercise, perhaps walking, jogging, swimming or cycling, contributes to members' general health and helps reduce feelings of depression (Griest et al., 1978). Exercise can also help indirectly by getting members out of the house and meeting people. An exercise of both body and mind contributes to a total overall betterment of Group members.

Relaxation

To help relieve personal stress, members might wish to have Group relaxation at the end of the meetings. Relaxation methods do vary in their effects, so are not universally indicated (Palmer, 1992). Feedback is important, as is the willingness to try more than one method. There are many different relaxation tapes which can be helpful and methods to be learned, methods such as meditation, autogenic training and massage. Bringing someone to one Group to demonstrate the correct methods of massage proved useful and made a pleasant change.

Health promotion

There is a case for members taking up a more healthy lifestyle to reduce stress. The reduction of smoking, drinking, and appropriate weight loss accompanied by physical exercise are all potential life-enhancers. A change to a more healthy diet might also prove to be of use (Ivancevich and Matteson, 1988). Such health measures should not be pressed, as some members drink and smoke to cope with life, and the thought of doing without them can itself be stressful.

Outside help

Members can benefit from individual help for themselves at times, and coming to the Group should not be seen as necessarily sufficient in itself. Indeed, some members might be suffering from such severe stress that symptoms such as forgetfulness, agoraphobia or depression can prevent them from getting to the meetings. Some members should be encouraged to seek help elsewhere as well as coming to the Group; individual and Group help can then reinforce each other and maximise the help given.

REVIEW OF SUPPORT WORK

Introduction

What has been provided so far in this book are various ways in which support in the Group can be maximised. However, using these facilitative suggestions will not necessarily improve the help offered. In view of this, it is imperative to know whether members really are being supported. But first, the following points should be considered.

Group atmosphere

Simply using ideas about support delivery is insufficient if little note is taken of the atmosphere, the feelings in the Group. There is always the danger that emphasis is placed by facilitators on the cognitive aspects of their work, without reference to feelings. All the ideas in this book need to be sensitively used, otherwise they may well prove unhelpful.

The Group atmosphere should be positive and members should enjoy themselves, even when serious and difficult subjects are faced. Members should be interacting, the sessions should be appropriately challenging, and all this requires variations from time to time in the work done.

Overall planning

Variations in the work have to be set in the context of overall planning. The facilitator must consider the stage of the Group's life, the work in part addressing the developmental needs as perceived by the facilitator. The expressed needs and desires of members have to be borne in mind, along with the ability of the Group to satisfy them. Finally, account has to be taken of what is judged to be the most helpful amount of facilitative intervention.

Empowerment

Members have to be empowered, partly so that they may benefit from support. Active steps are required to take and use support, otherwise it is little more than a quick and very transient way of feeling better. For empowerment, two aspects need to be worked on.

1. Members have to become self-sufficient to some extent. They have to become themselves, regain or re-establish their own individuality and confirm their own identity. Methods such as disengagement, awareness of roles and taking care of oneself are all useful, but not to be overlooked is the simple attendance and participation in the meetings. Doing things, interact-

ing with others, expression of feelings and reflection are of the essence.

2. Members have to look to externalising what happens within the Group. Support which only lasts for the duration of the meetings is not enough; support should help members in their families. Making people reliant on the Support Group is a poor way of helping.

Feedback

Ensuring these two points have been put into action, the Group needs to know whether its efforts are useful and the time spent has been conducive to learning. The Group also needs to know if members are being helped in the meetings and if this help is being transferred to the home. This can be done informally, but from time to time the facilitator is advised to suggest more formal methods.

MONITORING, REVIEWING AND MANAGEMENT

Introduction

Whatever the form of support given, it is essential to ensure that Group members really are being supported. What is required are methods that allow honest feedback, without members feeling personally threatened by the process. If these are built into the Group's programme from the very beginning, then they are seen as normal activities and are likely to be accepted as such. The methods used are monitoring, reviews and evaluation.

Monitoring

Initial ideas. Monitoring is very much within the remit of the facilitator and consists of assessing ongoing work in the Group and discovering how the Group members are feeling. This is often done at the end of the meeting and can be helpful, but it is not advisable to leave it so late, since little can then be done about any expressed dissatisfaction. Such late checking is likely to appear to be no more than showing concern for the sake of it.

The facilitator finds out how members feel, asking for both positive and negative feelings. Just being able to express feelings helps members, and hearing the feelings of the others can bring more trust to the Group. However, permanent improvements occur only if what is said is taken on board and some action is taken.

Facilitation. The facilitator must be self-monitoring. This is done formally through facilitator support and supervision, but the process to some extent should also be ongoing. In practice, this means the facilitator should occasionally reflect on the following principal areas of concern:

1. Being aware of oneself; what possible personal agendas might be imported into the meeting; being a real person as well as carrying out a professional role; being sensitive to one's own thoughts and feelings, and being aware of oneself as a person in relation to the others.

2. Being aware of the facilitation role, especially in relation to how the Group generally and individual members in particular might be seeing and reacting to it.

3. The facilitator should think about possible difficulties or problems that have arisen during the meeting. Immediate action might be called for, or action at a later date. Sometimes situations seem unclear, so time is needed to see how they develop.

4. The facilitator might also consider how things are developing in the meeting; in content, in belief systems and in general feelings. This is not to censor what happens, but at times intervention might be required to ensure that members will feel supported by the end of the session.

5. The facilitator might also consider what learning is or could be taking place. This applies to the facilitation itself, to what the facilitator is gaining from the meeting and what the members and the Group as a whole are gaining.

Ongoing meetings. Meetings, as entireties, should also be monitored and the basis of this should be the recording of sessions. The simplest method is the writing up of notes by the facilitator after the meeting. These can be sent out to members in summarised form, as frequently they will want to reflect on what was said in meetings. The notes can also be used by facilitators as part of their supervision and for deciding on possible changes in facilitation. Another method is to make a sound recording of the Group meetings. The tapes are especially useful as a learning tool for the facilitator. Using the tapes, attention can be given to whether there were matters left unfinished from the meeting. These may be discussions which ran out of time, or topics that were ended but not covered completely. Finally, if members are left with unresolved feelings this might also need following up.

Records are useful in that they can formalise any decisions made at the meeting. This includes the substance of the decision, who is to carry out the action, and the agreed timescale.

Recordings might be used for the facilitator to reflect upon between meetings. Sometimes having time and being detached from the meeting allows second thoughts about what took place. Particular aspects that might be picked up include:

1. Discovering misconceptions and misunderstandings in the meeting.

2. Locating where there seem to have been omissions or things not said.

3. Seeing whether there are feelings expressed that appear surprising, understated or inappropriate in some way.

4. Finding parts of the meeting which somehow do not feel right.

5. Checking whether the recording leads to any new perceptions of what happened.

6. Checking whether there is a greater understanding.

Reviews

Introduction. Reviews are different from monitoring in that they involve members commenting on the meetings. The emphasis is very much on discovering whether members see the Group and its meetings as being personally supportive. This can be done semi-formally by members taking time to discuss various relevant Group aspects, or members might prefer to answer a questionnaire privately and have the answers summarised by the facilitator for discussion.

Limitations of reviews. In helping processes in general, there has been much more attention given to the consumer's or client's views of and feelings about helping processes (Mayer and Timms,

1970). The drawback with clients' views is that, in general, clients have goodwill towards service providers (Robinson, 1978) and feel it disloyal to criticise any helper who is pleasant or nice (Cohen, 1971). In fact, one of the difficulties for members is to differentiate between who the helpers are and what they do (Reid, 1967).

So we should be careful about accepting members' views uncritically, whether they are good or bad. On the other hand, reviews and evaluations can be helpful in that feedback can lead to further improved behaviour change in both members and facilitators (Posavac and Carey, 1980).

Content of reviews.   The reviews cover four main areas. First, the members themselves, and how they experience the benefits of attending the Group. Personal evidence may be given through:

(a) A decrease in stress. This may be shown by less obsessional thinking about drug use, better communication and hence fewer arguments at home, and more regular sleep patterns.

(b) Less affective distress, in that feelings are more easily identified and expressed.

(c) Improved anxiety management, in that members feel less worried in general and are less preoccupied with the drug user.

(d) Members think their understanding of drug use and drug users, of the functioning of the family, and of what is happening to themselves has increased.

(e) Members find decisions and actions easier to make and to take, and this is accompanied by a feeling of greater self-confidence and the ability to consider their own welfare as well as that of others.

Second, the Group meetings, and how successfully they help, from the individual's point of view. This may be taken to cover, among other factors:

(a) Whether the member has been able to say what he or she wanted to say, and was given adequate time to do so.

(b) Whether the member has received sufficient attention and has been listened to during the meetings.

(c) Whether what takes place at meetings is relevant to the member's needs.

(d) What, for the member and for the Group meetings, would lead to improvements.

Third the facilitation, if it takes place, should also be assessed by the Group members and by the facilitator. The facilitator's assessment is not irrelevant, as comparison with the Group's view can be enlightening. Some idea of the members' views can be found in the answers to the following questions:

(a) Is the facilitator too controlling?

(b) Should the facilitator be more active at meetings?

(c) Could the facilitator help members to understand things better?

(d) Is the facilitator understanding of Group members?

(e) Is the facilitator non-judgemental?

(f) Does the facilitator favour some members over others in the Group?

(g) Should the facilitator be more professional or more informal and personal?

(h) What improvements can be made to the facilitation?

(i) Should employing another facilitator be considered?

The fourth area of interest is the Group in general. Members are asked to decide:

(a) Do they want the Group to continue as at present?

(b) If the members want change, what sort of changes are required?

Reviews might be done every six to twelve months, depending on how frequently the Group meets. An additional meeting may be required to discuss the results of the review.

EVALUATIONS

Introduction

Evaluations are designed to give an impartial and substantiated picture of the quality of support delivered by the Group meetings. Evaulations might be composed by facilitators, or Groups might have evaluations imposed on them. Whatever the case may be, having some perspective on the process is important. It can help to attend to the following points:

1. What do we want to find out?
2. Why do we want to find that out?
3. When do we need the information?
4. How can we get the information?
5. Where can we get the information?
6. Who is the information for?

These may be applied to evaluations (Patton, 1985) as it is essential that the answers are clear, especially for imposed evaluations.

Wherever possible, evidence is quantified or assessed qualitatively, and this is done through examining the following:

Anxiety reduction. Evidence for actual anxiety reduction is mainly physical or psychological. The weakness in substantiation is that most of the evidence comes from self-reports, perhaps supplemented by medical reports, and this gives a debatable picture.

The physical signs can be seen in a lessening of long-term stress related symptoms. These can include lowered blood pressure, and a lessening in frequency, severity or duration of the following where they occur: peptic ulcers; eczema; asthma attacks; psoriasis; muscular pains; headaches; epileptic attacks; gastric upsets. Anxiety reduction can also see a rise in weight to the person's more usual level.

The psychological signs can be cognitive, affective or behavioural. The cognitive improvements can result in a reduction in obsessional, blocked, or rigid thinking. Decision making is easier. Actions are seen more positively, and failure is viewed more positively.

The affective improvements include increased enjoyment, less guilt and anger, and a freer expression of feelings.

Behavioural improvements cover normalised sleep patterns, increased social activity, increased sexual interest, better communication, decreased alcohol and nicotine use, a better diet, and a decrease in prescribed drug use.

Self-esteem. Self-esteem is difficult to measure with any accuracy, yet it is important as a basis for confidence and the ability to make decisions and to act. The following list gives a rough guide, to be done not as a questionnaire but in the Group. It can be liberating, especially as members can say what changes they have noticed in one another.

(a) Do you feel better? (Smile or laugh more?)

(b) Do you take things less personally?

(c) Do you admit your mistakes?

(d) Do you examine ideas rather than just accepting them?

(e) Do you look at the consequences of actions rather than doing what is 'right'?

(f) Do you try for the best option rather than the best solution?

(g) Do you take care of yourself?

(h) Do you forgive others?

(i) Do you have sufficient control in your life?

(j) Can you be assertive?

(k) Can you say 'no'?

Dealing with difficulties. Changes for Group members can be seen in how they deal with difficulties. These are usually centred in the home, but the facilitator and the rest of the Group can also give indirect evidence as to whether a particular member is managing better. Some indication is given with regard to dealing with difficulties by answering the following questions:

(a) Can you properly identify what is important and what is not?

(b) Can you stand back from situations and not intervene?

(c) Do you listen to other points of view?

(d) Can you act in a detached manner?

(e) Do you have to win arguments?

(f) Can you accept actions you do not agree with?

Evaluations can be linked with reviews as this gives a more rounded description of what is happening in the Group meetings. However, improvements also have to be linked to other factors that might be affecting the member. These might be changes in the drug user's situation, such as his or her receiving medical help, leaving home, being sent to prison, or becoming a parent. On the other hand, there might be changes largely unconnected with the drug user which affect the member. These might be marital separation, financial problems, moving house or the death of a close relative.

Evaluation is not going to be a very accurate exercise and it is easy to pick holes in the process. However this in no way diminishes its usefulness. Accountability is reinforced, some idea of the success in attaining the Group aim is obtained, and the meetings can be improved. Moreover, members find the actual process of evaluation helpful; it is indirectly a way of increasing mutual support.

CONCLUDING IDEAS

Introduction

The intention of this book has been to look at some ways of increasing mutual support through Groups. In practice, each Support Group is different, just as its members are all different. How Groups develop depends on how members want them to develop; there is no set or best way. As long as members are conscious of what they are doing and of the path they are taking, then different directions are quite acceptable.

Practical matters

Some members get support by dealing with practical matters, those relating to drug use. For instance, what should be done if a user overdoses in the house. Knowing First Aid, how to attend to vital signs and put drug users into the recovery position, knowing whether to move the person and what to do with used syringes, is best explained by demonstration, something the local Red Cross group will do.

Visiting drug clinics, Courts or prisons can be further ways of gaining information and also gaining familiarity with agencies that might be completely foreign to members. The visits can be arranged so a doctor, lawyer or Governor can explain the set up and answer questions.

It is helpful if members have some knowledge of relevant legal matters, such as the rights of those arrested, the rights of relatives to see those in custody, the laws, rules and rights regarding prescribing and being prescribed drugs, and the law about people using drugs in their homes or drugs being found there. Information given by someone from a Citizen's Advice Bureau or a Community Legal Centre is probably best.

Information about HIV infection – not just the risks of infection but the helping and care of those infected – may be required by members, and help can be obtained from the local AIDS agency or Helpline.

Social events

From time to time Support Groups will organise their own social events, such as nights out, Christmas celebrations or anniversaries of the first meeting. These events not only lighten the general tone of the Group but have specific advantages in themselves. They are a good way of helping to build up trust in the Group and allow members to get away from any Group roles they habitually play out. It is helpful if the facilitator can be present on at least some of these occasions.

A possible danger of having too many social events is that they can end up as a way of avoiding real support work. Another difficulty is that of confidentiality. This can easily be overlooked when members are no longer in a formal meeting. Nevertheless, these drawbacks can be overcome and social events can act as a way of deepening working relationships.

Contact with other groups

After a time, Groups can fall into routine ways of working and become inward in their perspectives. For this reason it can be useful if the Group makes links with other Support Groups, through informal contact or through formal contact and cooperative alliances. Contact might include the visiting of other Groups to see how they operate and to maximise support.

It is worth taking time to reflect on contacts that are made, and to think about what it means to be a Group member. Members get increased self-esteem not only through being part of the Group but also through identifying with it. However, this identification may extend to seeing their Group as being better than others (Blake and Mouton, 1962), rather than accepting that all Groups are different. Superior attitudes can lessen members' ability to learn from each other.

Alliances and Groups

One way of decreasing the risks of inter-group difficulties is to join or form an alliance of Support Groups, which can help to determine inter-group relationships. Groups who see themselves as having the same goals will experience less rivalry (Sherif, 1966). Such an alliance would have additional benefits in that it could, as a representative of the constituent groups, act as an information or a pressure group to local Health Boards or Social Services Departments. This applies equally to representation on an overtly political level to Parliament and its relevant committees.

What is not so obvious at first is that any substantial funding usually involves a degree of political control, albeit under the guise of keeping a check on how the money is spent. This is likely to make the Group or the support organisation more political on a local level. This might or might not be acceptable to the members, but it will probably require a slight modification of the Group's basic aim.

Groups and professionalisation

Support Groups are often started by volunteers who, in time, look for some financial help, perhaps even a full-time job and salary. This means their perspective on the Group is likely to be influenced by personal financial considerations. We should also remember that if some members are given paid full-time jobs, they may experience resentment from other unpaid volunteer members. This can lead to open strain when paid Group members see themselves as the 'professionals', and the voluntary helpers see themselves as the people with true commitment.

These points may seem obvious enough but in practice there tends to be less clarity. Everyone might be committed to the idea of providing more and better support. The question is how should this be done. Funding authorities might like closer monitoring and the keeping of more detailed records. The Group then has to decide whether to become more management orientated and have the capacity to help more people through increased funding, or to reject such terms of funding and keep the family feel of a purely voluntary Group. Sometimes there has to be a balance of these competing claims.

As Groups develop and the quality of their service is improved, a balance might have to be struck between the people involved, such as the fund-raisers, paid Group members, Group volunteer helpers and the members themselves. The difficulty is to ensure that the last category, the Group members, do have the major say in decisions made. Also, if Groups decide to get together and form local or national alliances, then a balance between local autonomy and centralism has to be struck.

Expansion of the Group

Over time there might be an increase in Group membership and this might require that there be more than one Group. The original Group might also act as a base for expansion into other problematic drug related areas. Both changes would require managerial input. Members should also be aware that as an organisation grows, so the perception of it by the general public will change. Equally, the Group needs to take a long look at itself, and not drift into a randomly evolved entity.

Politicisation

More radical changes in the Group can come through having a different view of its aims and objectives. Seeing support working might make them decide to take more direct action on drug use. Members might refuse to accept the status quo and move to a more active approach, such as the practising of advocacy skills or the role-playing of meetings with doctors or drugs workers. There might be further radicalisation by lobbying for drug related causes, or moving to direct action which might include local campaigns against dealers in the neighbourhood, campaigns for changes in prescribing policies or the provision of Rehabilition Centres. Alternatively, the Group might want to provide local drug education for young people.

Whatever the Group decides to do, members should be aware of the tendency towards such radicalisation and understand that it is different from support.

Final conclusions

Drug Family Support Groups have sprung up nationally, reflecting a need felt by family members to gain help for themselves, help which is not forthcoming from other sources. Almost all of these Groups have been self-help Groups, a fact which underlines members' positive attitudes to doing something about their plight, despite limited official help and recognition.

A potential drawback to such Support Groups is one shared by all services: namely, that all forms of helping can be harmful. To minimise potential harm, there are three interlocking aspects of service provision which require careful monitoring and reviewing, with a view to possible action if necessary.

1. Understanding, which is both understanding by members of themselves as a functioning part of the Group and their family, and understanding of drug use and drug users.

2. Ethics, which covers members taking responsibility for themselves and their actions, being themselves and not hiding behind a role, and accepting others for themselves and being aware of their needs.

3. The aim which members must hold to. It applies to all Group members, is mutual, and extends from the Group to members' families. It is based on regular meetings, which are best if facilitated.

The use of different support work methods helps to increase support, so helping members and, indirectly, the family. This in turn means the family will be able to help the drug user when the member does stop using drugs and requires support to stay off (Klingeman, 1992). With the advent of HIV infection, the role of the family may grow from support to caring, and the pressures are such that family support is even more important.

The positive aspects of support may not always be apparent, nor is it possible to say that attendance at the Group has improved matters, but as one mother commented:

'Ever since I've been coming here, Rachel has not been so bad. I don't know whether that's because I think she behaving better or whether she really is better. Frankly, I don't care. The main thing is that the two of us have been getting on and that's made it enjoyable for the two of us.'

And her daughter's comment was:

'No matter what, a junkie's best friend is her Mum.'

So if family members are supported, they feel better in themselves, are able to come to terms with drug use, and thus function better. This has a knock-on effect and can help the drug user, which feeds back to help the family and the Group member. This reinforces support and allows members to lead better and fuller lives.

BIBLIOGRAPHY

All publishers in London unless indicated otherwise

Achterberg, J., Lawlis, G., Simonton, O. and Matthews-Simonton S. (1977) Psychological factors and blood chemistries as disease outcome predictors for cancer patients. *Multivariate Experimental Clinical Research* Vol. 3 p. 107.

AIDS and Drug Misuse: Part 2, (1989) Report by the Advisory Council on the Misuse of Drugs. HMSO.

Alexander, B. and Dibb, G. (1975) Opiate addicts and their parents. *Family Process* Vol. 14 p. 499.

Andersen, T. (1991) *The Reflecting Team.* New York: W. W. Norton.

Archer, R., Hormuth, S. and Berg, J. (1982) Avoidance of self-disclosure; an experiment under conditions of self-awareness. *Personality and Social Psychology Bulletin* Vol. 8 p. 122.

Argyle, M. (1981) *Social Skills and Health.* Methuen.

Auvine, B., Densmore, B., Extrom, M., Poole, S. and Shanklin, M. (1977) *A Manual for Group Facilitators.* Wisconsin: Centre for Conflict Resolution.

Aveline, M. and Dryden, W. (eds) (1988) *Group Therapy in Britain.* Milton Keynes: Open University Press.

Bahr, H. and Harvey, C. (1980) Correlaters of morale among the newly wed. *Journal of Social Psychology* Vol. 110 p. 219.

Bales, R. (1953) The equilibrium problem in small groups, in Parsons, T., Bales, R. and Shils, E. (eds) *Working Papers in the Theory of Action.* New York: The Free Press.

Bales, R. (1958) Task roles and social roles in problem-solving groups, in Maccoby, E., Newcomb, T. and Hartley, E. *Readings in Social Psychology.* New York: Holt.

Bannister, D. and Fransella, F. (1980) *Inquiring Man.* Penguin.

Barkow, J. (1977) Human ethology and intra-individual systems. *Social Science Information* Vol. 16 p. 133.

Beattie, M. (1992) *Codependent No More.* Minnesota: Hazelden.

Beck, A., Rush, A., Shaw, B. and Emery, G. (1979) *Cognitive Therapy of Depression.* New York: Guilford Press.

Beker, P., McLellan, T., Childress, K. and Garibi, P. (1993) Role reversals in families of substance users: a transgenerational phenomenon. *International Journal of the Addictions* Vol. 28(7) p. 613.

Belle, D. (1982) The stress of caring: women as providers of social support, in Goldberger, L. and Breznitz, S. (eds) *Handbook of Stress*. New York: Free Press.

Bengston, V., Gellar, J. and Ragan, P. (1977) Stratum contrast and similarities in attitudes towards death. *Journal of Gerontology* Vol. 32 p. 76.

Benson, J. (1991) *Working More Creatively With Groups*. Routledge.

Berkman, L. (1985) The relationship of social networks and social support to morbidity and mortality in Cohen, S. and Syme, S. (eds) *Social Support and Health*. New York: Academic Press.

Berkman, L. and Syme, L. (1979) Social networks, host resistance and mortality. *American Journal of Epidemiology* Vol. 109 p. 186.

Bertcher, H. and Maple, F. (1977) *Creating Groups*. Sage Publications.

Bion, W. (1961) *Experiences in Groups*. Tavistock.

Blake, R. and Mouton, J. (1962) Overevaluation of own group's product in intergroup competition. *Journal of Abnormal and Social Psychology* Vol. 64 p. 237.

BMJ [*British Medical Journal*] Leader article: (1985) Media drugs campaign may be worse than a waste of money. Vol. 290 p. 416.

Bomboy, R. (1974) *Major Newspaper Coverage of Drug Issues*. Washington, DC: Drug Abuse Council.

Borman, L. (1982) Introduction, in Helping people to help themselves: Self-help and Prevention. *Prevention in Human Services*. New York: Haworth. Vol. 1(3) p. 3.

Boud, D., Keogh, R. and Walker, D. (eds) (1985) *Reflection: Turning Experience into Learning*. Kogan Page.

Bowen, M. (1976) Family reaction to death, in Guerin, P. (ed.) *Family Therapy: theory and practice*. New York: Gardner.

Bowers, W. and Gauron, E. (1981) Potential hazards of the co-therapy relationship. *Psychotherapy: Theory, Research and Practice* Vol. 18 p. 225.

Bowlby-West, L. (1983) The impact of death on the family system. *Journal of Family Therapy* Vol. 5 p. 279.

Boyce, W., Kay, M. and Uitti, C. (1988) The taxonomy of social support: an ethnographic analysis among adolescent mothers. *Social Science and Medicine* Vol. 26 p. 1079.

Boyle, C. (1970) Differences between patients' and doctors' interpretation of some common medical terms. *British Medical Journal* (2) p. 286.

Brown, A. (1992) *Groupwork*. Aldershot, Hants: Ashgate Publishing.

Brown, B. (1993) History of drug user counselling. *International Journal of the Addictions* Vol. 28(12) p. 1243.

Brown, G. (1974) Meaning, measurement and stress of life events, in Dohrenwend, B.S. and Dohrenwend, B.P. (eds) *Stressful Life Events: their Nature and Effects*. New York: Wiley.

Brown, G. and Harris, T. (1978) *The Social Origins of Depression: A Study of Psychiatric Disorder in Women*. Tavistock.

Brown, R. (1992) *Group Processes*. Oxford: Blackwell Publishers.

Browne, K. and Freeling, P. (1967) *The Doctor–Patient Relationship*. Edinburgh: Livingstone, pp. 23 and 25.

Buunk, B. and Hoorens, V. (1992) Social support and stress. *Journal of Clinical Psychology* Vol. 31 p. 445.

Byrne, P. and Long, B. (1976) *Doctors Talking to Patients*. HMSO.

Cartwright, A. (1964) *Human Relationships in Hospital Care*. Routledge & Kegan Paul.

Cartwright, A. and Anderson, R. (1981) *General Practice Revisited*. Tavistock.

Cartwright, A. and O'Brien, M. (1976) Social class variations in General Practitioner consultations, in Stacey, M. (ed.) *Sociology of the NHS, Sociological Review Monograph No. 22* Warwick: University of Keele.

Chelune, G. (1976) Reactions to male and female disclosure at two levels. *Journal of Personality and Social Psychology* Vol. 34 p. 1000.

Chesler, M. and Barbarin, O. (1984) Difficulties in providing help in a crisis: relationships between parents of children with cancer and their friends. *Journal of Social Issues* Vol. 40(4) p. 113.

Clark, M. (1983) Recipient–donor relationship and reaction to benefits, in DePaulo, B., Nadler, A. and Fisher, J. (eds) *New Directions in Helping*. Vol. 2. New York: Academic Press.

Cobb, S. (1976) Social support as a moderator of life stress. *Psychosomatic Medicine* Vol. 38 p. 300.

Cohen, A. (1971) Consumer view: retarded mothers and the social services. *Social Work Today* 1(12) p. 35.

Cohen, S. and Syme, S. (1985) *Social Support and Health*. New York: Academic Press.

Cohen, S. and Wills, T. (1985) Stress, social support and the buffering hypothesis. *Psychol. Bull.* Vol. 98. p. 317.

Coleman, A. (1976) How to enlist the family as an ally. *American Journal of Drug and Alcohol Abuse*. Vol. 3(1) p. 167.

Coleman, A., Kaplan, J. and Downing, R. (1986) Life-cycle and loss: the spiritual vacuum of heroin addiction. *Family Process* 25: p. 5.

Comstock, C. (1982) Preventative processes in self-help groups: parents anonymous, in Helping people to help themselves: Self-help and Prevention. *Prevention in Human Services*. New York: Haworth, Vol. 1(3) p. 47.

Costanza, R., Derlega, V. and Winstead, B. (1988) Positive and negative forms of social support: effects of conversational topics on coping with stress among same-sex friends. *Journal of Experimental Social Psychology* Vol. 24 p. 182.

Cox, T. (1978) *Stress.* Baltimore: University Park Press.

Coyne, J., Wortman, C. and Lehman, D. (1988) The other side of support: emotional over-involvement and miscarried helping, in Gottlieb, B. (ed.) *Marshaling Social Support: Formats, Processes and Effects.* Newbury Park, Ca.: Sage.

Coyne, R. (1974) Effects of facilitator directed and self-directed group experiences. *Couns. Educ. Superv.* Vol. 13 p. 184.

Dakof, G. and Taylor, S. (1990) Victims' perceptions of social support. What is helpful from whom? *Journal of Personality and Social Psychology* Vol. 58 p. 80.

Dallos, R. (1993) *Family Belief Systems, Therapy and Change.* Milton Keynes: Open University Press.

Davis, L. and Proctor, E. (1989) *Race, Gender, and Class: Guidelines for Individuals, Families and Groups.* New Jersey: Prentice Hall.

Dean, J. and Rud, F. (1984) The drug addict and the stigma of addiction. *International Journal of the Addictions* Vol. 19(8) p. 859.

De Haes, W. (1988) 'Drug education? Yes, but how?' *Addictive Behaviours,* Edinburgh: Scottish Health Education Group.

Derlega, V., Metts, S., Petronio, S. and Margulis, S. (1993) *Self-disclosure.* Newbury Park, Ca.: Sage Publications.

Derlega, V., Winstead, B., Wong, P. and Hunter, S. (1985) Gender effects in an initial encounter: a case where men exceed women in disclosure. *Journal of Social and Personal Relationships* Vol. 2 p. 25

Dorn, N. and South, N. (eds), (1987) *A Land Fit For Heroin?* Basingstoke: Macmillan Education.

Douglas, T. (1970) *A Decade of Small Group Theory, 1960–70.* Bookstall Publications.

Douglas, T. (1991) *A Handbook of Common Groupwork Problems.* Tavistock.

Dunning, D. and Parpil, M. (1989) Mental addition versus mental subtraction in counterfactual reasoning. *Journal of Personality and Social Psychology* Vol. 61 p. 521.

Dyregrov, A. (1990) Parental reactions to the loss of an infant child: a Review. *Scandinavian Journal of Psychology* Vol. 31 p. 266.

Edelwich, J. and Brodsky, A. (1992) *Group Counseling for the Resistant Client.* New York: Lexington Books.

Egan, G. (1973) *Face to Face.* Pacific Grove, Ca.: Brooks Cole Publishing.

Egan, G. (1986) *The Skilled Helper.* Pacific Grove, Ca.: Brooks Cole Publishing, p. 68.

Eldred, C. and Washington, M. (1976) Interpersonal relationships in heroin use by men and women and their role in treatment outcome. *International Journal of the Addictions* Vol. 11 p. 117.

Ellinwood, E., Smith, W. and Vaillant, G. (1966) Narcotic addiction in males and females: a comparison. *International Journal of the Addictions* Vol. 1 p. 33.

Elliott, R. (1985) Helpful and nonhelpful events in brief counseling interviews: an empirical taxonomy. *Journal of Counseling Psychology* Vol. 32 p. 307.

Epstein, N., Bishop, D. and Levin, S. (1978) The McMaster model of family functioning. *Journal of Marriage and Family Counselling* Vol. 4 p. 19.

Festinger, L. (1954) A theory of social comparison processes. *Human Relations* Vol. 7 p. 117.

Fiedler, F. (1967) *A Theory of Leadership Effectiveness*. New York: McGraw-Hill.

Fink, P. (1981) The relative's group: treatment for parents of adult schizophrenics. *International Journal of Group Psychotherapy* Vol. 31(4) p. 453.

Fisher, J., Goff, B., Nadler, A. and Chinsky, J. (1988) Social psychological influences on seeking help and support from peers, in Gottlieb, B. (ed.), *Marshaling Social Support: Formats, Processes, and Effects*. Newbury Park, Ca.: Sage Publications, p. 267.

Folkman, S. and Lazarus, R. (1980) An analysis of coping in a middle-aged population. *Journal of Health and Social Behaviour* Vol. 21 p. 29.

Folkman, S., Schaefer, C. and Lazarus, R. (1979) Cognitive processes as moderators of stress and coping, in Hamilton, V. and Warburton, D. (eds) *Human Stress and Cognition: An Information Processing Approach*. Chichester: John Wiley and Sons, p. 265.

Fontana, D. (1989) *Managing Stress*. British Psychological Society and Routledge.

Fram, D. and Hoffman, H. (1973) Family therapy in the treatment of the heroin addict, in *Fifth National Conference on Methadone Treatment* Vol. 1. New York: National Association for the Prevention of Addictions to Narcotics.

Francis, V., Korsch, B. and Morris, M. (1969) Gaps in doctor–patient communication. *New England Journal of Medicine* Vol. 280 p. 535.

Freedman, J. and Fraser, S. (1966) Compliance without presure: the foot-in-the-door technique. *Journal of Social Psychology* Vol. 4 p. 195.

Fuller, R. (1982) The story as the engram: is it fundamental to thinking? *Journal of Mind and Behavior* Vol. 3 p. 127.

Galinsky, M. and Schopler, J. (1977) Warning: groups may be dangerous. *Social Work*, March 1977.

Garcia, S. (1993) Maternal drug abuse: Laws and ethics as agents of just balances on therapeutic intervention. *International Journal of the Addictions* Vol. 28(13) p. 1311.

Gardiner, G. and McKinney, K. (1991) The great American War on Drugs. *Journal of Drug Issues* Vol. 21 p. 605.

Garfield, S. (1990) Issues and methods in psychotherapy process research. *Journal of Counselling and Clinical Psychology* Vol. 58 p. 273.

Gibson, D., Sorensen, J., Wermuth, L. and Bernal, G. (1992) Families are helped by drug treatment. *International Journal of the Addictions* Vol. 27(8) p. 961.

Gilhooly, M. (1987) Senile dementia and the family, in Orford, J. (ed.) *Coping with Disorder in the Family*. Croom Helm.

Giordano, J. (1976) Community mental health in a pluralistic society. *International Journal of Mental Health* Vol. 6.

Glass, I. (1989) Undergraduate training in substance abuse in the United Kingdom. *British Journal of Addiction* Vol. 84 p. 197.

Glass, I. (ed.) (1991) *Addiction Behaviour*. Routledge.

Glassner, B. and Loughlin, J. (1987) *Drugs in Adolescent Worlds*. Basingstoke: Macmillan Press.

Gleeson, A. (1991) Family therapy and substance abuse. *Australian and New Zealand Journal of Family Therapy* 12 p. 91.

Goffman, E. (1968) *Notes on the Management of Spoiled Identity*. Penguin.

Goldfried, M. and Robins, C. (1982) On the facilitation of self-efficacy. *Cognitive Theory and Research* Vol. 6 p. 36.

Goldstein, P., Abbot, W. and Page, W. (1977) Tracking procedures in follow-up studies of drug abusers. *American Journal of Drug and Alcohol Abuse* Vol. 5 p. 21.

Gold-Steinberg, S. and Buttenheim, M. (1993) Telling one's story in an incest survivors group. *International Journal of Group Psychotherapy* Vol. 43(2) p. 173.

Goodstadt, M. (1980) Drug Education: A turn on or a turn off? *Journal of Drug Education* Vol. 10 p. 89.

Goodyear, R. (1981) Terminations as a loss experience for the counsellor. *Personnel Guide* Vol. 59(6) p. 347.

Gottlieb, B. (ed.), (1981) *Social Networks and Social Support*. Beverley Hills, Ca.: Sage Publications.

Gottlieb, B. (1983) *Social Support Strategies: Strategies for Mental Health Practice*. Beverley Hills, Ca.: Sage Publications.

Graubard, S. (ed.) (1990) *Living with AIDS*. Cambridge, Mass.: The MIT Press.

Griest, H., Klein, M., Eischens, R. and Faris, J. (1978) Antidepressant running. *Behavioural Medicine* Vol. 5(6) p. 19.

Hagstrom, W. (1965) *The Scientific Community.* New York: Basic Books.

Haley, J. (1978) *Problem-solving Therapy.* New York: HarperCollins.

Handy, C. (1988) *Understanding Voluntary Organisations.* Penguin.

Hanson, B., Beschner, G., Walters, J. and Bovelle, E. (1985) *Life with Heroin.* Lexington, Mass.: Lexington Books.

Hare, A. (1962) *Handbook of Small Group Research.* New York: The Free Press

Harrison, L. (1992) Substance misuse and social work qualifying training in the British Isles. *British Journal of Addiction* Vol. 87 p. 635.

Hartford, M. (1971) *Groups in Social Work.* New York: Columbia University Press.

Hartnoll, R. (1992) Research and the help-seeking process. *British Journal of Addiction* Vol. 87 p. 429.

Harwin, J. (1982) The excessive drinker and the family: approaches to treatment, in Orford, J. and Harwin, J. (eds) *Alcohol and the Family.* Croom Helm.

Hazan, C. and Shaver, P. (1987) Romantic love conceptualised as an attachment process. *Journal of Personality and Social Psychology* Vol. 52 p. 511.

Heitler, J. (1973) Preparation of lower-class patients for expressive group psychotherapy. *Journal of Consulting and Clinical Psychology* Vol. 43 p. 251.

Heller, K. (1979) The effects of social support: Prevention and treatment implications, in Goldstein, A. and Kaufer, F. (eds) *Maximising Treatment Gains: Transfer Enhancement in Psychotherapy.* New York: Academic Press, p. 335.

Heller, K., Gott, M. and Jeffery, C. (eds) (1987) *Drug Use and Misuse.* Chichester: John Wiley and Sons, in association with the Open University.

Hinricksen, G., Revenson, T. and Shinn, M. (1985) Does self-help help? An empirical investigation of scoliosis peer support groups. *Journal of Social Issues* Vol. 41 p. 65.

Hirsch, B. (1981) Social networks and the coping process: Creating personal communities, in Gottlieb, B. (ed.) *Social Networks and Social Support.* Beverley Hills, Ca.: Sage Publications.

Hodge, J. (1985) *Planning for Co-Leadership.* Newcastle-upon-Tyne: Grapevine Publications.

Hollander, E. (1958) Conformity, status, and idiosyncrasy credit. *Psychological Review* Vol. 65 p. 117.

Hollander, E. (1982) *Principles and Methods of Social Psychology.* Oxford: Oxford University Press.

Hooley, J., Orley, J. and Teasdale, J. (1986) Levels of expressed emotion and relapse in depressed patients. *British Journal of Psychiatry* Vol. 148 p. 642.

Hooper, E., Comstock, L., Goodwin, J.M. and Goodwin, J.S. (1982) Patient characteristics that influence physician behaviour. *Medical Care* Vol. 20 p. 630.

Illich, I. (1976) *Limits to Medicine: Medical Nemesis: the expropriation of health.* Penguin.

Ivancevich, J. and Matteson, M. (1988) Promoting the individual's health and well-being in Cooper, C. and Payne, R. (eds) *Causes, Coping and Consequences of Stress at Work.* New York: John Wiley and Sons.

Janis, T. (1983) The role of social support in adherence to stressful decisions. *American Psychologist* Vol. 38 p. 143.

Jenkins, H. (1989) Precipitating crisis in families: patterns that connect. *Journal of Family Therapy* Vol. 11 p. 99.

Julien, R. (1992) *A Primer of Drug Action.* New York: W.H. Freeman & Co.

Kahn, R. and Antonucci, T. (1980) Convoys over the life course: Attachments, roles, and social support, in Baltes, P. and Brim, O. (eds) *Life-span Development and Behaviour* Vol. 3. New York: Academic Press.

Kaplan, J. (1983) *The Hardest Drug.* Chicago: Chicago University Press.

Kassorla, I. (1984) *Go For It: How to Win at Love, Work and Play.* New York: Dell.

Katschnig, H. and Konieczna, T. (1987) Psychosocial treatment of schizophrenia, in Strauss, J., Baker, W. and Brenner, H. *The Philosophy and Practice of Self-help for Relations of the Mentally Ill.* Toronto: Hans Huber.

Katz, D. and Hermalin, J. (1978) Self-help and prevention, in Hermalin, J. and Morell, J. (eds) *Prevention Planning in Mental Health.* Newbury Park, Ca.: Sage Publications.

Kelly, G. (1955) *The Psychology of Personal Constructs.* New York: Norton.

Kelner, M. and Bourgeault, I. (1993) Patient control over dying. *Social Science and Medicine* Vol. 36(6) p. 757.

Kessler, R. and McLeod, J. (1985) Social support and mental health in community samples, in Cohen, S. and Syme, S. (eds) *Social Support and Health.* New York: Academic Press.

Klingeman, H. (1992) Coping strategies of spontaneous remitters from the problem use of alcohol and heroin in Switzerland.

International Journal of the Addictions Vol. 27(12) p. 1559.

Kobak, R. and Hazan, C. (1991) Attachment in marriage: effects of security and accuracy of working models. *Journal of Personality and Social Psychology* Vol. 60 p. 861.

Kobasa, S., Maddi, S., Puccetti, M. and Zola, M. (1985) Effectiveness of hardiness, exercise and social support as resources against illness. *Journal of Psychosomatic Res.* Vol. 29 p. 525.

Koffinke, C. (1991) Family recovery issues and treatment resources, in Daly, D. and Raskin, M. (eds) *Treating the Chemically Dependent and Their Families.* Newbury Park, Ca.: Sage

Kokkevi, A. and Stephanis, C. (1988) Parental rearing patterns and drug abuse. *Acta Psych. Scand.* Vol. 78 Suppl. 344 p. 151.

Kosten, T., Jalali, B. and Kleber, H. (1983) Complementary marital roles in male heroin addicts. *American Journal of Drug and Alcohol Abuse* Vol. 9 p. 155.

Kottler, J. (1992) *Compassionate Therapy.* San Francisco: Jossey-Bass Publishers.

Kubler-Ross, E. (1973) *On Death and Dying.* Tavistock Publications.

Kuipers, L., Lef, J. and Lam, D. (1992) *Family Work for Schizophrenia.* Gaskell, p. 36.

Labrecque, M., Blanchard, C., Ruckdeschel, J. and Blanchard, E. (1991) The impact of family presence on the physician–cancer patient interaction. *Social Science and Medicine* Vol. 33(11) p. 1253.

Lansdown, R. and Benjamin, G. (1985) The development of the concept of death in children aged 5–9 years. *Child: Care, Health and Development* Vol. 11 p. 13.

Large, T. (1989) Some aspects of loneliness in families. *Family Process* Vol. 28 p. 25.

Lazarus, R. (1966) *Psychological Stress and the Coping Process.* New York: McGraw-Hill.

Lazarus, R. (1983) The costs and benefits of denial, in Breznitz, S. (ed.) *Denial of Stress.* New York: International Universities Press, p. 1.

Lazarus, R. and Launier, R. (1978) Stress-related transactions between person and environment, in Pervin, L. and Lewis, M. (eds) *Perspective in International Psychology.* New York: Plenum Books.

Leavy, R. (1983) Social support and psychological disorder: a review. *Journal of Community Psychology* Vol. 11 p. 3.

Lehman, D., Ellard, J. and Wortman, C. (1986) Social support of the bereaved: recipients' and providers' perspectives on what help fits. *Journal of Consulting and Clinical Psychology* Vol. 54 p. 438.

Levine, B. (1985) Adolescent substance abuse: toward an integration of family systems and individual adaptation theories. *American Journal of Family Therapy* 13 p. 3.

Levy, L. (1981) The National Schizophrenia Fellowship: a British self-help group. *Social Psychiatry* Vol. 16 p. 129.

Levy, L. (1982) Mutual support groups in Great Britain: a survey. *Social Science and Medicine* Vol. 16 p. 1265.

Lewis, R. (1978) Emotional intimacy among men. *Journal of Social Issues* Vol. 34 p. 108.

Ley, P. (1988) *Communicating with Patients: Improving Communication Satisfaction and Compliance*. Croom Helm

Ley, P. and Spelman, M. (1967) *Communicating with the Patient*. Staples Press.

Lieberman, M. (1990) A group therapist perspective on self-help groups. *International Journal of Group Psychotherapy* Vol. 40(3) p. 251.

Lieberman, S. and Black, D. (1982) Loss, mourning and grief, in Bentovim, A., Barnes, G. and Cooklin, A. (eds) *Family Therapy: Complementary Frameworks of Theory and Practice*. New York: Grune and Strattan.

Lindenfield, G. and Adams, W. (1984) *Problem-solving Through Self-help Groups*. Ilkley, West Yorks: Self-Help Associates.

Lindsey, A., Norbeck, J., Carrieri, V. and Perry, E. (1981) Social support and health outcomes in post masectomy women: a review. *Cancer Nursing*, October, p. 377.

Linn, M., Sandifer, R. and Stein, S. (1985) Effects of unemployment on mental and physical health. *American Journal of Public Health* Vol. 75 p. 502.

Locker, D. and Dunt, D. (1978) Theoretical and methodological issues in sociological studies of consumer satifaction with medical care. *Social Science and Medicine* 12(4) p. 283.

Lockley, P. (1995) *Counselling Heroin and Other Drug Users*. Free Association Books.

McCubbin, H. and Patterson, J. (1982) Family adaption to crisis, in McCubbin, H. and Patterson, J. (eds) *Family Stress, Coping and Social Support*. Springfield, Ill.: Charles C. Thomas.

McGrath, J. (1984) *Groups: Interaction and Performance*. New York: Prentice Hall.

McIntosh, V. and Zirpoli, E. (1982) Fighting parents' hopelessness. *International Journal of Group Psychotherapy* Vol. 32(1) p. 75.

McKay, M. and Fanning, P. (1987) *Self-esteem*. Oakland, Ca.: New Harbinger Publications.

McKinlay, J. (1979) Epidemiological determinants and political determinants of social policies regarding public health. *Social Science and Medicine* Vol. 13A p. 541.

MacLeod, A., Williams, J. and Bekerian, D. (1991) Worry is reasonable: the role of explanations in pessimism about future personal events. *Journal of Abnormal Psychology* Vol. 100 p. 478.

McMahon, N. and Link, P. (1984) Co-therapy: The need for practical pairing. *Journal of Psychology* Vol. 29 p. 385.

McNab, R. (1990) What do men want? Male ritual initiation in group psychotherapy. *International Journal of Group Psychotherapy* Vol. 40(2) p. 139.

McNeill-Taylor, L. (1983) *Living with Loss: A Book for the Widowed*. Glasgow: Fontana.

Madanes, C. (1981) *Strategic Family Therapy*. San Francisco: Jossey-Bass

Madanes, C., Dukes, J. and Harbin, H. (1980) Family ties of heroin addicts. *Archives of General Psychiatry* 3: p. 889.

Maddison, D. and Raphael, B. (1973) Conjugal bereavement and the social network. *Proceedings of Symposium on Bereavement*, New York, November 1973.

Maguire, P. (1985) Barriers to psychological care of the dying. *British Medical Journal* Vol. 291 p. 1711.

Masson, J. (1990) *Against Therapy*. Fontana.

Maton, K. (1988) Social support, organisational characteristics, psychological well-being, and group appraisal in three self-help group populations. *American Journal of Community Psychology* Vol. 16 p. 53.

Mayer, J. and Timms, N. (1970) *The Client Speaks*. Routledge.

Meehl, P. (1960) The cognitive activity of the clinician. *American Psychologist* Vol. 15 p. 19.

Megginson, D. and Pedler, M. (1991) *Self-development: A Facilitator's Guide*. Maidenhead: McGraw-Hill.

Minuchin, H. (1982) *Family Therapy Techniques*. Cambridge, Mass: Harvard University Press

Mischel, W. (1973) Towards a cognitive social learning reconceptualisation of personality. *Psychology Review* Vol. 80 p. 252.

Mistry, T. and Brown, A. (1991) Black/White co-working in groups. *Groupwork* Vol. 4(2)

Moos, R. (1974) *Evaluating Treatment Environments: A Social Ecological Approach*. New York: Wiley.

Morland, R. (1985) Social categorisation and the assimilation of new members. *Journal of Personality and Social Psychology* Vol. 48 p. 1173.

Moscovici, S. (1980) Toward a theory of conversion behaviour, in

Berkowitz, L. (ed.) *Advances in Experimental Psychology* Vol. 13, New York: Academic Press, p. 209.

Mowrer, O. (1984) The mental professions and mutual help programs: cooptation or cooperation, in Gartner, A. and Riessman, F. (eds) *The Self-help Revolution.* New York: Human Sciences Press, Ch. 11.

Mullender, A. and Ward, D. (1991) *Self-directed Groupwork: Users Take Action for Empowerment.* Whiting and Birch.

Murphy, P., Cramer, D. and Lillie, F. (1984) The relationship between curative factors perceived by patients in the psychotherapy and treatment outcome: an exploratory study. *British Journal of Medical Psychology* Vol. 57 p. 187.

Nagy, M. (1948) The child's theories concerning death. *Journal of Genetic Psychology* Vol. 73 p. 3.

National Commission on Marihuana and Drug Abuse, (1973) *Drug Use in America: problem in perspective.* Washington, DC: US Government Printing Office, p. 376.

Needle, R., McCublin, H., Wilson, H., Reinech, R., Lazar, A. and Mederer, H. (1986) Interpersonal influences in adolescent drug use: The role of older siblings, parents and peers. *International Journal of the Addictions* Vol. 21 p. 739.

Newcomb, M. and Bentler, P. (1989) *Consequences of Adolescent Drug Use.* Newbury Park, Ca.: Sage Publications.

Nichols, K. and Jenkinson, J. (1991) *Leading a Support Group.* Chapman and Hall.

Nisbet, R. (1984) Death, in Shneidman, E. (ed.) *Death: Current Perspectives.* Palo Alto, Ca.: Mayfield.

Nungesser, L. and Bullock, W. (1988) *Notes on Living Until we Say Goodbye.* New York: St Martin's Press.

Olson, D. and McCubbin, H. (1983) *Families: What Makes Them Work?* Beverley Hills, Ca.: Sage Publications.

Orford, J. (1987) *Coping with Disorder in the Family.* Croom Helm.

Palazzoli, M. (1980) Why a long interval between sessions? The therapeutic control of family therapist system, in Andolphi, M. and Zwerling, I. (eds) *Dimensions of Family Therapy.* New York: Guilford.

Palmer, S. (1992) Guidelines and contra-indications of teaching relaxation as a stress management technique. *Journal of the Institute of Health Education* Vol. 30(1) p. 25.

Palmer, S. and Dryden, W. (1995) *Counselling for Stress Problems.* Sage, p. 169.

Parkes, C. (1975) *Bereavement.* Penguin Books.

Parkes, C. and Weiss, R. (1983) *Recovery from Bereavement.* New York: Basic Books.

Patrick, D., Morgan, M. and Charlton, J. (1986) Psychosocial support and change in the health status of physically disabled people, in Patrick, D. and Scambler, G. (eds) *Sociology as Applied to Medicine*. Bailliere Tindall.

Patton, M. (1985) *Practical Evaluation*. Beverley Hills, Ca.: Sage Publications.

Pearlin, L. and Schooler, C. (1978) The structure of coping. *Journal of Health and Social Behaviour* Vol. 19 p. 2.

Pearson, R. (1990) *Counseling and Social Support*. Beverley Hills, Ca.: Sage Publications.

Pekkanen, J. (1976) The impact of promotion of physician's prescribing patterns. *Journal of Drug Issues* Vol. 6 No.1.

Pennebaker, J., Hughes, C. and O'Heeron, R. (1987) The psychophysiology of confession: linking inhibitory and psychosomatic processes. *Journal of Personality and Social Psychology* Vol. 52 p. 781.

Pennebaker, J. and O'Heeron, R. (1984) Confiding in others and illness rate among spouses of suicide and accidental death victims. *Journal of Abnormal Psychology* Vol. 93 p. 473.

Perera, K., Tulley, M. and Jenner, K. (1987) The use of benzodiazepines among drug addicts. *British Journal of Addiction* Vol. 82 p. 511.

Perez, J. (1986) *Counseling the Alcoholic Group*. New York: Gardner Press.

Petronio, S. (1991) Communication boundary management: a theoretical model of managing disclosure of private information between marital couples. *Communication Theory* Vol. 1 p. 311.

Petronio, S. and Martin, J. (1986) Ramifications of revealing private information: a gender gap. *Journal of Clinical Psychology* Vol. 42 p. 499.

Plant, M. and Plant, M. (1992) *Risk-takers*. Routledge.

Pollock, G. (1989) *The Mourning–Liberation Process* Vol. 1. New Haven, Ct.: International University Press.

Posavac, E. and Carey, R. (1980) *Program Evaluation: Methods and Case Studies* Englewood Cliffs, NJ.: Prentice Hall, p. 15.

Reid, W. (1967) Characteristics of casework interventions. *Welfare in Review* Vol. 5 No. 8.

Reiss, D. (1981) *The Family's Construction of Reality*. Cambridge, Mass.: Harvard University Press.

Reiss, D. (1990) Patient, family and staff responses to end-stage renal disease. *American Journal of Kidney Diseases* Vol. 15 p. 194.

Roback, H., Purdens, S., Ochoa, E. and Bloch, F. (1992) Guarding confidentiality in client groups. *International Journal of Group Psychotherapy* Vol. 42 p. 81.

Robinson, T. (1978) *In Worlds Apart*. Bedford Square Press.

Rogers, C. (1967) *On Becoming a Person*. Constable.

Rogers, C. (1973) *Becoming Partners: Marriage and its Alternatives*. Constable.

Rogers, R. and McMellin, C. (1989) *The Healing Bond: Treating Addicts in Groups*. New York: Norton.

Rogers, V. (1984) *Adult Learning Through Relationships*. New York: Praeger Publishers.

Romijn, C. and Platt, J. (1992) Family therapy for Dutch drug users. *International Journal of the Addictions* Vol. 27(1) p. 1.

Rook, K. (1984) The negative side of social interaction: impact on psychological well-being. *Journal of Personality and Social Psychology* Vol. 46 p. 1097.

Rosenthal, L. (1992) The new member: 'infanticide' in group psychotherapy. *International Journal of Group Psychotherapy* Vol. 42(2) p. 277.

Rosenthal, P. (1980) Short-term family therapy and pathological grief resolution with children and adolescents. *Family Process* Vol. 19 p. 151.

Rotter, J. (1966) Generalised expectations for internal versus external control of reinforcement. *Psychological Monograph: General and Applied* Vol. 80(1).

Rueveni, U. (1979) *Networking Families in Crisis: Intervention Strategies with Families and Social Networks*. New York: Human Services.

Sainsbury, E. (1975) *Social Work with Families*. Routledge and Kegan Paul, p. 72.

Sarason, I., Sarason, B. and Pierce, G. (1990) Social support: the search for theory. *Journal of Social and Clinical Psychology* Vol. 9 p. 133.

Sarnoff, I. and Zimbardo, P. (1961) Anxiety, fear and social facilitation. *Journal of Abnormal and Social Psychology* Vol. 62 p. 597.

Satir, V. (1967) *Conjoint family therapy*. Souvenir Press (1978) p. 4.

Schachter, S. (1959) *The Psychology of Affiliation*. Stanford, Ca.: Stanford University Press.

Schaps, E., Di Bartolo, R., Palley, C. and Chugin, S. (1981) A review of 127 drug abuse prevention programmes. *Journal of Drug Issues* Vol. 11(1).

Scheidlinger, S. (1982) On scapegoating in psychotherapy. *International Journal of Group Psychotherapy* Vol. 32(2) p. 131.

Scheier, M. and Carver, C. (1985) Optimism, coping and health. *Health Psychology* Vol. 4 p. 219.

Scheier, M. and Carver, M. (1992) Effects of optimism on psychological and physical well-being. *Cognitive Therapy and Research* Vol. 16 (2) p. 201.

Schlesinger, S. (1986) Substance misuse training in nursing, psychiatry and social work. *International Journal of the Addictions* Vol. 21(4&5) p. 595.

Schussler, G. (1992) Coping strategies and individual meanings of illness. *Social Science and Medicine* Vol. 34 (4) p. 427.

Schwartzman, J. (1975) The addict, abstinence and the family. *American Journal of Psychiatry* Vol. 132 p. 154.

Seldin, N. (1972) The family of the addict: a review of the literature. *International Journal of the Addictions* Vol. 7 p. 97.

Seligman, M. (1975) *Helplessness.* San Francisco: Freeman.

Seymour, R. and Smith, D. (1987) *Guide to Psychoactive Drugs.* New York: Harrington Park Press.

Shaver, P. and Liebling, B. (1976) Explorations in the drive theory of social facilitation. *Journal of Social Psychology* Vol. 99 p. 259.

Sherif, M. (1966) *Group Conflict and Cooperation.* Routledge and Kegan Paul.

Silver, R. and Wortman, C. (1980) Coping with undesirable life events, in Gerber, J. and Seligman, E. (eds) *Human Helplessness: Theory and Implications.* New York: Academic Press.

Slovic, P., Fischhoff, B. and Lichtenstein, S. (1976) Cognitive and societal risk-taking, in Carroll, J. and Payne, J. (eds) *Cognition and Social Behavior.* Hillsdale, New York: Lawrence Erlbaum.

Snyder, S. (1986) *Drugs and the Brain.* New York: W.H. Freeman & Co.

Solomon, M. (1973) A developmental conceptual premise for family therapy. *Family Process* Vol. 12 p. 179.

Spear, S. (1991) Impact of chemical dependency on family health states. *International Journal of the Addictions* Vol. 26(2) p. 179.

Stanton, M. and Todd, T. (1982) *The Family Therapy of Drug Abuse and Addiction.* New York: Guilford Press.

Stasser, G. and Davies, J. (1977) Opinion change during group discussion. *Journal of Personality and Social Psychology* Vol. 88 p. 252.

Stedeford, A. (1981) Couples facing death: 11: Unsatisfactory communication. *British Medical Journal* Vol. 283 p. 1098.

Stephan, F. and Misler, E. (1952) The distribution of participation in small groups: an exponential approximation. *American Sociological Review* Vol. 17 p. 598.

Stimson, G. (1987) British drug policies in the 1980s, in Heller, T., Gott, M. and Jeffery, C. (eds) *Drug Use and Misuse.* Chichester: John Wiley and Sons in association with the Open University.

Stimson, G. and Oppenheimer, E. (1982) *Heroin Addiction.* Tavistock Publications.

Strang, J. and Stimson, G. (1990) *AIDS and Drug Misuse*. Routledge.

Stuart, R. (1980) *Helping Couples Change: A Social Learning Approach to Marital Therapy*. New York: Guilford, p. 194.

Suls, J. and Fletcher, B. (1985) The relative efficacy of avoidant and non-avoidant coping strategies: a meta-analysis. *Health Psychology* Vol. 4 p. 249.

Taylor, S., Wilbur, M. and Osnos, R. (1966) The wives of drug addicts. *American Journal of Psychiatry*. Vol. 123.

Teichman, C. (1973) Emotional comparison and affiliation. *Journal of Experimental Social Psychology* Vol. 9 p. 591.

Telfer, I. and Clulow, C. (1990) Heroin misusers: what they think of their General Practitioners. *British Journal of Addiction* Vol. 85 p. 137.

Tobler, N. (1986) Meta-analysis of 143 adolescent drug prevention programs. *Journal of Drug Issues* Vol. 16 p. 537.

Tolsdorf, C. (1976) Social networks, support and coping mechanisms. *Family Process* Vol. 15 p. 407.

Toseland, R., Rossiter, C., Peak, T. and Hill, P. (1990) Therapeutic process in peer led and professionally led support groups for caregivers. *International Journal of Group Psychotherapy* 40(3) p. 279.

Tuckman, B. and Jensen, M. (1977) Stages of small group development revisited. *Group and Organisational Studies*. Vol. 2 p. 419.

Turk, D. and Kerns, R. (1985) The family in health and illness, in Turk, D. and Kerns, R. *Health, Illness and Families: A Life-span Perspective*. New York: Wiley.

Turkat, D. (1980) Social networks: theory and practice. *Journal of Community Psychology* Vol. 3(4) p. 268.

Vachon, M., Lyall, W., Roger, J., Freedman, K. and Freedman, S. (1980) A controlled study of self-help intervention for widows. *American Journal of Psychiatry* Vol. 137 p. 1380.

Vasey, M. and Borkovec, T. (1992) A catastrophizing assessment of worrisome thought. *Cognitive Therapy and Research* Vol. 16 p. 505.

Vaux, A. (1983) Variations in social support associated with gender, ethnicity and age. *Journal of Social Issues* Vol. 41(1) p. 89.

Videka-Sherman, L. (1982) Coping with the death of a child. *Journal of Orthopsychiatry* Vol. 52 p. 688.

Waitzkin, H. and Stoekle, J. (1972) The communication of information about illness. *Advances in Psychosomatic Medicine* Vol. 8 p. 180.

Wald, P. and Abrams, A. (1972) *Dealing with Drug Abuse: A Report to the Ford Foundation*. New York: Praeger Publishers.

Walster, E, Walster, W. and Berscheid, E. (1978) *Equity: Theory and Research*. Boston: Allyn and Bacon.

Wegner, D., Schneider, D., Carter, S. and White, T. (1987) Paradoxical effects of thought suppression. *Journal of Personality and Social Psychology* Vol. 53 p. 5.

Wermuth, L. and Scheidt, S. (1986) Enlisting family support in drug treatment. *Family Process* Vol. 25 p. 25.

Whitaker, D. (1985) *Using Groups to Help People*. Routledge & Kegan Paul.

White, M. and Epston, D. (1990) *Narrative Means to Therapeutic Ends*. New York: W.W. Norton.

Wilcox, B. (1981) Social support in adjusting to marital disruption, in Gottlieb, B. (ed.) *Social Networks and Social Support*. Beverley Hills, Ca.: Sage Publications, p. 97.

Williams, H. (1993) A comparison of social support and social networks of black parents and white parents with chronically sick children *Soc. Sci. Med.* Vol. 37(12) p. 1509.

Williams, W. and Polak, P. (1979) Follow-up research in primary prevention: a model of adjustment in acute grief. *Journal of Clinical Psychology* Vol. 35 p. 35.

Wills, T. (1978) Perceptions of clients by professional helpers. *Psychological Review* Vol. 65 p. 117.

Wills, T. (1985) Supportive functions of interpersonal relationships, in Cohen, S. and Symes, S. (eds) *Social Support and Health*. New York: Academic Press.

Wiseman, J. (1980) The 'have treatment': The first step in trying to cope with an alcoholic husband. *Family Relations* Vol. 29 p. 541.

Yalom, I. (1985) *The Theory and Practice of Psychotherapy*. New York: Basic Books.

Yelding, D. (ed.) (1990) *Caring for Someone with AIDS*. Hodder and Stoughton.

Youniss, J. and Smollar, J. (1985) *Adolescent Relations with Mothers, Fathers, and Friends*. Chicago: University of Chicago Press.

Zahn, M. and Ball, J. (1972) Factors related to the care of opiate addiction among Puerto Rican addicts. *International Journal of the Addictions* Vol. 7 p. 237.

Zinker, J. (1978) *Creative Process in Gestalt Therapy*. New York: Vintage Books.

Zola, I. (1975) In the name of health and illness. *Social Science and Medicine*. Vol. 9 p. 83.

INDEX

Index by Judith Lavender